THE COMPREHENSIVE INTERVENTION MODEL

THE COMPREHENSIVE INTERVENTION MODEL

NURTURING SELF-REGULATED READERS THROUGH RESPONSIVE TEACHING

Linda Dorn, Carla Soffos, and Adria Klein

Stenhouse
PUBLISHERS

Portsmouth, New Hampshire

Library of Congress Cataloging-in-Publication Data

Names: Dorn, Linda, author. | Soffos, Carla, author. | Klein, Adria, author.

Title: The comprehensive intervention model : nurturing self-regulated readers through responsive teaching / Linda Dorn and Carla Soffos.

Description: Portsmouth, New Hampshire : Stenhouse Publishers, 2021. | Includes bibliographical references and index. |

Identifiers: LCCN 2019057763 (print) | LCCN 2019057764 (ebook) | ISBN 9781625312891 (paperback) | ISBN 9781625312907 (ebook)

Subjects: LCSH: Reading (Primary) | Reading--Remedial teaching. | Response to intervention (Learning disabled children)

Classification: LCC LB1525. D654 2020 (print) | LCC LB1525 (ebook) | DDC 372.4--dc23

LC record available at https://lccn.loc.gov/2019057763
LC ebook record available at https://lccn.loc.gov/2019057764

Cover design, interior design, and typesetting by Thomson Digital

Printed in the United States of America

This book is printed on paper certified by third-party standards for sustainably managed forestry.

26 25 24 23 22 21   4371   9 8 7 6 5 4 3 2

DEDICATION

This book is dedicated in loving memory to Linda Dorn and her life-long commitment to education. We also dedicate this book to all administrators, Reading Recovery professionals, literacy coaches, and teachers who work tirelessly to adhere to their educational commitment while also refining their teaching practices.

CONTENTS

VIDEO TABLE OF CONTENTS

(Continued)

(Continued)

PREFACE

Knowledge is transformative. The goal of teaching is to create the conditions that activate what the learner already knows and to build bridges through scaffolding that enable the learner to transform the old knowledge into something new.

–Linda Dorn

The power of professional development is a clear message of Linda Dorn and Carla Soffos in this completely revamped and expanded book, which is a follow-up to their outstanding *Interventions That Work: A Comprehensive Intervention Model for Preventing Reading Failure in Grades K–3* (2011). In their earlier book, Richard Allington noted that the authors clearly understood that Response to Intervention meant whole-school reform and that all professionals would be involved in creating an intervention plan that was both comprehensive and systematic. In further support of this point, Allington and Peter Johnston emphasized that the CIM design "recognizes that expertise is not only individual teacher expertise, but also systemic expertise, the latter reciprocally providing the conditions for the former (2015, viii). From this view, the CIM focuses on the refinement of teacher expertise through teacher training, ongoing professional development, and engagement in the "Comprehensive Literacy Learning Network" (CLLN), a virtual network that includes real-time observations of intervention lessons, followed by intellectual discourse with colleagues from across the United States, aimed at fostering continuous improvement. Through these multifaceted experiences, teachers acquire the skills and knowledge for leading comprehensive and systemic changes within their schools.

In the design for this new book, Dorn and Soffos have refined all of the layers of intervention from the previous text, and added entirely new chapters on Comprehension Focus Groups for both elementary and upper-grade students and on the Strategic Processing Intervention model for students identified with particular challenges. This expanded and revised book is not only about the K–3 CIM model but also about the "beyond," where Dorn and Soffos discuss what is both new and critically important from the latest research.

Another essential component that they have developed and field-tested is the Language Phase that has been embedded into all the interventions. This understanding of the importance of language as the first self-extending system that transfers across all learning is based on Clay's theory of language and literacy processing moving forward together, linked and patterned from the start. I was invited to provide theory into practice support for the added Language Phase and support for English Acquisition Learners across all of the interventions, and am honored to have joined them in this work.

Additionally, they elaborated on the theory and research on the goal of transfer of learning. Thus, this new book includes revised Guide Sheets for all interventions, updated planners including the Language Phase, new examples, additional formative assessments, expanded writing prompts, and much more. Everyone will find invaluable the more than fifty video links, including links to examples of each of the interventions from the original *Interventions that Work* (*ITW*) video series, which teachers will be able to access as part of the new book. I can't think of any other book that has impacted teaching in the last decade as much as the original *ITW*, and I see this new text by Dorn and Soffos as guiding teachers and school systems K-12 for the next decade.

In the original *ITW* book, Allington recommended starting with Chapter 9, to frame the work with school-based case studies, and then reading the book from the beginning. In the last chapter of this new book, Chapter 10, Dorn and Soffos discuss the "Ten Principles of CIM Professional Development Design" and share the stories of literacy educators from four states who have implemented the CIM as a systemic Response to Intervention approach. They focus on how professional development serves to empower teachers with the knowledge and strategies to make effective data-based decisions for accelerating student learning. With this in mind, I suggest that teachers take the same approach by starting with Chapter 10, to learn from the real-world experiences of other educators, then begin reading from the beginning. Because of the work of Dorn and Soffos, all of us will be better teachers for the sake of our students.

As readers of this book are likely to know, Linda Dorn lost her battle with cancer in September 2019. Her legacy of learning will influence generations to come. Carla Soffos and I are committed to continuing and expanding the work she and Linda Dorn began over twenty years ago. We invite you to join us on this learning journey to provide the most current understandings for educators to meet the needs of all learners.

Adria Klein, Ph.D.
Saint Mary's College of California

ACKNOWLEDGMENTS

Let us begin our acknowledgments with a brief history of the Comprehensive Intervention Model and its many contributors. We first developed the small-group interventions in 1995, originally documented in the first edition of *Apprenticeship in Literacy: Transitions Across Reading and Writing.* Over the years, we have constantly refined the interventions based on teacher feedback and student achievement. In 2005, we expanded the original three interventions (Interactive Writing, Writing Aloud, and Guided Reading Plus) to encompass two new interventions (Comprehension Focus Groups and Writing Process) and clustered the collection under the Comprehensive Intervention Model (CIM). Then in 2011, with the focus on Response to Intervention (RTI), we revised the CIM to represent a portfolio of decision-making layered interventions based on a four-tiered RTI concept, and we added the Targeted Intervention to the CIM portfolio. Five years later, we expanded the portfolio to include the Strategic Processing Intervention, and we initiated teacher training classes and research partnerships with several schools. Throughout this history, we have collaborated with teachers and university colleagues across the United States on the development, refinement, and assessment of the CIM as a theoretical framework for responding to student needs. It has been an amazing journey, and we are very aware that without the ongoing support of so many literacy educators, the CIM would not exist as a decision-making design.

For sure, we are indebted to so many people that it is impossible for us acknowledge everyone. Our professional lives have been enriched by classroom teachers, interventionists, special educators, literacy coaches, administrators, university colleagues, and others—all committed educators who have shared their teaching experiences with us in both face-to-face and virtual learning contexts. Through the Comprehensive Literacy Learning Network (CLLN), we have interacted with teachers across the country who have taught intervention lessons in real time, while more than 200 educators observed their teaching and learning interactions and problem-solved with one another. These educators exemplify the spirit of collaboration and reflective practice in their quest for continuous improvement. To all these outstanding individuals, we offer our deepest appreciation and admiration for all they do to guarantee the literacy success of the children they teach.

All artifacts in this book are authentic resources created by literacy coaches and interventionists who are members of the CIM network. We owe special thanks to these educators: Brian Reindl for developing numerous resources, including the observation protocols and for assisting us with the refinement of the Planners and Guide Sheets; Michelle Amend for her dedication and commitment to this model and for providing us with ongoing feedback from the large number of teachers she supports in Wisconsin; Jianna Taylor for reformatting the intervention planners; Rena Comer for sharing her SPI video lessons; Julie Eckberg for creating the letter-pattern charts; and Carolyn Miller for sharing her video lessons of the Comprehension Focus Group intervention. Also, we offer thanks to Cindy Owens for her collaboration on a three-year study to examine the effects of the SPI training design on teachers' self-efficacy and the accelerated growth of children with dyslexia.

Additionally, we are grateful to the educators who contributed their stories of the CIM implementation, along with valuable resources to support other teachers in implementing and assessing their own CIM programs. We have included these stories and resources in Chapter 10. Special thanks to Vicki Wong, Janeen Zuniga, Molly Bozo, Dana Myers, Peggy Eklog, Amy Oakley, Candice Sayre, Jennifer Soehner, and Cindy Owens. Without the input of these dedicated and visionary leaders, this book would be missing an important section—the application of the CIM to the school context.

Our acknowledgments would not be complete without recognizing our university colleagues who have collaborated with us on the CIM development and research. These special people include Salli Forbes, Janet

Behrend, Debra Semm Rich, Mary Ann Poparad, Debra Hogate, Lori Taylor, Judy Embry, Lindy Harmon, Sue Duncan, Kent Layton, Stephanie Copes, and Wendy Satterfield. Also, we acknowledge Wiley Blevins for his valuable feedback on the word study chapter.

Further, we extend our special thanks to Bill Varner, Emily Hawkins, Shannon St. Peter, Stephanie Levy, Alicia Burns, and the Stenhouse editorial team for their commitment to our professional work. Since 1995, with our first book, the Stenhouse family has been there for us, believing in what we do, and giving us a voice to reach more teachers through our books.

In closing, we offer our deepest gratitude to God for giving Linda the strength to write even as she was battling cancer. During the past two years, we have become more aware than ever of how blessed we are to have so many literacy friends who prayed for Linda's recovery and sent a constant flow of cards and positive thoughts, along with numerous artifacts to support the intervention practices in the book. In recognition of these blessings, we present the new Comprehensive Intervention Model book as a theory-based framework for empowering teachers to make evidence-based decisions to accelerate students' literacy development.

INTRODUCTION

The research on early intervention is clear. We know that most reading difficulties can be prevented through high-quality instruction. However, this is not as simple as providing a student with extra support; rather, it requires a diagnostic process to determine the problem and to use the student's strengths to scaffold the weaknesses. Unfortunately, many schools are lured into using packaged programs as quick fixes. This solution is flawed because a packaged program is not personalized instruction nor can it identify what a student knows; therefore, it can only take a prescriptive approach to remediate weaknesses. Duffy and Israel (2009) cautioned, "One of the major reasons instruction cannot be packaged and prescribed in advance is the growing understanding that 'being explicit' does not mean students are passive recipients of explanations" (671). Rather, teachers must be experts in designing instruction that taps into students' existing knowledge and engages their minds in strategic activity for learning something new. Expert teaching, as described by Allington (2002b), requires "knowing not only how to teach strategies explicitly but also how to foster transfer of the strategies from the structured practice activities to students' independent use of them while engaged in reading . . . (744). The goal of transferring strategies renders the use of scripted instructional materials a questionable approach.

Simply put, thinking is an active process, and learning is co-constructed during meaningful interactions with more knowledgeable persons. Using instructional scaffolds as the tool, the teacher plays a critical role in shaping the student's literacy knowledge. The Comprehensive Intervention Model (CIM) provides a theoretical framework for aligning instructional support for low-progress readers across classroom and supplemental settings, while intentionally teaching for the transfer of knowledge and strategies for different purposes and on different tasks. The CIM framework includes a combination of (a) high-quality, differentiated classroom instruction, (b) a portfolio of evidence-based interventions, (c) a seamless assessment system at an individual and system level, and (d) school-embedded professional learning for increasing teacher efficacy and building capacity in schools.

Since 1991, we have collaborated with educators across the country in the development, implementation, and refinement of the small-group interventions. Over the years, we've observed hundreds of low-progress readers with a range of reading problems, and we've collected data on their responsiveness to different interventions. As a result, we realize that no single intervention can address the diverse needs of all students; therefore, we have created a portfolio of small-group interventions for accentuating particular literacy areas in literacy processing. Each intervention in the portfolio includes authentic reading and writing opportunities that mirror high-quality classroom instruction while allowing teachers to make data-based decisions on the best intervention for highlighting the strengths and needs of individual learners. The CIM stresses instructional congruency and seamless assessments across classroom and supplemental programs with built-in structures for promoting collaboration among teachers.

In all our publications, we have stressed the importance of teacher decision making based on a strong theory of learning that is continuously refined through systematic observations of students' literacy behaviors. We believe that a strong theory, along with keen observation skills and high-quality instructional resources, provides teachers with the data for making evidence-based decisions about their students' learning. In the pages of this book, we demonstrate how teachers have applied the CIM as a theoretical model of teaching and learning for accelerating the literacy gains of their low-progress students. In support of teacher learning, we have included a wealth of downloadable resources for assessing and implementing the CIM as a Response to Intervention method. In the next section, we provide a brief overview of each chapter.

A PREVIEW OF THE CHAPTERS

We encourage teachers to begin with Chapter 10 to learn from educators who have implemented the Comprehensive Intervention Model as a systemic approach to literacy improvement. Next, we suggest reading Chapter 1 for a theoretical explanation of the CIM as a Response to Intervention method, including an overview of evidence-based practices in literacy instruction, followed by Chapters 2 and 3 on the CIM portfolio and assessments used in diagnosing and monitoring student progress in response to specific interventions. Then, with this background in place, teachers can select different chapters to focus on specific interventions, while also referring to Chapter 4 on classroom alignment and Chapter 7 on word study as essential components of all interventions. The processing continuums in various chapters should be revisited over and over again as teachers keep the focus on executive control functions, transferability, and flexible strategies for promoting automaticity and efficiency on tasks that gradually increase in difficulty and complexity.

In Chapter 1, we present the cognitive theories and evidence-based practices that support the CIM as a Response to Intervention (RTI) process. We ground these practices in a multifaceted approach that addresses the relationship between metacognition, self-regulation, executive control, and social and emotional learning. Here, we set the purpose for embedding these cognitive and social-learning processes into all interventions in the CIM portfolio. We advocate for a complex theory that views knowledge as transformative, whereby the goal of teaching is to create the conditions that activate what the learner already knows and to build bridges through scaffolding that enable the learner to transform the old knowledge into something new.

In Chapter 2, we describe RTI as a comprehensive, data-driven decision-making process for identifying students with learning and behavioral difficulties and providing a series of more intensive instructional interventions over extended periods of time. An effective RTI process provides a framework for distinguishing between students with low achievement (based on poor instruction, poverty, and other environmental factors) and students with reading disabilities. As a decision-making model, the CIM uses a four-tiered, layered approach for monitoring a student's responsiveness to intervention. Within the portfolio design, all interventions encompass evidence-based practices that are differentiated to accommodate student needs, thus allowing the teacher to make data-based adjustments with regard to intensity, duration, and targeted instruction. Consequently, the different interventions can be layered or mixed to promote the student's accelerated growth in reading.

In Chapter 3, we present the components of a Comprehensive Assessment System (CAS) as an RTI process. One goal of RTI is to develop more valid procedures for assessing and identifying students who are at risk of reading failure. Intervention and assessment are dynamic processes; that is, the teacher designs a responsive intervention based on the student's strengths and needs, then assesses the student's capacity to learn from instruction. If a student is not responding to intervention, the problem is with the teaching, not with the student. Simply put, the student's learning provides a mirror on the teacher's instruction. The CAS offers teachers a process for examining teaching and learning through multiple measures and across different contexts (classroom and intervention). The ultimate goal of intervention is the acceleration of students' learning gains; therefore, if a student is not making the expected progress, the teacher should apply three decision rules to determine the appropriateness of the intervention.

In Chapter 4, we emphasize the classroom literacy program as the first line of defense against reading failure. We discuss how classroom instruction and interventions are intentionally aligned within a layered design of evidence-based practices. An integrated workshop framework in the classroom provides a scaffold for differentiating instruction for all students. Within this framework, classroom teachers are able to deliver more individualized support for low-progress readers, while intervention teachers provide an additional layer of targeted instruction that matches student needs. The purpose of an integrated workshop is to permit the alignment, coordination, and congruency of instructional goals across varied settings. The language workshop serves as the foundation for reading and writing workshops and aligns with the language phase of all interventions in the CIM portfolio. This chapter takes a close look at the features of reading and writing workshops and explains how teachers provide small-group interventions to enable low-progress learners to benefit from classroom instruction.

Chapter 5 details how a writing intervention can be used to increase reading achievement. The Assisted Writing intervention includes two types: Interactive Writing and Writing Aloud. The Interactive Writing intervention is designed for emergent and beginning early writers, and the Writing Aloud intervention is for readers who need assistance with the writing process. Teachers make decisions about the most appropriate intervention to match the student's needs. Teachers should use the Assisted Writing intervention planners and guide sheets to design scaffolded instruction for lifting students' knowledge and strategies to higher levels of literacy processing.

In Chapter 6, we present the three phases of the Guided Reading Plus (GRP) intervention at the emergent, early, and transitional levels, along with specialized procedures for implementing the intervention as a component of the CIM design. During phase one (language), the teacher focuses on the students' listening and speaking comprehension through an interactive read-aloud with a complex text that is revisited over several days for a deeper analysis. During phase two (reading), the teacher provides targeted instruction in word study, followed by opportunities for the students to apply word-solving strategies during their guided reading component. During phase three (writing), the teacher prompts the students to write about the reading from the guided reading discussion. The GRP intervention aligns with high-quality classroom instruction while providing targeted instruction in word study, strategy use, and writing about reading.

Chapter 7 focuses on the word study component of the interventions. Here, we present change over time in the development of the phonological and orthographic systems, along with instructional activities that align with the processing continuum. The goal of an effective word study component is achieved when students use strategies to solve words quickly and efficiently during their reading and writing of meaningful texts. Teachers should refer to this chapter when planning for the letter- and word-learning activities that are included in all interventions in the CIM portfolio. Also, teachers should refer to the reading processing continuum in Chapter 1 to promote students' ability to integrate visual and phonological sources with meaning and structure sources as they read to comprehend the author's message.

In Chapter 8, we share the principles that validate the Comprehension Focus Group (CFG) as an effective intervention for transitional and above readers. We emphasize the evidence-based practices that are grounded in the three phases of the CFG framework. In support of the transfer principle across classroom and intervention settings, we revisit the essential strategies for high-impact minilessons (first introduced in Chapter 3) and apply these strategies to the minilesson component of the CFG intervention. The chapter provides examples of intervention planners and videos of CFG lessons to support teachers as they plan for and implement the CFG intervention with their older readers.

In Chapter 9, we shift our attention to the Strategic Processing Intervention (SPI) for students with more severe reading problems, including dyslexia. First, we provide an overview of the research on phonological processing, followed by reminders that students must integrate their word knowledge with other sources of information as they read for meaning. An underlying principle of the SPI relates to teaching and assessing for transfer; therefore, the SPI planner is organized to nurture students' capacity to acquire, consolidate, and generalize phonological information across lesson components for purposes of constructing meaning. To support teachers, the chapter includes assessments, planners, guide sheets, activities, and video lessons.

In the final chapter, we share the stories of literacy educators from California, Washington, Wisconsin, and Missouri who have implemented the CIM as a systemic RTI method. In each case, professional development is the vehicle for empowering teachers with specialized knowledge for increasing the literacy gains of low-progress readers. To illustrate the processes of systemic change, we provide teachers with an implementation continuum for planning and assessing implementation variables in their own schools. The chapter is full of authentic resources, including video examples that document how literacy educators have implemented comprehensive and systemic changes that have led to increases in students' literacy achievement.

Throughout the book, we have emphasized the teacher as the heartbeat of the CIM. The teacher must understand how students learn and be able to provide the best instruction possible. Furthermore, an intervention model must be based on what we know about high-quality classroom instruction. As teachers acquire more knowledge about literacy processing and they observe the changes in their students' learning, they develop a sense of moral purpose (Fullan 1993) that drives their decision making. And as teachers collaborate with other teachers around changes in students' learning in response to their teaching, they refine their theories of how students learn. This book is organized to support teachers with the theories and evidence-based practices in reading instruction and assessment, along with the tools for implementing the CIM portfolio and the resources for implementing comprehensive and systemic changes in literacy improvement. With this in mind, we welcome teachers to provide us with feedback on their CIM implementations in order to continuously improve our teaching of the students who need us the most.

Chapter 1

LEARNING TO READ IS A COMPLEX PROCESS

Research has shown that effective interventions can prevent future reading failure, thus placing low-performing students on track for college and career readiness. As educators in the twenty-first century, we have access to a wealth of evidence-based resources to continually improve our expertise in teaching low-performing readers. The goal of education is to engage students' minds in using what they know to transform old knowledge into new information. To do this, readers must understand how to set goals, apply flexible strategies, and construct meaning from text-based experiences. At the same time, teachers must keep a watchful eye on students' literacy progress and be prepared to provide the best intervention when necessary. Equally important, the intervention should be grounded in social and cognitive learning theories, evidence-based practices, meaningful materials, and opportunities for students to apply flexible strategies to comprehend texts of increasing complexity.

Gersten et al. (2001) proposed that "inefficiency rather than deficiency most accurately characterizes the problems experienced by students with learning disabilities" (p. 280). This inefficiency typically results in random, guessing reactions that are in contrast to the reflective and intentional thinking associated with proficient readers (see Table 1). Strategy-based interventions are designed to foster the development of self-regulated processes, specifically, the reader's capacity to use knowledge, skills, and strategies for learning from text-based experiences.

High-progress readers use flexible strategies to initiate efficient problem-solving plans, to monitor their actions, and to redirect their thinking when meaning is threatened. All of these critical behaviors involve metacognition. An essential component of higher-level thinking, metacognition is shaped by three psychological functions (Luria 1980; Vygotsky 1978):

- Conscious awareness (I know what I know.)
- Selective attention (I can focus on what is important.)
- Voluntary memory (I need to remember this.)

Self-regulation is a key component of the broader concept of metacognition. Self-regulated learners exhibit more control over their cognitive, emotional, and motivational processes, which, in turn, allows them to adjust their actions and goals to achieve a particular outcome. Like metacognition, executive functioning relates to the overall regulation of thinking and behavior, that is, the higher-order processes used by learners to plan, sequence, adjust, and sustain their behavior toward achieving a desired goal. Simply put, metacognition, self-regulation, and executive functioning are neural processes that work together in flexible ways to enable readers to learn from varied experiences.

At the same time, the learner's emotions serve a regulatory function: they provide signals about when to keep working, when to stop, when to change course, what is important to remember, and what is not (Immordino-Yang and Damasio 2007). In the report *How People Learn II: Learners, Contexts, and Cultures*, researchers from the National Academies of Science, Engineering, and Medicine emphasize the complexity of learning within social contexts:

> Understanding the integration and interplay of these various levels of processing is important to understanding how learners orchestrate their learning in the context of their complex cognitive and social environments (National Academies of Science, Engineering, and Medicine 2018, 70).

Clearly, such a complex and transformative process requires a knowledgeable teacher who understands how to create opportunities for students to develop, refine, and transfer their decision-making capabilities for different purposes on wide-ranging tasks.

Table 1.1.   Behaviors of High-Progress and Low-Progress Readers

High-Progress Readers	Low-Progress Readers
Flexible problem-solving strategies for solving problems within text	Haphazard or guessing reactions to problems within text
Persistent and motivated actions	Tendency to give up easily and seek help
Intentional and purposeful goals for learning from text	No clear goal or purpose for learning from text
Strong monitoring systems, efficient self-correcting behaviors	Weak monitoring systems, poor self-correcting behaviors
Active engagement and self-directed actions	Passive engagement and dependency on others
Focus on meaning and big ideas	Focus on items and words
Retrieval of information in logical and meaningful ways	Retrieval of information in random ways
Ability to organize text in chunks of meaning and relationships	No organizational framework for understanding text relationships

To be effective, then, an intervention must enable low-progress readers to develop these higher-level psychological processes, thus shaping their ability to apply efficient and flexible strategies for learning. Research-based interventions, such as Reading Recovery (Clay 2016, D'Agostino and Murphy 2004), Interactive Strategies Approach (Scanlon and Anderson 2010), and Instructional Conversations (Goldenberg 1992), have shown that low-progress readers can acquire efficient strategies for regulating their thoughts as they read for meaning. However, it is essential that teachers are careful observers of students' literacy behaviors and are able to create the conditions that empower them to solve problems with greater efficiency and accuracy.

The purpose of this chapter is to build the theoretical context for supporting the Comprehensive Intervention Model (CIM) as a Response to Intervention (RTI) method for low-progress readers. We believe that a strong theory, along with keen observation skills and professional resources, provides teachers with the data for making evidence-based decisions about student learning. With this in mind, we have organized the chapter around two major goals. First, we provide a brief overview of the research on effective practices in literacy intervention with an emphasis on strategic activity and transfer. Here, we contextualize these instructional practices within a processing continuum that highlights observable changes over time in literacy behaviors that reflect cognitive shifts. Then, we present the theories of metacognition, self-regulation, and executive control functions, and the relationship among these neural processes in learning. In the following chapters, we share how the CIM provides a theoretical framework with specialized interventions and evidence-based practices for meeting the unique needs of learners with reading problems.

EFFECTIVE PRACTICES IN LITERACY INTERVENTION

A substantial body of evidence on early intervention has shown that students who are at risk for reading failure can be helped through explicit and intensive instruction in reading (Foorman et al. 2016; National Early Literacy Panel 2008; Neuman and Dickinson 2011). More specifically, research indicates that effective interventions are characterized by four features:

- Explicit instruction in the alphabetic principle and related processes, integrated with reading for meaning.
- Early intervention/prevention efforts in the early grades.
- Small-group and/or one-to-one intensive instruction.
- Teaching that is matched to the student's instructional level.

Successful interventions are designed to move low-progress readers into the normal range of reading performance within a short period of time. To accomplish this goal, an effective intervention is grounded in two learning theories:

- **Acceleration:** A rapid rate of progress that makes it possible for a low-progress learner to catch up with an average-progress learner over a short time period.
- **Scaffolding:** The degree of assistance provided by the teacher to enable the learner to accomplish a task that would be too difficult to perform alone.

In order to close the literacy gap, interventions should incorporate evidence-based practices and scaffolding techniques that promote accelerated learning, thus moving low-progress readers into the normal range of reading performance within a short amount of time. Furthermore, interventions must emphasize reading for meaning at all grade levels, with the expectation that students will demonstrate more advanced reading strategies for comprehending a broad range of high-quality texts as they progress through the grades (Adams 1994; Denton et al. 2006). Teachers can utilize six critical skills for reading development (Figure 1.1) and specific evidence-based recommendations that support reading comprehension (Figure 1.2) to implement effective practices for low-progress readers.

In the area of beginning reading programs, the What Works Clearinghouse practice guide identifies six critical skills for reading development (Shanahan et. al 2010):

- Word-level skills (phonemic awareness, word analysis strategies, sight word vocabulary, and practice to increase fluency while reading)
- Vocabulary knowledge and oral language skills (strategies to build vocabulary and strengthen listening comprehension)
- Broad conceptual knowledge (information-rich curriculum that develops the background knowledge necessary for good reading comprehension)
- Comprehension strategies (cognitive strategies for problem-solving within texts)
- Thinking and reasoning strategies (making inferences as text becomes more complex)
- Motivation to understand and work toward academic goals (persistence and mental effort to stay engaged in a task)

Figure 1.1   Six Critical Skills for Reading Development

The What Works Clearinghouse practice guide recommends five specific steps that teachers can take to successfully improve reading comprehension for low-performing readers (Shanahan et. al 2010):

- Teach students to use reading comprehension strategies.
- Teach students to identify and use the text's organizational structure to comprehend, learn, and remember content.
- Guide students through focused, high-quality discussions on the meaning of the text.
- Select texts purposely to support comprehension development.
- Establish an engaging and motivating context to teach reading comprehension.

Figure 1.2   Evidence-Based Recommendations That Support Reading Comprehension

The CIM portfolio of interventions builds on this body of evidence, alongside specific recommendations for reading improvement from four research reports:

- Critical skills in beginning reading programs (Foorman et al. 2016)
- Recommendations that support reading comprehension (Shanahan et al. 2010)
- Essential elements of research-based interventions (Scammacca et al. 2007)
- Recommendations for using writing to increase reading (Graham and Hebert 2010)

In keeping with these recommendations, the CIM acknowledges that reading is a complex neural process; therefore, teachers should select texts that engage readers' minds in accessing, integrating, and consolidating information, and they should be prepared to scaffold students as they practice problem-solving strategies with increasing speed and efficiency. Equally important, the CIM recognizes that children take different paths to common outcomes (Clay 2014) consequently, teachers should select interventions that are responsive to the unique strengths and needs of individual learners (Vellutino et al. 2008) and be ready to make adjustments based on observable changes in students' literacy behaviors.

CONSTRUCTING KNOWLEDGE THROUGH LITERACY EXPERIENCE

Learning is an active and transformative process that is stimulated by opportunities to acquire new knowledge in collaboration with others. Fischer (2008) described how learning takes place in recurring waves or scallops that reflect cycles as skills are constructed and reconstructed through strategic activity (also, see Siegler 1996, 2000). In a similar way, Tharp and Gallimore (1988) explained how the construction of knowledge is both generative and recursive as it is tested and solidified under different conditions; therefore, strategies are assembled to solve different problems for varied purposes (Singer 1994). The learner's problem-solving efficiency on diverse tasks can be mediated through teacher scaffolding at critical points in the processing cycle (Clay 2014). Critical behaviors are defined as overt evidence that the learner is engaged in cognitive processing, such as the following behaviors:

- Student pauses at a particular point, indicating awareness that a problem exists (monitoring).
- Student applies a strategy that depends on two or more sources of information (integrating).
- Student attempts to transfer some valid form of information to the problem (searching further).
- Student makes a correction, then rereads to confirm (correcting and confirming).
- Student demonstrates persistence toward reaching a meaningful solution (pursuing a goal).

From an intervention perspective, the teacher creates a supportive context and uses meaningful tools to engage the reader's mind in constructive activity. Constructive activity is cognitive: an intentional and strategic process for accomplishing a particular task. Strategic processes can be defined as neural actions for activating, assembling, integrating, and monitoring information for constructing new knowledge. It is essential for teachers to understand what students already know and to be able to prompt for strategic activity that links the known and unknown information.

With a focus on neural processing, Singer (1994) theorized that readers assemble cells of knowledge and organize these data into different working systems to deal with changes in purpose and/or task complexity. This

- **Attentional Control:** The ability to focus on particular information or a particular task regardless of distractions or fatigue.
- **Cognitive Flexibility:** The ability to consider multiple bits of information or ideas at one time and actively switch between them when engaging in a task.
- **Inhibition:** The ability to restrain one's normal or habitual responses (also called response inhibition or inhibitory control).
- **Initiation:** The ability to overcome inertia and begin a task.
- **Metacognition:** The ability to take a step back and reflect on thoughts, perspectives, and mental processes and assess their effectiveness.
- **Organization:** The ability to impose order on information and objects or to create systems for managing information or objects.
- **Planning:** The ability to decide which tasks are necessary to complete a goal, including understanding which ones are most important and the order in which the tasks should be completed to most effectively reach the goal.
- **Response to Feedback:** The ability to adjust one's behavior or alter one's plans in the face of new information.
- **Self-Regulation:** The ability to control one's own behavior and emotions in order to achieve goals.
- **Switching or Shifting:** The ability to change one's attentional focus from an initial idea to a new one (this is related to cognitive flexibility).
- **Working Memory:** The ability to hold information in mind to support the completion of tasks.

Figure 1.3   Executive Control Functions Associated with Strategic Activity, Efficiency, and Speed of Processing

strategic process is linked to executive control functions that involve intentional decision making as the reader sets goals, considers multiple sources of information, monitors outcomes, and self-corrects, when needed, to resolve conflict and construct meaning. Figure 1.3 summarizes the executive control functions associated with strategic activity and efficient processing in learning new information (Cartwright 2012, 26).

SOCIAL, EMOTIONAL, AND COGNITIVE LEARNING

The relationship of social, emotional, and cognitive learning to student achievement cannot be overstated. Obviously, students are willing to work harder if the content and skills they are learning are meaningful and relevant to their motivations and future goals. Yet, it is important to note that students must have the necessary background knowledge to arouse their attention, along with an awareness of particular strategies to sustain their search. Furthermore, students must gain a level of control over their own thinking, and they cannot exercise control while they remain unaware of what they know. As we stated earlier, metacognition is viewed as the foundation for developing self-regulation, executive control, and social and emotional learning (SEL). Here, we define the functions and interactive nature of the four cognitive processes that enable learners to build and expand their knowledge of the world (Durlak et al. 2011; Liew 2012):

- Metacognition: Awareness of one's own thinking.
- Self-Regulation: An internal plan to activate, monitor, and regulate one's actions, combined with the ability to use feedback for adjusting behavior in pursuit of the learning goal.
- Executive Control: Deliberate choices for making decisions, including choices about particular strategies for solving words and the amount of time to spend on specific aspects of the reading act.
- Social and Emotional Learning: The capacity to recognize and manage emotions, set and achieve positive goals, appreciate the perspectives of others, establish and maintain positive relationships, make responsible decisions, and handle interpersonal situations appropriately.

With a renewed focus on Social and Emotional Learning (SEL) in schools, Hoffman (2009) and others (e.g., Vadeboncoeur and Collie 2013) have stressed the need to reduce the emphasis on behavioral skills and individual assessments and to develop methods for embedding social and emotional experiences within the social practices of schools. From a Vygotskian perspective, SEL is part of a complex process of relationships that situates cognitive functions, emotional experiences, and human relationships within social and

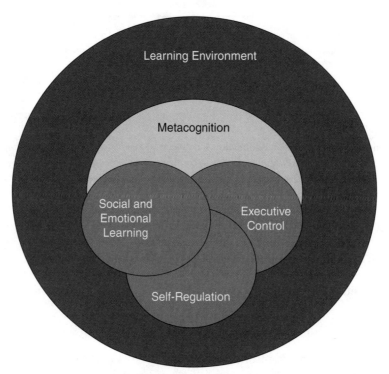

Figure 1.4   Interactions Between Metacognition, Self-Regulation, Executive Control, and Social and Emotional Learning Situated Within the Learning Environment

cultural environments (Vadeboncoeur and Collie 2013). In Figure 1.4, we illustrate the interaction between self-regulation, executive control function, and SEL, while emphasizing that these processes are grounded in metacognition and situated within the learning environment.

Based on this theory, all interventions in the CIM portfolio are designed to build students' metacognition and self-efficacy through scaffolded experiences with responsive teachers who understand the relationship of social and emotional factors to self-regulation and reading success.

READING IS A COMPLEX PROCESS

Throughout the chapter, we have emphasized the complexity of reading. In keeping with the complexity theory, a literacy processing system is defined as a well-orchestrated internal network of associative information that is strategically activated to construct meaning for a given event (Clay 1991). In other words, literacy processing represents a fast reaction of the brain to resolve an immediate problem—the rapid assembly of relevant strategies and background knowledge that is driven by the reader's motivation to learn from experience. This level of processing is related to greater flexibility in executive control functions, specifically, voluntary memory and strategic activity for setting goals and monitoring outcomes according to varied purposes and shifting circumstances. When learners apply problem-solving strategies across reading and writing situations, their brains build neural connections or pathways among these related sources. In this way, if readers are unable to access the needed information through one system, they can take an alternative route to solve the problem. Here, the teacher's role in lifting the reader's processing activity to higher levels is dependent on the teacher's ability to notice changes (including patterns of change) in students' literacy behaviors and to create opportunities for readers to develop flexible strategies for solving problems with greater ease and automaticity. In Table 1.2, we provide teachers with a processing continuum for observing changes over time in literacy processing behaviors, and we encourage teachers to design instruction that

Table 1.2.   Literacy Processing Continuum of Change over Time in Reading Behaviors of Emergent to Beyond Transitional Readers: Reading Multiple Types of Texts for Different Purposes

Emergent Text Reading Levels: A–D/E, and Decodable Texts Kindergarten	**Beginning Early** Text Reading Levels: E – F/G, Decodable Texts, and Grade Level Texts Early First Grade	**Late Early** Text Reading Levels: G/H, Decodable Texts, and Grade Level Texts Mid-First Grade	**Transitional** Text Reading Levels: I–M and Grade Level Texts End of First Grade – End of Second Grade	**Beyond Transitional** Grade Level Texts Third Grade and Beyond
Goal	**Goal**	**Goal**	**Goal**	**Goal**
Use meaning, structure, and orthographic/visual sources of information within simple texts to increase attention to print in an **integrated** way. • Points to words in a one-to-one match throughout two to three lines of text; understands that print carries the message; later removes finger and uses only as needed. • Notices errors (self-monitors); *cross-checks* multiple sources of information (checks to make sure the reading makes sense, sounds right, and looks right). • Rereads when needed to cross-check visual information with meaning and structural cues.	Use meaning, structure, and orthographic/visual sources of information within text along with relevant background and strategic knowledge in an **integrated** way to support ongoing comprehension of texts. • Notices errors (self-monitors); initiates multiple attempts to self-correct; *integrates* multiple sources of information to make a self-correction (checks to make sure the reading makes sense, sounds right, and looks right). • Rereads when needed to cross-check visual information with meaning and structural cues.	Use meaning, structure, and orthographic or visual sources of information within text along with their relevant background and strategic knowledge in an **integrated** way to support ongoing comprehension of texts. • Notices errors and self-monitors with greater ease; initiates multiple attempts to self-correct; *integrates* multiple sources of information (checks to be sure the reading makes sense, sounds right, and looks right). • Rereads when needed to cross-check visual information with meaning and structural cues.	Use meaning, structure, and orthographic or visual sources of information within text along with their relevant background and strategic knowledge in an **orchestrated** way to support ongoing comprehension of texts. • *Orchestrates* multiple sources of information (meaning, structure, and visual cues); reads texts with greater accuracy and more efficient self-correction.	Use meaning, structure, and orthographic or visual sources of information within text along with their relevant background and strategic knowledge in an **orchestrated** way to support ongoing comprehension of texts. • *Orchestrates* multiple sources of information (meaning, structure, and visual cues); reads texts with greater accuracy and more efficient problem-solving and self-correction. • Uses knowledge of letters, consonant blends and digraphs, long vowel patterns, r-controlled vowels, diphthongs, prefixes, and suffixes to solve words with fluency and greater accuracy.

(Continued)

Table 1.2. *(Continued)*

Emergent	Beginning Early	Late Early	Transitional	Beyond Transitional
Text Reading Levels: A–D/E, and Decodable Texts	Text Reading Levels: E - F/G, Decodable Texts, and Grade Level Texts	Text Reading Levels: G/H, Decodable Texts, and Grade Level Texts	Text Reading Levels: I-M and Grade Level Texts	Grade Level Texts
Kindergarten	Early First Grade	Mid-First Grade	End of First Grade – End of Second Grade	Third Grade and Beyond
• Uses knowledge of letter-sound relationships to initiate an efficient decoding strategy at the point of difficulty; searches through unknown one-syllable words with easy **predictable letter–sound relationships** in a left-right sequence, blends letters into sounds; repeats words to confirm if needed. • Uses knowledge of letter-sound patterns to read other words and to check on reading. • Reads known words with added inflectional endings. • Reads known high-frequency words with fluency. • Self-corrects using known high-frequency words and other print cues. • Uses simple punctuation to regulate phrasing and fluency (prosody).	• Uses knowledge of letter-sound relationships to initiate an efficient decoding strategy at the point of difficulty; searches through unknown one-syllable words with easy predictable letter–sound relationships in a left-right sequence; blends letters into sounds including **consonant blends and digraphs;** repeats word to confirm if needed. • Uses knowledge of letter-sound relationships to initiate an efficient decoding strategy at the point of difficulty; searches through unknown one-syllable words in a left-right sequence; blends letters, consonant blends, and digraphs into sounds including **long vowel pattern words with final e;** repeats to confirm if needed. • Reads known words with simple inflectional endings. • Reads known high-frequency words with fluency. • Self-corrects using known high-frequency words and other print cues. • Uses simple punctuation to regulate phrasing and fluency (prosody).	• Uses knowledge of letter-sound relationships to initiate an efficient decoding strategy at the point of difficulty; searches through unknown one-syllable words in a right to left to right sequence; blends letters, consonant blends, and digraphs into sounds including **long vowel patterns;** repeats to confirm if needed. • Uses known letters, consonant blends and digraphs, and long vowel patterns to decode and read **two- and some three-syllable words including compound words;** repeats to confirm if needed. • Reads **contractions and possessives.** • Reads known words with more complex inflectional endings. • Reads known high-frequency words with fluency. • Self-corrects using known high-frequency words and other print cues. • Uses simple punctuation to regulate phrasing and fluency (prosody).	• Uses knowledge of letter-sound relationships to initiate an efficient decoding strategy at the point of difficulty; searches through unknown words in a left-right sequence; blends letters, consonant blends, digraphs, and long vowel patterns into sounds including **r-controlled vowels, irregular vowel patterns, and diphthongs.** • Uses known word patterns to decode and read words including **complex multisyllabic** words with efficiency and accuracy. • Uses knowledge of syllable division strategies to support decoding and reading of multisyllabic words. • Uses morphemic units including **prefixes and suffixes** to read and understand word meanings. • Reads known complex high-frequency words with fluency and ease. • Self-corrects using known high-frequency words and other print cues. • Uses more complex punctuation to regulate phrasing and fluency (prosody).	• Uses knowledge of syllable division strategies to decode and read multisyllabic words with greater efficiency and accuracy. • Uses morphemic units including prefixes and suffixes to read and understand word meanings. • Reads complex high-frequency words with fluency and ease. • Self-corrects using known high-frequency words and other print cues. • Uses complex punctuation to regulate phrasing and fluency (prosody).

Note: Bolded words indicate the phonetic or word-learning principles the students have learned in the word study component of the intervention. During the reading, the teacher observes for the transfer of the learning from one activity setting to another and uses data to plan for additional word study lessons to support strategic activities on texts.

simultaneously activates and extends students' knowledge to higher levels of processing. (See Resource A.1, Literacy Processing Continuum of Change over Time in Reading Behaviors of Emergent to Beyond Transitional Readers: Reading Multiple Types of Text for reproducible copy.)

Certainly, learning to read is a complex process that involves different parts of the brain in consolidating knowledge sources and making thoughtful decisions that deepen one's understanding of text-based experience (Clay 1991; Paris, Wasik, and Turner 1991; Willingham 2017). In light of this complexity, dual coding theory helps to explain how readers integrate multisensory modalities to represent knowledge (Sadoski and Paivio 2004, 2007, 2013). All representations derive from sensory experiences and can be classified as either verbal or nonverbal codes that are activated by context and mediated by motor. Here, information is organized in associative structures of interrelated knowledge, which the reader can then galvanize through strategic processes to make sense of a particular phenomenon. Motor structures, including spatial and sequential components, play a central role in learning, particularly when motor movements are associated with verbal descriptions. In light of this information, teachers can prompt students to use language to describe the spatial orientation and sequential path of movement as they simultaneously construct the letter (see Chapter 7 and Resource G.2, Language for Describing the Path of Movement for Learning Letters). The importance of language and motor in higher-order cognitive processes is supported by the research on dual coding theory.

Flexible strategic thinking, in contrast to rigid beliefs, can be empowering for learners, since it allows them to grow their intellect through associations. We know that skilled readers attend to multiple sources of information, including word-level phonological information and meaningful contextual information, whereas low-progress readers tend to fixate on decoding (phonological features) without attending to meaning (Pressley 2002). Cartwright (2012) proposed that inflexibility is a hallmark of struggling readers; therefore, interventions should include literacy tasks that require readers to classify phonological and meaning cues simultaneously, thus nurturing their capacity for cognitive flexibility.

All interventions in the CIM portfolio require teachers to understand cognitive theories and create the conditions that enable low-progress readers to develop metacognition, cognitive flexibility, and self-regulatory behaviors for learning from experience. Efficiency, speed, and accuracy are the outcomes of effective literacy processing. To achieve these goals, the learner must be able to integrate and evaluate multiple sources of information for interpreting the deeper meanings within the text. The CIM portfolio of interventions includes explicit procedures for coordinating multisensory modalities (visual, auditory, motor) supported by verbal (language) and nonverbal (images, graphic organizers, pictures, etc.) cues, in tandem with cognitive strategies, to build associative networks of generalizable knowledge.

TEACHING FOR TRANSFER

The ultimate goal of an intervention is to empower students to regulate their learning for task-specific purposes. Students must understand that knowledge can be transferred to different contexts and for different purposes and goals (McKeough, Lupart, and Marini 1995; Perkins and Salomon 2012). Too often, we find students who do not understand that knowledge is generalizable; consequently, they view each learning opportunity as a novel experience. When teachers teach for transfer, they enable students to use what they know to learn new information; and teachers collaborate with one another to promote the students' transfer of knowledge across multiple settings. Self-regulation and transfer are dependent on the reader's control of three knowledge sources (Meichenbaum and Biemiller 1998; Paris, Lipson, and Wixson 1994).

- **Declarative Knowledge:** Knowledge of the literacy task.
- **Procedural Knowledge:** Knowledge of steps/procedures for carrying out the literacy task.
- **Strategic Knowledge:** Knowledge of flexible strategies for performing the literacy task in varied contexts and for different purposes.

The CIM includes a framework for aligning instruction across classroom and supplemental settings. Transfer is facilitated as the student learns the new task in an environment with reduced distractions and tailored support, then applies the knowledge to an environment with normal distractions and distributed support. In the CIM, the following steps are used to promote transfer.

- Student receives instruction in a small reading group from the classroom teacher within the classroom setting.
- Student receives an intervention from an intervention specialist who provides highly tailored support, precision teaching, and expert scaffolding. The intervention occurs in a setting with limited distractions, thus enabling the student to develop conscious awareness, selective attention, and strategies for problem-solving in connected texts.
- Classroom and intervention teachers observe the student's ability to transfer knowledge across the two contexts. If transfer is not occurring, the teachers examine instructional factors (e.g., text levels, teaching prompts) that could impact the student's ability to generalize knowledge.

Transfer must be taught explicitly; therefore, teachers should design activities that promote transfer: the capacity of learners to generalize their knowledge for solving problems on diverse tasks in varied situations (Perkins and Salomon 1988, 2012). If transfer is not emphasized, struggling readers might develop contextual dependency; in other words, they might understand that their knowledge can be utilized in different contexts and for different purposes. Generalizable knowledge reflects the learner's ability to think beyond the isolated items and organize information in meaningful relationships that represent big ideas.

All interventions in the CIM portfolio include a predictable framework, with specialized procedures and language prompts, that emphasizes transferable knowledge across a range of language, reading, and writing tasks. At the same time, the effectiveness of the intervention is dependent on the teacher's skill in adjusting degrees of scaffolding that enable students to apply flexible strategies for dealing with complexity within continuous texts.

A SYSTEM DESIGN FOR PROMOTING TRANSFER

In supporting struggling readers, the need for instructional alignment of reading programs is more important than ever. Johnston, Allington, and Afflerbach (1985) proposed that instructional alignment between programs could be an important factor in a student's acceleration in a reading intervention. Simply put, instructional alignment occurs when classroom and intervention teachers create mutual plans for using common materials and instructional activities across varied contexts in order to support the reading development of struggling learners. In a fragmented reading program, according to Johnston, Allington, and Afflerbach, the student's instruction in one program may interfere with learning in another setting, such that the student becomes confused about the nature of the task and how it should be solved. For decades, Allington and Johnston (1989), in their reviews of supplemental programs for low-performing readers, have argued that incongruent programs and isolated practices contribute to the problems of struggling readers. More recently, a study by Wonder-McDowell, Reutzel, and Smith (2011) concluded that struggling readers who participated in instructionally aligned programs outperformed a similar group who did not. Taken together, the research suggests that aligned instruction creates a scaffold that enables struggling readers to transfer knowledge, skills, and strategies across multiple settings.

What can teachers do to promote transfer? The challenge is to make transfer more likely by design rather than by happenstance. To meet this challenge, a design should include four essential elements:

- **Coordination (alignment and seamlessness):** Coordination is achieved through the intentional effort to align programs, curriculum, and assessments to maximize learning by enabling students to transfer their knowledge, skills, and strategies across varied contexts and for different purposes.

- **Congruency (similarity):** Congruency relates to the similarity of instructional practices, approaches, and language, which enables students to focus their attention on higher-level strategies for integrating, predicting, testing, and constructing new knowledge in different situations.
- **Common Language (mutual understandings):** Common language for instructional activities enables teachers to go beyond the procedural components and focus on the underlying theories and rationales that support students' learning. Without a common language of instruction, misconceptions can occur and teacher decision making can be impaired.
- **Collaboration (working together):** Collaboration is an intentional process that engages teachers in joint activities and decision-making processes aimed at creating conditions for students to transfer their knowledge, skills, and strategies to similar tasks in diverse settings.

As an RTI method, the CIM provides students with opportunities for consistent, repetitive practice across various situations that nurture their automaticity and deeper understandings. The students' success will depend on two interrelated factors:

- The effectiveness of universal instruction in the general education classroom, plus the classroom teacher's ability to differentiate instruction for low-performing students.
- The effectiveness of interventions for students with persistent reading difficulties, plus the intervention teacher's ability to scaffold students' independence on tasks that gradually increase in complexity and difficulty.

CLOSING THOUGHTS

In this chapter, we highlighted cognitive theories of metacognition, self-regulation, executive control, social and emotional learning, and transfer as related to students' success in reading. As we illustrated in Figure 1.4, these processes do not exist in isolation; rather, they work together to shape students' capacity to learn from the environment. Literacy learning is viewed as a complex interactive and transformative process whose development is determined by the social and cultural context. From this perspective, a literacy intervention should be multifaceted to address the dynamics among cognitive processing, emotional reactions, and the social environment in reading acceleration. At the same time, a literacy intervention should incorporate evidence-based practices in literacy instruction, provided by a knowledgeable teacher who understands how to adjust support to accommodate shifts in students' learning behaviors.

So, why did we begin the book with a focus on theory? Simply put, the teacher's theory of learning will have a direct influence on the types of interventions she provides for low-progress readers. If the teacher perceives students' behaviors through a deficit lens (i.e., a focus on what the student does not know), the teacher is more likely to implement a remediation approach that emphasizes a sequence of decoding activities, including restricted texts that focus on the phonics code. The problem with this approach is that students may get better at decoding but still lack comprehension, more advanced language skills, and flexible strategies for regulating their reading on more complex texts. In contrast, if the teacher views students' behaviors through a constructivist lens (i.e., a focus on what the student already knows), the teacher is more likely to implement an accelerative method that emphasizes the integration of multiple sources and the activation of flexible strategies for learning from texts that gradually increase in difficulty and complexity. With this approach, the students develop higher-level processing skills for monitoring and regulating their reading in order to comprehend the author's message. From a constructivist perspective, the interventions in the CIM portfolio require teachers to have a strong theory of how students learn and to be able to make moment-to-moment decisions that foster students' reading acceleration.

Chapter 2

A MULTITIERED SYSTEM OF COMPREHENSIVE INTERVENTIONS

Vygotksy's (1978) theory of positive differentiation has particular relevance for Response to Intervention (RTI). According to Gindis (2003, 213), Vygotsky's main premise was that "a child with a disability must be accommodated with experiences and opportunities that are as close as possible to the mainstreamed situation, but not at the expense of 'positive differentiation.' This should be based on a child's potential rather than on his or her current limitations."

The emphasis on potential rather than limitation is at the heart of RTI. At its best, RTI is a comprehensive, data-driven decision-making process for identifying children with learning and behavioral difficulties and providing them with a series of intensive instructional interventions over extended periods of time. It is the practice of providing high-quality instruction matched to student needs and using learning rate over time in tandem with levels of performance to make important educational decisions.

RTI was designed not just to identify and support low-progress students but also to help discern underlying challenges. Johnston (2010) explained that RTI was a logical response to at least four factors:

- The increasing number of students classified as having a specific learning disability (with associated costs).
- The documented effectiveness of early intervention efforts for reducing that number (and associated costs).
- The overrepresentation of minority students in special education.
- The demonstrable problems with IQ-achievement discrepancy assessments.

These four factors point to a distinction between two different groups of low-progress readers, those with reading disabilities and those with low achievement due to environmental factors. Similarly, Gersten and Dimino (2006) have proposed that, given the limited resources that schools possess, it is essential that students not be over-identified for reading disabilities and subsequently placed in intensive interventions that may not be necessary. Research has shown that most efforts to identify reading problems early in development, before formal reading instruction, over-predict reading disabilities (Felton 1992; Jenkins and O'Connor 2000), and that early intervention provides a tool for distinguishing between reading disabilities that are cognitive in nature and reading problems that are due to negative reading experiences, inadequate resources, and/or poor teaching (Clay 1987; Vellutino et al. 1996). An effective RTI process provides a framework for differentiating between these two groups of students.

In Chapter 1, we discussed how teachers' theories of how children learn to read directly influence the types of intervention they select for reading improvement. The CIM takes this basic relationship into account. It is not a scripted program; rather, it is a theoretical framework for implementing evidence-based practices in alignment with processing continuums of change over time in students' literacy behaviors. Consequently, the effectiveness of the intervention depends on the teacher's efficacy at making informed decisions based on the systematic observation of students' learning. Success depends also on the teacher's ability to provide responsive scaffolding that promotes self-regulation and independence. The purpose of this chapter is to build on the theories introduced in the previous chapter and present the CIM as an RTI method for low-progress readers.

COMPREHENSIVE INTERVENTION MODEL

The CIM is grounded in a multitiered, layered system of literacy interventions that increases in intensity and duration based on student needs. The process begins with high-quality classroom instruction and universal screening of all children and provides struggling learners with research-based interventions at increasing degrees of intensity to accelerate their rate of learning. Within this framework, teachers keep systematic data to measure how well the student is responding to intervention, while keeping in mind that rate of growth (acceleration) is the best measure of student responsiveness to instruction. An effective RTI framework includes five essential features:

- Maximizes the effect of core instruction for all students.
- Provides a data-based problem-solving framework for assessing and monitoring student progress over time in response to instruction/intervention.
- Requires classroom and specialty teachers to collaborate on specific ways to scaffold students for success on grade-level curriculum.
- Uses evidence-based and well-delivered interventions with degrees of intensity and duration to meet the unique needs of low-performing readers.
- Results in more accurate identification of students with reading disabilities.

The CIM is based on the philosophy that low-progress readers need consistent instruction that is layered across classroom and supplemental programs. Students with reading difficulties should engage in the same high-quality curriculum as their classmates, although teachers should differentiate the content by providing extra time, adapting specific methods of teaching, and providing additional adult assistance. The CIM interventions are designed to offer "positive differentiation" (Gindis 2003) by varying the degree of intensity and the duration of services.

The CIM uses a layered approach within a four-tier framework for aligning classroom instruction, supplemental interventions, and special education (Dorn and Henderson 2010; Dorn and Schubert 2010; Dorn and Soffos 2015). The interventions are not delivered in a rigid, lockstep manner; instead, the RTI team makes data-driven decisions about the most appropriate intervention (based on intensity, duration, size of group, and teacher expertise) for meeting the unique needs of the individual learners. To remediate reading failure, teachers must understand the challenges faced by poor readers:

- Low-progress readers must unlearn inefficient and inappropriate responses that are preventing them from making literacy progress. Unfortunately, many of these responses have become habituated reactions to problems, thus interfering with the new learning. The situation can be further exacerbated by inappropriate interventions delivered by unqualified staff.
- Low-progress readers must make giant leaps in their learning in order to catch up with their average peers. This can be an upward struggle for low-progress readers. As classroom instruction improves in quality, the reading levels of average readers will also increase, and the achievement gap between the poor and average readers could actually widen. When this occurs, some student may need a temporary intervention to close the gap.
- Low-progress readers must maintain their gains after the intervention has ceased, often in spite of other social or economic issues that can impact literacy. This means that low-performing readers will need sensitive observation and flexible support for at least one year beyond the intervention period.

The CIM includes multiple layers of intervention to promote and sustain reading progress over time. If the student is not responding to intervention, the problem may be with the teaching, not with the student. This diagnostic model requires teachers to use data in systematic ways, including observations of how students are learning on different tasks across changing contexts (classroom, Title 1, special education). The layered framework views all teachers as intervention specialists, including classroom teachers, supplemental teachers, and special education teachers (see Figure 2.1).

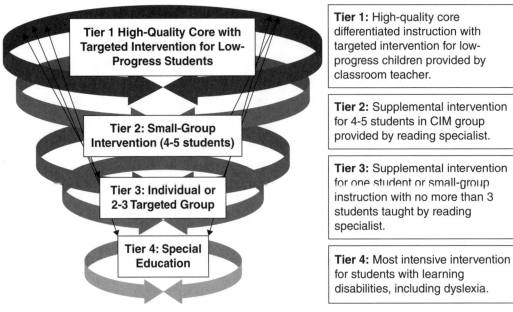

Tier 1: High-quality core differentiated instruction with targeted intervention for low-progress children provided by classroom teacher.

Tier 2: Supplemental intervention for 4-5 students in CIM group provided by reading specialist.

Tier 3: Supplemental intervention for one student or small-group instruction with no more than 3 students taught by reading specialist.

Tier 4: Most intensive intervention for students with learning disabilities, including dyslexia.

Figure 2.1   Layers of Literacy Support Within the Four-Tier Decision-Making Framework

TWO WAVES OF LITERACY DEFENSE

First Wave. The child's best defense against reading failure is a high-quality classroom literacy curriculum delivered by a responsive and knowledgeable classroom teacher. Core instruction should be differentiated to meet the diverse needs of learners and should include evidence-based practices that support reading achievement, such as the following:

- Integrated curriculum that promotes the transfer of knowledge, skills, and strategies across reading, writing, and content areas.
- Clear models and demonstrations with guided practice and explicit feedback.
- In-class grouping strategies with small-group and individualized support to meet student needs.
- Opportunities for volume reading to increase amount of reading experience, as well as vocabulary, content knowledge, and strategy development.
- Effective classroom management with established procedures and high levels of time on task.
- Explicit, systematic, and differentiated instruction, including phonics, comprehension, vocabulary, and writing.
- Balance of rigor and support to ensure students are able to accomplish challenging tasks, with assistance, as needed, from a more knowledgeable person.

School teams can use a modified version of the Environmental Scale for Assessing Implementation Levels (ESAIL) to assess the school's learning climate and literacy curriculum (Scott et al. 2015; see Resource B.1, Environmental Scale for Assessing Implementation Levels (ESAIL), for reproducible form). These resources recognize that the first line of defense for preventing reading difficulties resides in the classroom.

Second Wave. Students who are not responding to high-quality, differentiated classroom instruction (generally 10 to 15 percent of the class) are considered at risk for reading failure and are placed immediately in a more intensive, targeted intervention, where their progress is carefully monitored. The CIM portfolio includes a range of small-group interventions with predictable routines and research-based activities to meet the diverse needs of low-progress readers. As part of the second wave of literacy defense, each intervention is expertly designed to help children acquire skills and strategies for learning from texts of increasing complexity and difficulty.

EARLY TO LATE INTERVENTIONS

Early Intervention (Emergent to Early Transitional Readers). Early readers are generally classified as kindergarten to second-grade students. Students who exhibit characteristics of reading difficulties are provided with early intervention as soon as possible. The premises of early intervention are logical:

● Intervene before confusions turn into habituated or automatic reactions.

● Provide intensive, short-term services that focus on problem-solving strategies in continuous texts.

● Make data-driven decisions about the intensity of interventions, the duration period, and the need for follow-up support.

Early intervention is a preventative measure for enabling beginning readers to develop an effective processing system for learning to read. At this level, intervention focuses on the acquisition of phonological and orthographic knowledge, along with strategic knowledge for constructing meaning within texts that gradually increase in difficulty over time. This period of early reading development changes as students transition to silent reading (Clay 2016).

Later Intervention (Beyond Transitional Readers). Beyond transitional readers are classified as those at third grade and above. With appropriate interventions, readers at risk in the upper grades can become successful readers. However, there are two major challenges to overcome:

● Years of unproductive reading practices can create resistance, passivity, and lack of motivation.

● Interventions may take longer to yield positive results.

At this level, interventions focus on strategic activities for reversing reading failure, including vocabulary and comprehension strategies for inferring deeper meanings within texts. Addressing these challenges requires schools to redesign their classroom programs in four significant ways:

● Implement a model of differentiated instruction, including whole-group, small-group, peer-group, and one-to-one interactions.

● Build students' background knowledge of content through multiple tools, including traditional texts, digital resources, videos, and creative projects.

● Teach comprehension strategies and vocabulary strategies for understanding complex topics.

● Provide literacy interventions, including small-group and one-to-one, for students who are lagging behind.

A DECISION-MAKING FRAMEWORK

For decades, many schools have used a discrepancy model for identifying students with learning disabilities. This deficit approach assumes that the problem lies within the child, while ignoring the fact that external factors (e.g., flawed assessments, inappropriate materials, limited opportunities, poor instruction) may be the root cause of reading difficulties (Spear-Swerling and Sternberg 1996). As a result, many children are identified as learning disabled based on an inefficient school system (Aaron 1997; Allington 2002a).

Clay (1987) argued that learning-disabled and low-achieving readers are virtually indistinguishable groups. She insisted that there is no evidence to suggest that children with learning disabilities should be taught any differently than children with reading difficulties. Many of the programs developed for poor readers, generally by specialists in the field of reading, might also be highly appropriate for children with learning disabilities.

Critical factors that increase the likelihood of success for small-group interventions have been cited in numerous research reports (Allington 2002a, Mathes and Torgeson 1998, Scanlon and Vellutino 1996, Schwartz 2005; Vellutino et al. 2008). The small-group interventions in the CIM portfolio were developed, evaluated, and refined in partnership with literacy colleagues across the country (Dorn, Doore, and Soffos 2015). Literacy components within the CIM include (a) phonemic awareness, (b) phonics, (c) oral language, (d) fluency, (e) vocabulary, (f) comprehension, and (g) writing.

Within the CIM framework, teachers employ data-driven decision-making processes, including selecting books, prompting for strategies, and teaching for independence and transfer. In essence, the CIM is characterized by ten features:

- Decision-making framework with predictable lesson components.
- Balance of rigor and support.
- Evidence-based practices that reflect a high-quality classroom curriculum.
- Acceleration versus remediation.
- Brisk and targeted pacing.
- Reading and writing reciprocity.
- Metacognition, goal-setting, and strategic processing.
- Explicit teaching, clear modeling, guided practice, and transfer.
- Authentic texts to promote motivation and sustained attention.
- Built-in assessment (dynamic) with progress-monitoring intervals for checking on growth in relation to average students.

THE PORTFOLIO OF INTERVENTIONS

The CIM portfolio includes a collection of six small-group interventions for kindergarten to secondary level: (1) Guided Reading Plus (GRP), (2) Interactive Writing (IW), (3) Writing Aloud (WA), (4) Comprehension Focus Group (CFG), (5) Strategic Processing Intervention (SPI), and (6) Targeted Interventions (TI). (See Table 2.1 and Resource B.2, Comprehensive Intervention Model (CIM) Portfolio of Interventions.)

Table 2.1.   CIM Portfolio of Small-Group Interventions and Alignment to Classroom

Intervention	Role of Reading	Role of Writing	Alignment to Classroom
Guided Reading Plus (GRP) Emergent to Beginning Transitional Levels	Reading strategies, fluency, word-solving strategies, comprehension, vocabulary development	Writing about reading, word-solving/spelling strategies, composing and planning strategies, reading and writing reciprocity	Guided Reading Group Word Study and Vocabulary Writing About Reading Interactive Read Aloud
Assisted Writing Group • Interactive Writing Emergent to Beginning Early Levels	Concepts of print, reading and writing reciprocity, letter and word knowledge, early reading strategies	Concepts of print, fluent composing, word-solving strategies, early revising and editing strategies, composing meaningful messages, phonological awareness, reading and writing reciprocity	Interactive Writing Shared Reading Guided Reading Word Study and Vocabulary

(Continued)

Table 2.1. (*Continued*)

Assisted Writing Group • Writing Aloud Beginning Early to Beyond Transitional Level	Reading and writing reciprocity, vocabulary, word-solving strategies, text structure	Writing for different audiences, revising and editing strategies, text structure, writing craft, vocabulary and language conventions, spelling strategies	Interactive Read Aloud Word Study and Vocabulary Writing Process Guided Reading Group
Targeted Interventions • Literacy Task Cards • Writing Process • Close Reading Strategies Emergent to Transitional and Beyond Levels	Language development, decoding skills, cognitive flexibility, comprehension strategies	Writing strategies Writing process Spelling	Language Workshop Reading Workshop Writing Workshop Word Study and Vocabulary
Comprehension Focus Group (CFG) Late Transitional and Beyond	Text structures, writing craft, reading strategies, close reading, integration of knowledge, ideas, and concepts, complex vocabulary, language conventions	Writing strategies and processes (planning, composing, revising, editing), text structure, writing craft, vocabulary, language conventions, reading and writing reciprocity	Language Workshop Literature Discussion Groups Reading Workshop Writing Workshop Research Projects
Strategic Processing Intervention (SPI) Early to Beyond Transitional Level	Reading strategies, fluency, word-solving strategies, comprehension, vocabulary development	Writing about reading, word-solving/spelling strategies, composing and planning strategies, reading and writing reciprocity	Language Workshop Reading Workshop Writing Workshop Word Study and Vocabulary

The small-group interventions can be taught by classroom teachers (Tier 1), supplemental teachers (Tiers 2 and 3), and special education teachers (Tier 4). The intensity of each intervention is determined by group size, which can range from two to ten students. In some cases, specifically with SPI or TI, the teacher may deliver a one-to-one intervention for special needs. Following diagnostic assessment, an intervention team is convened, and teachers collaborate on the most appropriate intervention to meet the unique needs of the students (see Chapters 3 and 10 for video examples). Each intervention can be implemented within or outside of the classroom as a supplemental intervention.

Guided Reading Plus Intervention. The GRP is designed for early readers who are building foundational skills for learning to read. The addition of writing and word study to the reading intervention is especially important for struggling readers. Writing plays a special role in lifting reading achievement, as writing slows down the reading process and increases the reader's orthographic and phonological knowledge through motor production. The GRP intervention enables struggling readers to read for understanding, practice efficient decoding strategies, use what they know about reading to assist with their writing, and vice versa.

Interactive Writing Intervention. The IW intervention is designed for beginning readers at the emergent to early levels. The physical act of writing slows down the reading process; and if the writing is meaningful, it promotes the integration of three language systems: (a) comprehension of ideas (meaning system); (b) expression of ideas (language system); and (c) facility with mechanics (graphophonemic and motor systems). The teacher creates opportunities to shape children's knowledge and skills in the following areas:

- Building phonological awareness and concepts about print.
- Composing and transcribing a meaningful message.
- Applying rereading strategies to predict and monitor reading.
- Articulating words slowly and hearing and recording letters in words.
- Using simple resources as self-help tools (e.g., ABC chart, personal dictionary).
- Becoming fluent with correct letter formation.
- Building a core of high-frequency words.
- Cross-checking sources of information.

Writing Aloud Intervention. The WA intervention is designed for students who are reading at the transitional level or beyond, but are experiencing difficulty with the writing process. The goal is to assist students in understanding that writing includes a process of generating ideas, drafting a message, revising, editing, and preparing a piece for a particular audience. The WA intervention includes five elements:

- Explicit teaching through strategy-based minilessons
- Group compositions
- Individual writing
- Teacher conferences
- Student reflection and self-assessments

Comprehension Focus Group Intervention. The CFG intervention is designed for readers who have transitioned into silent reading. Each intervention consists of a series of reading and writing lessons with a specific focus, delivered over a period of weeks. The intervention is organized around units of study that require readers to apply higher-level comprehension strategies to analyze relationships within and across texts. Reading and writing are viewed as reciprocal processes; therefore, students are taught to use their knowledge from reading to support their writing and vice versa. The CFG intervention consists of three phases: (a) the language phase, (b) the reading phase, and (c) the writing phase.

Strategic Processing Intervention. The SPI incorporates the four essential elements of research-based reading interventions: (1) phonological awareness, decoding, and word study, (2) independent reading of progressively more difficult texts, (3) writing activities, and (4) comprehension practice with meaningful texts

(Scammacca et al. 2007). Additionally, the SPI emphasizes listening and speaking comprehension through read-aloud activities, plus formative assessments at designated intervals to monitor students' capacity to transfer knowledge, skills, and strategies to new texts.

The SPI includes three language-based phases that work together to build students' control of oral and written language. Each phase is thirty to forty-five minutes long, depending on the size of the group, and includes systematic activities that align with evidence-based practices for teaching children with reading difficulties. Additionally, the SPI includes an assessment phase at two-week intervals for monitoring students' ability to transfer knowledge and skills to new tasks.

Targeted Interventions. TIs are designed to emphasize particular areas where students may need more precise, direct instruction. These interventions can be delivered as short-term stand-alone lessons within the CIM portfolio. For example, if a student's learning rate in the GRP intervention is lower than expected as a result of decoding errors, the student could receive a TI for a short duration. Word-level interventions should be carefully monitored to determine the student's ability to transfer knowledge of letters, sounds, and words to reading and writing in continuous texts.

The Phonics Task Cards are a targeted intervention that employs a systematic sequence of phonological and orthographic activities with opportunities for students to perform specific tasks in both assisted and unassisted settings. Based on the processing continuum of simple to more complex actions, the word-solving tasks require students to process multiple sources of information, and also to write about their problem-solving steps in a learning log. Because this is a targeted intervention, the teacher models the task procedures while simultaneously using descriptive language and standard tools to communicate the task goals. To ensure that students understand the task, the teacher provides them with two or three new examples, observes their behaviors, and scaffolds them accordingly to facilitate their success. In the final steps of the intervention, the teacher reviews the task procedures, checks to make sure each student understands the learning goal, introduces the new task card, and sends students off to work independently on the new task. The overall goal of the Phonics Task Cards is to develop self-regulated learners with a focus on metacognition and transfer. In Videos 2.1, 2.2, and 2.3, we share how three readers at different levels use the Phonics Task Cards to orchestrate multiple actions for planning, monitoring, searching, and self-correcting their thinking while maintaining a focus on the learning goal.

Video 2.1   In the next three videos, the phonics tasks are systematically designed to promote self-regulated learners with the capacity to initiate plans, monitor their actions, and work toward a solution. The teacher introduces the task procedures and associated language, followed by opportunities for students to carry out the actions with teacher scaffolding. 2.1 shows an emergent reader, 2.2, an early reader, and 2.3, a transitional reader.

Video 2.2

  Video 2.3

In support of the research on cognitive flexibility (Cartwright 2012), teachers can create task cards that require students to classify information simultaneously according to phonological and semantic properties (See Figure 2.2).

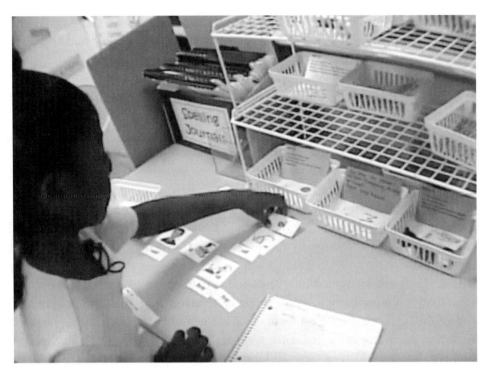

Figure 2.2   During the targeted intervention, an early reader works independently on a phonics task for learning vowel patterns.

Integration and flexibility are critical aspects of self-regulated thinking. Other types of targeted interventions include Writing About Reading, studying vocabulary, analyzing text structure, and practicing comprehension strategies. In all cases, the targeted interventions emphasize the integration of the oral and written language systems. (See Resource B.3, Planner for Targeted Interventions, for reproducible form.)

MATCHING INTERVENTIONS TO STUDENTS

The portfolio approach is validated by the belief that children possess unique strengths and needs; therefore, an intervention should be carefully selected to match the particular student. The identification of students with reading difficulties is a complex process that requires a comprehensive literacy diagnosis (see Dorn and Henderson 2010b). The diagnosis consists of a battery of literacy assessments, including classroom observations. Following the literacy diagnostic, the intervention team (e.g., classroom teachers, specialists, administrators) meets to discuss the student's progress and select the most appropriate intervention for the student.

Once the student is selected to receive an intervention, the team completes an RTI Planner. (See Figure 2.3; see also Resource B.4, Response to Intervention Planner for Aligning and Layering Interventions, for reproducible form.) The RTI Planner is a collaborative tool for aligning and layering services across classroom and supplemental programs. For example, if a student's diagnostic indicates a weakness in phonics, the student's classroom intervention (Tier 1) might include a ten-minute word study lesson prior to the guided reading lesson for three days a week; and the supplemental intervention (Tier 2 or 3) might be GRP with careful attention to the development of word knowledge in both reading and writing. The RTI Planner serves as a chronological record of any intervention that a student receives (classroom, small-group, or one-to-one) and outlines the plan for instruction, the monitoring of that plan, and the intensity and duration of the intervention (Meyer and Reindl 2010). In Chapter 3,

RTI Plan for Aligning and Layering Literacy Interventions

Student_____ Grade _____ Classroom Teacher_____ Date_____

		Degrees of Intensity			
		Individual or Small Group	**Small Group**	**Whole Class**	**Independent Work**
Classroom: Tier I	**Universal**	☐ Reading Conference ☐ Writing Conference	☐ Guided Reading Group ☐ Word Study ☐ Vocabulary Study ☐ Literature Discussion Group ☐ Writing About Reading ☐ Reading and Writing Conferences	☐ Strategy Lessons ☐ Interactive Read Aloud ☐ Shared Reading ☐ Integrated Workshop Lessons/Minilessons ☐ Spelling/Phonics/Word Study ☐ Vocabulary Studies	☐ Familiar/Independent Reading ☐ Writing ☐ Phonics or Vocabulary Tasks ☐ Literature Extensions ☐ Research Projects ☐ Internet Projects
	Intervention	**1:1 or Small Group (2-3)** ☐ Targeted Intervention	**Small Group (4-5)** ☐ Word Study ☐ Writing About Reading ☐ Assisted Writing Group ☐ Vocabulary Study ☐ Targeted Intervention	**Plan/Monitoring/Duration**	
Intervention Specialist	**Tier II**	**Small Group (4-5)** ☐ Guided Reading Plus Group ☐ Comprehension Focus Group ☐ Assisted Writing Group		**Plan/Monitoring/Duration**	
	Tier III	**Individual** ☐ Targeted Intervention ☐ Strategic Processing Intervention	**Small Group (2-3)** ☐ Guided Reading Plus Group ☐ Comprehension Focus Group ☐ Assisted Writing Group ☐ Targeted Intervention ☐ Strategic Processing Group	**Plan/Monitoring/Duration**	
Special Education	**Tier IV**	**Individual** ☐ Targeted Intervention ☐ Strategic Processing Intervention	**Small Group (2-5)** ☐ Guided Reading Plus Group ☐ Comprehension Focus Group ☐ Assisted Writing Group ☐ Strategic Processing Intervention Group ☐ Targeted Intervention	**Plan/Monitoring/Duration**	

Layers of Support/Expertise

Team Members Present: _____

Next Meeting:_____

Figure 2.3 Response to Intervention Planner for Aligning and Layering Interventions

we share how teachers are using the RTI planner to align instructional support for a struggling reader across classroom and intervention settings.

CLOSING THOUGHTS

In this chapter, we have proposed that students with reading difficulties often develop inefficient systems for regulating their reading, and that intervention can prevent or reverse these reading problems. The goal of intervention is to create a learning context that enables students to acquire metacognitive strategies for planning, monitoring, and self-correcting their reading. These strategies are grounded in higher-level psychological processes of consciousness, attention, and voluntary memory. An intervention should focus on the development of self-regulation and transfer rather than on the acquisition of simple items of knowledge.

The CIM is a theoretical framework for layering interventions across classroom and intervention settings, ensuring consistency for the most fragile learners. The portfolio of interventions is grounded in the theory that struggling readers have unique needs, and that a range of interventions provides options for matching the intervention to the learner.

The portfolio is based on four principles:

- Teachers select the most appropriate intervention to meet student needs.
- Intervention aligns with high-quality classroom instruction.
- Student progress is closely monitored across interventions and classroom instruction.
- Intervention teams collaborate on student learning and make data-based decisions for continued improvement.

The heartbeat of the CIM is the responsive teacher who understands that if a child is not responding to intervention, the problem is with the intervention, not the child. In the following chapters, we present details for implementing the CIM as a process for meeting the unique needs of struggling readers.

Chapter 3

A COMPREHENSIVE ASSESSMENT AND INTERVENTION SYSTEM

In this chapter, we discuss the role of assessments in the CIM within the CIM portfolio, assessment and instruction are viewed as reciprocal and recursive processes. The teacher uses assessment to design the best intervention for the student, while assessing the effectiveness of the intervention according to how well the student is responding. Response to Intervention serves two purposes:

- It provides intervention for students who are at risk of school failure.
- It develops more valid procedures for identifying students with reading disabilities.

Students at risk of reading failure may exhibit haphazard behaviors when responding to problems, making accurate assessment difficult; therefore, the assessment process should involve multiple perspectives and sources of data. In order to make valid decisions about instruction and intervention, teachers must be sensitive observers of literacy behaviors—specifically, of how students respond to instruction—and they must be able to adjust their teaching to accommodate students' learning. To be able to make useful observations and subtle adjustments, teachers must first understand two basic facts:

- Learning occurs along a psychological continuum of simple to more complex processing.
- The student's capacity to learn is shaped by instructional opportunities with a knowledgeable and responsive teacher.

All interventions in the CIM are designed to accelerate student reading achievement through the process of scaffolding. The idea of scaffolding comes from the work of Lev Vygotsky. Vygotsky (1978) maintained that intellectual development occurs as children work in two complementary learning zones:

- **Zone of Actual Development (ZAD) (or Actual Level).** This is where the child can accomplish a learning task independently.
- **Zone of Proximal Development (ZPD) (or Potential Level).** This is where the child is able to accomplish a task but requires the assistance and guidance of a more knowledgeable person. The ZPD is the area of the child's potential development, but success depends on the teacher's ability to structure appropriate tasks and use language that lifts the child's understanding to a higher level.

According to Vygotsky, the child's cognitive, linguistic, and social functioning in educational settings are not innate abilities or disabilities; rather, these processes are formed during instructional interactions with a more knowledgeable person. Vygotsky insisted that the assessment of the child's ability to learn through collaborative activity is a better predictor of future cognitive functioning than measures of independent performance through traditional assessments (Kozulin et al. 2003).

In this chapter, we keep Vygotsky's insight in mind as we discuss the role of assessments in the CIM. First, we describe how schools can create a Comprehensive Literacy Diagnostic (CLD) as an RTI assessment and intervention process. Then we provide details for the various assessments that are part of the CLD, including the use of dynamic assessment for determining the child's capacity to perform higher-level tasks during scaffolded experiences.

Table 3.1.   Three Types of Assessments in a Comprehensive Literacy Diagnostic

Pre- and Post-Intervention	During the Intervention	At Designated Points
Comprehensive portfolio of all assessments, including standardized measures, classroom observations, and work samples, to inform decision about intervention	Daily ongoing formative assessments for analyzing how well the student is responding to intervention. Also, as needed, dynamic assessment to determine optimal level of challenge.	Progress-monitoring assessments at preestablished intervals for monitoring the student's growth in comparison to average-performing peers.

A COMPREHENSIVE LITERACY DIAGNOSTIC

A CLD is a portfolio of literacy assessments that serves three purposes as an RTI method:

- It identifies students at risk of reading failure.
- It matches students to the appropriate intervention.
- It monitors students' responsiveness to the intervention (see Dorn and Henderson 2010b).

This comprehensive process greatly reduces the problem of misidentification and the dangers that go with it: providing intervention to students who do not need it (false positives) and denying intervention to students who do need it (false negatives) (Pedhazur and Schmelkin 1991).

The CLD includes three types of assessments, which are administered at designated periods: (1) pre- and post-assessments to determine the student's actual level of development prior to and after the intervention, (2) ongoing formative assessments to determine the student's potential to learn from the intervention, including dynamic assessments, as needed, to determine optimal level of challenge, and (3) progress monitoring assessments to measure the student's rate of learning on instructional tasks administered at frequent intervals (see Table 3.1).

PRE- AND POST-INTERVENTION: DIAGNOSTIC ASSESSMENTS

The assessment process begins with the classroom teacher, who recommends a student for diagnostic assessment based on the student's difficulty in the classroom literacy program. The school's reading specialist administers the appropriate assessments to determine the student's strengths and needs. For example, a kindergarten student with at-risk behaviors in the classroom might be identified for further testing on several diagnostic measures, such as the Observation Survey, Emergent Writing Assessment, Record of Oral Language, word recognition, and a phonological assessment. Other examples of diagnostic assessments for struggling readers include text reading assessment, comprehension measure, fluency scale, spelling assessment, and writing assessment.

The diagnostic assessments are administered at pre- and post-intervention periods; therefore, alternative versions of each assessment must be available. Diagnostic assessment requires an in-depth analysis of a student's literacy behaviors in order to identify strengths and needs in specific areas. Prior to intervention, the teacher compiles the information into a diagnostic summary with specific recommendations for intervention. After the intervention, the post-test version of the assessment is administered and results are documented, including specific recommendations for monitoring the student's progress over a designated period.

COMPREHENSIVE ASSESSMENT PORTFOLIO

Following diagnostic testing and prior to intervention, the RTI team collects other assessments to create a comprehensive portfolio of the student's learning. These supplemental assessments may include both formative and summative measures. Formative assessments provide evidence of the student's ability to learn from classroom instruction and include measures such as observation checklists, selected work samples, running records, and informal rubrics. Summative assessments provide evidence of the student's ability to accomplish particular tasks with proficiency and without assistance. The RTI team examines the full range of assessments to determine whether the student needs an intervention. If so, the team discusses the purpose of each intervention and selects the most appropriate intervention for the student. As discussed in Chapter 2, the team uses the RtI Plan for Aligning and Layering Interventions to align interventions across classroom and supplemental layers. (See Resource B.4, for the form.) The Intervention Planner provides a record of the student's interventions (classroom, small-group, or one-to-one) over time and outlines the plan for instruction, how the plan will be monitored, and the intensity and duration of the intervention.

DURING THE INTERVENTION: DYNAMIC ASSESSMENTS

Dynamic Assessment (DA) occurs as needed during the intervention. Since DA is intertwined with teaching, the student's ability to respond to instruction is observed carefully during the process of learning. The goal of DA is to discover whether and how much the learner will change under the influence of scaffolding activities (Lidz and Gindis 2003). Essentially, DA is interactive and open ended, and generates information about the responsiveness of the learner to intervention. From an RTI perspective, DA is especially relevant because it embeds intervention within the assessment procedure.

Dynamic Assessment occurs in the student's zone of proximal development; therefore, the teacher must understand how to scaffold the student's learning in order to accomplish new tasks. With DA, teaching is embedded into the assessment, thus providing evidence of how much help a student might need to tackle a similar task. If the teacher has to provide too much help, the task might be too difficult. In our forthcoming book, *Teaching for Transfer*, we illustrate how teachers can use DA procedures to determine the optimal (challenge) level at which a student can read with scaffolding. This method is especially beneficial for identifying challenging texts for older readers who are participating in the CFG intervention.

The DA process can be used to assess a student's potential to learn a new strategy or principle based on what the student already knows. For example, when planning for word study instruction, the teacher can create a structured protocol to assess the student's ability to transfer a spelling principle to a new word with varying degrees of teacher scaffolding. Here are the steps in the process:

- The teacher assesses the student's independent knowledge of spelling patterns based on a standardized spelling measure (e.g., Ganske 2000; Gunning 2000, 2012).
- Then the teacher moves to a higher level on the spelling continuum to assess the students' optimal level.
- The teacher reminds the student of what they already know that is relevant to the new learning, then provides an explicit explanation of the new pattern to be learned.
- The teacher engages the student in guided practice with the new concept, scaffolding as needed to promote understanding.
- If the student is able to perform the task with minimal assistance, the teacher introduces a new word with the same pattern and provides varying degrees of assistance to determine the student's learning potential.
- The teacher assesses the student's ability to learn from assisted instruction.

Formative assessments in the form of running records and writing samples provide authentic data for planning instruction on a day-by-day, student-by-student basis. The teacher uses running records to analyze how a student is responding to the intervention, and also to inform the teacher's decisions about book selections and teaching prompts. At the same time, writing samples provide the teacher with data on a student's ability to transfer information across reading and writing goals. Most importantly, ongoing formative assessments provide the teacher with critical data for documenting the student's control and flexibility of knowledge across multiple literacy tasks.

PROGRESS MONITORING ASSESSMENTS

Progress monitoring assessments provide evidence of how well the student is responding to the intervention. The assessments are designed to measure the student's ability to accomplish independently a literacy task that relates to the intervention (Afflerbach and Klein, 2020). A well-designed progress monitoring assessment includes four features:

- It focuses on integration and strategies for problem-solving within texts.
- It occurs on new material (e.g., a new book or a new writing task).
- It includes a standardized administration (e.g., book introduction, purpose for reading, or writing prompt).
- It takes place at designated intervals that align with benchmark points of average achievement.

Progress monitoring assessment occurs at predetermined intervals during the course of the intervention (generally every four weeks), and it assesses a student's ability to read an unseen text. Teachers can use text reading levels as a valid measure for progress monitoring (see Dorn, Doore, and Soffos 2015). The first step is to determine benchmarks for beginning, quarterly, and end-of-year text reading levels. Then the student's beginning text reading level is plotted, and an AIM line (benchmark standard) is drawn from the beginning-of-year benchmark to end-of-year grade-level expectation for text reading level. This AIM line marks the path a teacher will need to take in order to move a student from their current level of performance to grade-level norms. By drawing a line from a student's current benchmark to end-of-year expectations, the teacher can determine whether the student is progressing (accelerating) enough to reach grade-level norms by the end of the school year. As long as the student's performance is at or above the AIM line, the teacher can be reasonably assured that the intervention is instructionally appropriate. (See Resource C.1a, b, c, and d, AIM Lines for Grades One to Four.)

The student's growth along the AIM line is assessed through progress monitoring at frequent intervals. In Figure 3.1, we provide an example of a student's responsiveness to intervention over a one-year period. At the beginning of second grade, the student scored significantly below the average reading level and was recommended for the Guided Reading Plus (GRP) intervention. The GRP intervention included six text reading level assessment points for progress monitoring throughout the year. The AIM line revealed a significant dip in reading acceleration at week 18; therefore, the RTI team met to discuss adjustments to the student's intervention plan. Upon further examination of the student's writing journal, the team concluded that writing was a weak area for the student and recommended that the Writing Aloud (WA) intervention be alternated with the GRP intervention (i.e., one week for GRP followed by one week for WA). In this example, the teacher's decision to combine a more targeted writing intervention with the reading intervention increased the student's rate of learning on text reading levels.

If the intervention fails to alter the trajectory of the student's progress, the intervention team reconvenes to engage in continued and collaborative problem-solving. This problem-solving process includes the following steps:

- Identifying any additional information that may need to be collected.
- Determining how to best obtain that information.
- Interpreting and evaluating the new information against previous information.
- Adapting or designing instruction within the portfolio of interventions to ensure the student's literacy growth.

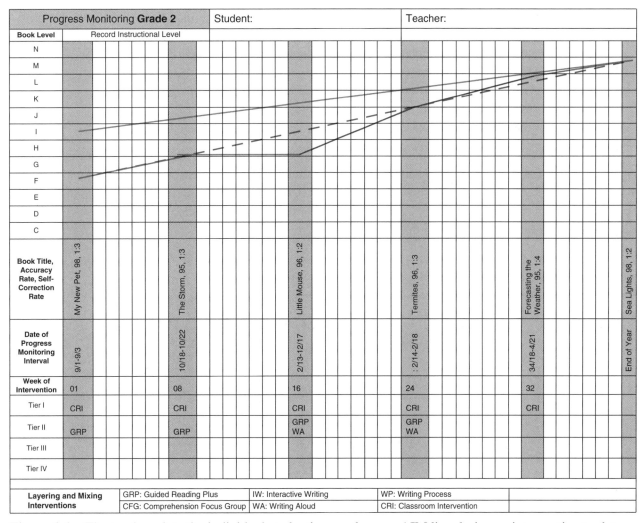

Progress Monitoring **Grade 2**		Student:		Teacher:			
Book Level	Record Instructional Level						

Book Title, Accuracy Rate, Self-Correction Rate

	My New Pet, 98, 1:3	The Storm, 95, 1:3	Little Mouse, 96, 1:2	Termites, 96, 1:3	Forecasting the Weather, 95, 1:4	Sea Lights, 98, 1:2

Date of Progress Monitoring Interval	9/1-9/3	10/18-10/22	2/13-12/17	: 2/14-2/18	34/18-4/21	End of Year
Week of Intervention	01	08	16	24	32	
Tier I	CRI	CRI	CRI	CRI	CRI	
Tier II	GRP	GRP	GRP WA	GRP WA		
Tier III						
Tier IV						

Layering and Mixing Interventions	GRP: Guided Reading Plus	IW: Interactive Writing	WP: Writing Process	
	CFG: Comprehension Focus Group	WA: Writing Aloud	CRI: Classroom Intervention	

Figure 3.1   The teacher plots the individual student's growth on an AIM line during an intervention to determine the effectiveness of the intervention in narrowing the literacy gap on benchmark criteria. In this example, the student began the intervention significantly below the benchmark and reached the benchmark at the end of the school year.

Based on the student's response patterns as charted on the text reading AIM line at progress monitoring points, teachers should consider the impact of a specific intervention in accelerating the student's reading gains toward the benchmark goal. Using a decision-making framework, teachers should adjust or revise the intervention according to three decision rules, laid out by Batsche et al. (2005):

1. **Positive response to the intervention:**
   - Continue the intervention with the current benchmark goal.
   - Continue the intervention with the benchmark goal increased.
   - Fade the intervention to determine if the student has acquired functional independence.
2. **Questionable response to the intervention:**
   - Determine whether the intervention was implemented as designed (See Resources C.10a, b, c, d, e, and f, for Observation Protocols).
   - If it was not, examine areas where the intervention was compromised and initiate strategies for implementing the intervention with integrity.

- If it was, increase the intensity of the intervention for a short period of time to assess impact. If the student's response rate improves, continue with the intervention. If the response rate does not improve, meet with RTI team to determine a more appropriate intervention for the student.

3. **Poor response to the intervention:**
   - Determine whether the intervention was implemented as designed.
   - If it was, meet with the RTI team to examine student data for problem areas.
   - Select a new intervention based on student needs with benchmarks, goals, and frequent progress monitoring.

Electronic AIM Lines. An electronic AIM line can provide teachers with a tool for triangulating and analyzing student data for shifts in learning patterns over time, thus enabling teachers to make data-based decisions that result in the student's accelerated growth. In Chapter 10, we share details, including video applications, for how CIM teachers can use an electronic AIM line to monitor the progress of their students. Below, in Figure 3.2, we provide an illustration of the electronic AIM line.

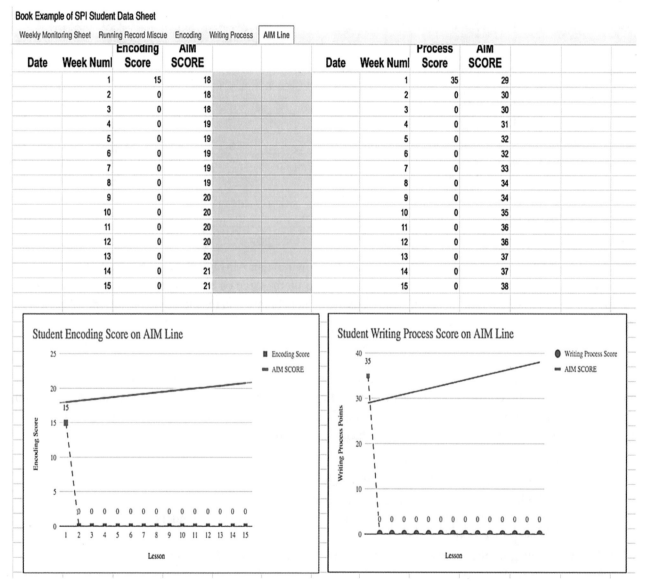

Figure 3.2   CIM teachers use an electronic AIM line to analyze reading and writing data for shifts in literacy processing over time.

ASSESSMENTS IN THE COMPREHENSIVE INTERVENTION MODEL

In this section, we provide details for each assessment in the CIM, including how a range of literacy assessments is aggregated into a CLD for each child. Teachers should select the most appropriate assessments to create a comprehensive diagnostic portfolio for the individual student, thus providing the RTI team with a valid measure for studying change over time in the student's learning in response to a specific intervention. Some of the assessments may be used for multiple purposes; for example, the writing prompt/rubric might be included in the pre-intervention portfolio and also used to monitor a student's progress during the intervention. Table 3.2 illustrates the assessment system for each intervention in the CIM.

Observation Survey of Early Literacy Achievement. The Observation Survey of Early Literacy Achievement was developed by Marie Clay to "capture some of the rapid change that occurs in early literacy awareness" (2019, 1). The survey includes six subtests: Letter Identification, Word Test, Concepts About Print, Hearing and Recording Sounds in Words, Writing Vocabulary Test, and text reading. The measures should not be used in isolation. Instead, teachers should examine the child's progress across all measures to identify strengths and areas of needs. After the survey, the teacher writes a diagnostic summary with recommendations for intervention.

Letter Identification, Sounds, and Handwriting. Teachers should keep a record of children's knowledge of letters and sounds, digraphs, and blends and sounds, plus children's ability to form the letters in the correct order (serial and sequential orders). In Resource C.2, Assessment Forms for Letter Identification, Sounds, and Handwriting, and Resource C.3, Assessment Forms for Beginning Blends and Digraphs, we provide several measures for assessing children's knowledge of orthographic and phonological information.

Emergent Writing Assessment. The emergent writing sample is designed to assess a child's ability to draw a picture, compose an oral message based on the picture, and use written symbols to represent the message. The assessment should be administered in a standardized format, according to the following procedures. (See Figure 3.3 for an example of an emergent writing assessment.)

- The teacher prompts the child to draw a picture. Some sample prompts could be to draw a picture of themselves or someone in their family, a picture of a favorite animal, a picture of a friend, or a picture of a favorite food. Tell the child that there will be a time limit and encourage them to work quickly. If a child says they cannot draw, encourage them by saying something like "Just do your best." Let the child know that you also want them to tell the story of the picture by writing it.
- After the child completes the drawing, tell the child that you would like them to write about their picture. Tell the child that you will not help them and that whatever they do will be just fine. If necessary, provide a separate sheet of paper for writing. If the child claims they cannot write, tell them to pretend to write. Try not to distract the child from writing by talking to them; however, if a child appears to need encouragement or further prompting, you should provide this extra support. Do not make comments about the child's writing (not even "You're doing a good job"). If you do not understand something that you observe, ask the child a quick question about it.
- When the child finishes, ask them to read the piece to you. Record what the child reads or pretends to read.
- Respond to the content of the writing in a specific and positive way—for example, "It sounds like you and Betsy had a wonderful time playing together."
- Use Clay's (1975) Writing Sample Assessment Rubric to score the writing.
- During the next two days, collect two additional pieces of writing from the child using the methods outlined above. Use the three assessments to diagnose the child's strengths and needs in writing.

Record of Oral Language. The Record of Oral Language (ROL) was developed by Clay et al. (2015b) to assess a student's knowledge and control over oral language structures. The ROL provides teachers with a tool for observing and recording a child's level of language performance, measuring progress over time, and isolating areas of difficulty. The ROL, as part of a literacy diagnostic, can be used to identify students for an Emergent Language and Literacy Intervention with an emphasis on oracy instruction.

Table 3.2. CIM Assessment and Intervention System

Intervention (Type, Level, & Setting)	Diagnostic Assessments (Pre-and Post-Intervention)	Comprehensive Literacy diagnostic (Pre-and Post-Intervention)	Dynamic Assessment (Ongoing Informal Assessments)	Progress Monitoring Assessments (Designated Intervals)
Guided Reading Plus Group Emergent – Transitional (pullout or push-in setting)	Text Reading Level (running records), Reading Behavior Checklist, Fluency Scale, Comprehension Guide, Writing About Reading Prompt and Checklist, Word Test, Phonological Assessment, Letter, Sound, and Handwriting Assessment	Summary of diagnostic assessments, classroom observation checklist, selected work samples, test results from district assessments, classroom rubrics/ checklist	Running records, known words in personal dictionary, writing journal or response log, anecdotal notes from reading and writing observations	Text Reading Level (running record), Reading Behavior Checklist, Fluency Scale, Comprehension Guide, Writing about Reading Prompt and Checklist
Assisted Writing-Interactive Writing Emergent – Beginning Early (pullout or push-in)	Text Reading Level (running records), Word Test, Writing Prompt with Rubric, Phonological Assessment, Letter, Sound, and Handwriting Assessment	Summary of diagnostic assessments, classroom observation checklist, selected work samples, test results from district assessments, classroom rubrics/ checklist	Writing journal, known words in personal dictionary, anecdotal notes from writing observations	Text Reading Level (running records), Reading Behavior Checklist, Writing Prompt And Checklist
Assisted Writing-Writing Aloud Group Late Early - Transitional (pullout or push-in)	Text Reading Level, Word Test, Writing Prompt with Rubric, Phonological Assessment		Writing samples, anecdotal notes from writing observations	Text Reading Level (running records), Reading Behavior Checklist, Fluency Scale, Writing Prompt and Checklist

(Continued)

Comprehension Focus Group Transitional and Beyond (pullout or push-in)	Text Reading (IRI & Miscue Analysis), Comprehension Guide, Writing About Reading Prompt and checklist	Summary of diagnostic assessments, classroom observation checklist, selected work samples, test results from district assessments, classroom rubrics/ checklist	Text Reading (running records), anecdotal notes from reading observations Writing samples, anecdotal notes from writing observations	Text Reading (IRI and Miscue Analysis), Fluency Scale, Comprehension Guide, Writing about Reading Prompt and Checklist
Strategic Processing Intervention Early to Transitional and Beyond	Text Reading Level (running records) or Text Reading (IRI & Miscue Analysis), Reading Behavior Checklist, Fluency Scale, Comprehension Guide, Writing About Reading Prompt and checklist, Phonological Assessment, Letter, Sound and Handwriting Assessment, Spelling Assessment and Norm-Referenced Assessments if needed	Summary of diagnostic assessments, classroom observation checklist, selected work samples from classroom, test results from district assessment, classroom rubrics/ checklist	Text Reading (running records), writing journal or response log, anecdotal notes from reading, writing	Text Reading Level (running records) or Text Reading (IRI & Miscue Analysis), Reading Behavior Checklist, Fluency Scale, Comprehension Guide, Writing About Reading Prompt and Checklist

Emergent Writing Prompt

Writing Prompt
"Draw a picture and write a story about it."

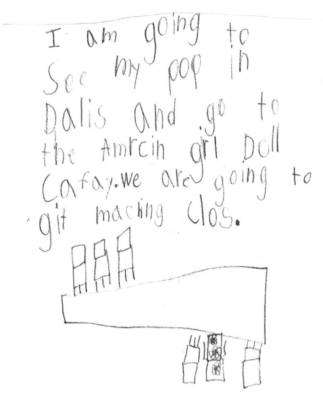

Figure 3.3   Example of Emergent Prompted Writing Assessment

Timed Word Writing Prompt. A quick assessment for determining a student's word knowledge is a ten-minute timed word-writing measure. The assessment is structured to provide insights into various aspects of the student's knowledge about print: (1) types of words the student writes, such as words from the environment (e.g., McDonalds), interesting words (e.g., dinosaur), and important words (e.g., names of friends or family); (2) words the student is able to write correctly (e.g., high-frequency words); and (3) words the student attempts to write, including strategies used to spell the words. As the student writes, the teacher records evidence of risk-taking behaviors, writing fluency, letter formation, and pattern knowledge. The assessment begins with general writing prompts: "Can you write your name?" "Can you write anyone else's name?" "Do you know any other words?" This interval is followed by more specific prompts for assessing a student's knowledge of commonly occurring words (e.g., *I, am, is, can, me, go, my, he, come, it*) from easy texts; this is not a dictated list but can help a student get started. The assessment continues for the full ten minutes (see Figure 3.4).

Phonological Awareness Assessment. Phonological awareness refers to an understanding of the sounds of speech as distinct from their meanings. This awareness proceeds along a developmental continuum that moves from less complex to more complex. Instruction along the continuum begins with rhyming activities, then progresses to blending and segmenting of words into onset and rime, and ultimately advances to blending, segmenting, and deleting phonemes.

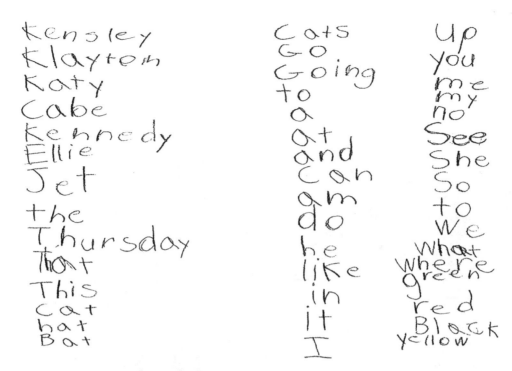

Figure 3.4   Example of Timed Word-Writing Assessment

An awareness of phonemes is necessary to grasp the alphabetic principle that underlies the system of written language. If children understand that words can be divided into individual phonemes and that phonemes can be blended into words, they are able to use letter–sound knowledge to read and build words. Researchers have shown that this strong relationship between phonological awareness and reading success persists throughout school (Blevins 2021, 2016; Adams 1994; Goswami and Bryant 1990).

Assessment in phonological awareness serves two purposes: (1) to initially identify students who appear to be at risk for difficulty in acquiring beginning reading skills, and (2) to monitor the progress of students who are receiving an intervention. Typically, kindergarten students are screened for risk factors in acquiring beginning reading skills in the second semester of kindergarten. Schools should select a good phonological measure as a component of the CLD.

Writing Prompt with Rubric. Many schools and states have included writing assessments as a routine measure of literacy achievement. The assessments are administered to all students in the classroom and include (1) a writing prompt, (2) standard procedures, and (3) a designated interval. If this classroom measure is available, it is included in the literacy diagnostic. For schools that do not have a preestablished writing assessment, we recommend they locate a good writing assessment for first- to third-grade students.

Running Record on Keystone Text. A well-designed text-reading measure can be a valuable tool for studying how an intervention is closing the literacy gap between low- and high-performing readers. Therefore, it is important for teachers to have access to high-quality leveled texts from multiple publishers to use for progress monitoring. With this in mind, we compiled a collection of exemplar texts from guided reading sets into a classroom assessment kit, which we call the Keystone Assessment Collection. The books represent a wide range of publishers, authors, text types, genres, formats, textures, sizes, and writing styles, and they can be used interchangeably for guided reading instruction and for progress monitoring.

To determine the validity of the Keystone Assessment Collection (Levels A–M) as a progress monitoring measure for the CIM, we conducted a study with forty-seven reading teachers from twenty-four schools across nine states, with 806 students in kindergarten through second grade. The students completed pre- and post-tests using

Writing About Reading Prompt: In your opinion, what lesson or moral did the lion learn from his experience with the mouse? Provide evidence from the text to support your opinion.

Title: *The Lion and the Mouse*   Guided Reading Level: M
Publisher: Hameray
Word Count: 112   Errors: 10   Genre: Fable

Introduction: The Lion and the Mouse is a fable, which means that a lesson or moral is going to be learned through the characters' actions and experiences. In this fable, the Lion considers himself to be king of the jungle and uses his size, teeth, and roar to scare all the other animals. However, the Lion soon learns an important lesson. Read aloud pages 1–5 to see what happens when the big lion meets up with one of the smallest animals, the mouse, in the jungle.

Take a running record on pp. 1–5. Then, ask the student to read the rest of the fable silently to find out if and how the lion's act of kindness was repaid and what both the lion and the mouse learn from the experience. Do a comprehension check.

Figure 3.5   Example of Keystone Book with Book Introduction, Assessment Procedures, and Writing About Reading Prompt

the Slosson Oral Reading Test (SORT) and the Keystone Assessment Collection. The Keystone pre- and post-scores proved to be highly (p<.001) correlated with the SORT-3 pre- and post-scores. These findings provide evidence that the Keystone Assessment Collection (Levels A–M) represents a valid and reliable method of estimating children's text level through an authentic, teacher-administered reading task (see Dorn, Doore, and Soffos 2015).

In Figure 3.5, we provide an example of a Keystone book with a standardized introduction, assessment procedures, and a Writing About Reading prompt. On the back of each book is a label that includes the guided reading level, the word count, the error count (to determine instructional level), the genre, the publisher, a short book introduction, and a Writing About Reading prompt. We encourage teachers to employ a similar process for monitoring the progress of intervention students on benchmark books in their class collections.

Text Reading Level Assessment. A text reading level assessment is administered to determine an instructional reading level for placement in an intervention. Teachers can select from several published assessments, which include leveled texts, standardized procedures for administration, and scoring rubrics for interpreting results. During text reading, the teacher records how the student applies strategies to solve problems within texts at three levels of difficulty: easy, instructional, and hard. The assessment also includes measures for assessing reading comprehension and fluency.

There are several reasons why teachers should include reading levels in an RTI assessment method (Dunn 2007). First, the reading level of a child in first grade is a predictor of future reading success. Second, a student's reading level can be charted over time and compared with grade-level peers (based on benchmark levels). Third, text reading levels have preestablished cut scores, which can be used for measuring individual reading growth from entry to exit, and also for comparing the individual scores with school and district scores. A well-designed text reading measure can be a valuable tool for studying how an intervention is closing the literacy gap between low- and high-performing readers.

Instructional Reading Levels. The teacher should determine the reading level at which a student can benefit most effectively from instruction. In instructional settings, research suggests that students do best when they know 95 to 98 percent of the words in the selection (Gambrell, Wilson, and Gantt 1981). As a general guide, we recommend that an accuracy rate of 90 to 94 percent would be appropriate for beginning readers, whereas, 95 to 98 percent would be expected for text level 28 and above. In an RTI process, the student's instructional level is especially important because (1) it indicates the point at which a student is most receptive to instruction, and (2) it focuses on the student's potential level of development (i.e., what the student can do with teacher assistance). The instructional level is determined by triangulating four sources of reading data: percentage of words read correctly (accuracy rate), strategies used at points of difficulty (monitoring, searching, and self-correcting behaviors), comprehension (purposeful reading), and fluency (rate and prosody). Accuracy rates for instructional texts are adjusted as students read materials that increase in complexity.

Teachers can use a standard protocol for measuring a student's instructional reading level, including procedures for assessing a student's ability to read for a particular purpose. This comprehension assessment is in contrast to methods that require students to answer a long list of comprehension questions. The reading protocol follows a set of standardized procedures:

- The teacher reads a scripted introduction that includes a purpose for comprehending a particular passage (e.g., to discover a relationship between multiple events or to locate content-specific information). The passage is approximately one hundred words.
- The teacher takes a running record of the student's oral reading behaviors, including evidence of how the student initiates problem-solving strategies on unknown words.
- After the reading, the teacher assesses the student's ability to read for a specific purpose, while prompting the student to provide evidence from the text to support their thinking.

For students at higher reading levels (generally transitional and above), the teacher adds a silent reading measure. The goal is to determine if a discrepancy exists between the student's oral and silent reading comprehension. As an RTI method, this is important data, since it could indicate that an instructional gap has occurred from lack of opportunities to develop silent reading competencies. Following the oral reading assessment, the teacher provides a scripted introduction to a new passage, gives the student a specific purpose for reading this section, and instructs the student to read silently approximately one hundred words. After the silent reading, the teacher assesses the student's ability to read for a particular purpose, while prompting the student to locate evidence from the text to support the comprehension goal.

Reading Behavior Checklist. The reading behavior checklist identifies critical reading behaviors that indicate print-solving strategies at the emergent, early, transitional, and fluent levels. At the emergent level, the reading behaviors include the following:

- Uses meaning and language to read simple texts.
- Points to words with one-to-one matching on one and two lines of print.
- Notices unknown words in text (self-monitors).
- Uses knowledge of some letter–sound relationships to initiate an action at point of difficulty.
- Articulates first letter in unknown words.
- Notices unknown words and searches for cues in pictures and print.
- Rereads to cross-check first letter with meaning and structure cues.

As students progress to higher levels, the reading behavior checklist focuses on more sophisticated problem-solving strategies, such as these:

- Solves multisyllabic words by noticing parts within words.
- Uses word meaning (e.g., prefixes, suffixes, roots, compound words) to solve unknown words.

In Chapter 1 (Table 1.2), we presented a reading continuum from emergent to transitional and beyond levels; in this chapter (Figure 3.6), we illustrate how a reading checklist and running record are used to analyze student progress at the transitional reading level. (See Resource C.4a, b, c, d, and e, Reading Processing Behavior Checklists for Emergent, Beginning Early, Late Early, Transitional, and Beyond Transitional Readers, for reproducible forms.) As the student reads a new text, the teacher takes a running record of the student's independent reading behaviors. After the reading, the teacher selects one or two teaching points and prompts the student to solve the reading problems. The reading checklist is used to document the student's processing at two levels: (1) what the student can do without assistance (actual level), and (2) what the student can do with assistance (potential level). It is important for teachers to identify the student's potential level of development, as this is the zone at which responsive teaching is aimed. The reading behavior checklist and the comprehension checklist (see next section) are analyzed together to determine how the student is responding to the intervention.

Comprehension Guides. Comprehension guides can be valid measures for assessing a student's literal comprehension after reading a new text. (See Resource C.5a, and b, Comprehension Guides for Fiction and Nonfiction Texts, for reproducible forms.) The student's deep-level comprehension is assessed through discussion groups and reading response logs (see Dorn and Soffos 2005). The comprehension guide is triangulated with the reading behavior checklist and the fluency scale to assess the student's reading competency on an instructional-level text. In Figure 3.7, we illustrate how the comprehension guide and the fluency scale are triangulated with the reading checklist for a late early reader.

Following the reading of a fiction text, the teacher prompts the student to discuss the purpose for reading. If the student needs further assistance, the teacher increases the level of support by asking specific questions from the comprehension guide. The measure includes an assessment of the student's comprehension behaviors:

- Identifies text structure.
- Identifies theme or message.
- Retells or summarizes important events.
- Analyzes the main character and discusses change over time in actions or motives.
- Asks questions, about characters' actions, events, vocabulary and word meanings, complex sentences or phrases, and/or puzzling parts of texts.

A structured comprehension guide is used to measure a student's ability to remember important details from an expository text. Following the reading, the teacher prompts the student to discuss the set purpose for

Transitional Reading Processing Behaviors
(Assessing Processing Behaviors to Check on Teaching and Learning)
End of First Grade – End of Second Grade
Grade Level Texts

Student: _Sara_   Date: _____

Book Title/Text Level: _Ninja Red Riding Hood_   Genre: _Fiction_

Accuracy Rate: _93%_   Self-Correction Ratio: _1:3_

Use meaning, structure and orthographic or visual sources of information within text along with their relevant background and strategic knowledge in an **orchestrated way** to support ongoing comprehension of texts.

Reading Behavior	Observed – Unprompted *Behaviors Observed During Reading; Record Behavioral Evidence from the Running Record*	Not Observed – Prompted *Behaviors Prompted for After Reading; Record Prompts and Student's Responses*
Orchestrates multiple sources of information (meaning, structure, and visual cues); reads texts with greater accuracy and more efficient self-correction.	Uses multiple sources of information to self-correct	
Uses knowledge of letter – sound relationships to initiate an efficient decoding strategy at the point of difficulty; searches through unknown words in a left-right sequence, blends letters, consonant blends and diagraphs and long vowel patterns into sounds including **r-controlled vowels, irregular vowel patterns, and diphthongs.**	Efficient decoding strategy used with consonant digraph and r-controlled pattern wh-irl	
Uses known word patterns to decode and read words including **complex multisyllabic words** with efficiency and accuracy.	Used knowledge to decode com·plain·ed	
Uses knowledge of syllable division strategies to support decoding and reading of multisyllabic words.	Accurately segmented multisyllabic words: Whirlwind, complained	Segmented compound word jack·knifed
Uses morphemic units including **prefixes and suffixes** to read and understand word meanings.	Attended to -ed suffix complained	
Reads known complex high-frequency words with fluency and ease.	No errors, fluent	
Self-corrects using known high-frequency words and other print cues.	No errors, fluent	
Uses more complex punctuation to regulate phrasing and fluency (prosody).	Attends to most punctuation	Needs to improve expressive reading of questions

Oral Reading Fluency Scale

Level 4	Reads primarily in large, meaningful phrase groups. Preservation of the author's syntax is consistent. Most of the story is read with expressive interpretation.	
(Level 3)	Reads primarily in three- or four-word phrase groups. The majority of phrasing seems to preserve the syntax of the author. Some expressive interpretation is present.	Some expression
Level 2	Reads primarily in two-word phrases with some three- or four-word groupings. Little or no expressive interpretation if present.	
Level 1	Reads primarily word by word. Occasional two-word or three-word phrases may occur. No expressive interpretation is present.	

Figure 3.6   Example of Running Record and Reading Processing Behavior Checklist for a Transitional Reader

RUNNING RECORD SHEET

Name: _____ Date: _____ D. of B.: _____ Age: _____ yrs _____ mths

School: _____ Recorder: _____

Text Titles		Errors / Running Words	Error Ratio	Accuracy Rate	Self-correction Ratio
Easy	_____		1: _____	_____ %	1: _____
Instructional	Little Red Riding Hood (unseen)	19/282	1: 15	93 %	1: 8
Hard			1: _____	_____ %	1: _____

Directional movement _____

Analysis of Errors and Self-corrections
Information used or neglected [Meaning (M), Structure or Syntax (S), Visual (V)]

Easy _____

Instructional Meaning and Structure are used predominantly for substitutions with some good visual problem-solving. Integration lead to a few self-corrections

Hard _____

Cross-checking on information (Note that this behaviour changes over time)

Page	Title	E (19)	SC (3)	Information used E MSV	SC MSV
	Little Red Riding Hood				
2.	✓✓R✓✓				
	✓✓✓✓✓✓				
	✓✓✓ ✓ ✓✓				
	✓✓ (W) Call-ed✓ / Called				
	✓✓✓✓				
3.	✓✓ ✓✓ ✓✓				
	✓✓ Grandma / Grandmother ✓✓	1		(msv)	
	(W) Ple-pl / Please T ✓✓✓✓	1			ms(V)
	✓ ✓✓✓ ✓✓✓				
	✓ (W) ✓ / off ✓				
	✓✓✓✓				

Figure 3.6   (*Continued*)

Comprehension Guide for Fiction Text
Assessing *Literal Level* Comprehension on an Instructional Level Text

Student: Sara   Name of Text: Ninja Red Riding Hood   Date: _____

Directions: After the teacher locates the student's instructional level, then the teacher checks on the student's comprehension on a first read by allowing the student to talk about the reading. The teacher uses sample prompts to stimulate the student's thinking about specific aspects of the text. As the student engages in a dialogue with the teacher, he/she records the student's response during the language exchange. The teacher uses the data collected to plan for comprehension instruction across various contexts.

Comprehension Goals	Sample Language Prompts to Stimulate Conversation *Encourage Textual Evidence to Support Thinking as Needed*	Student's Response	Suitable Responses ✓
Identifies text structure	⊙ *Is this a fiction or nonfiction text?*	Fiction—because there are talking pigs	✓
Identifies theme or message	⊙ *What do you think the author's message or possible life lesson or lessons might be?* ⊙ *What happened in the story that caused you to think that way?* • *How has the author's message or life lesson changed your theory of the world?*	She should not have trusted a stranger. The wolf wanted to eat her. If she hadn't talked to the wolf, none of this would have happened to her.	✓
Retells important events **OR** **Summarizes text**	• *What happened first, then, next and last in the story?* ⊙ *What was the problem in the story?* ⊙ *Was the problem solved? If so, how was it solved?* • *Can you describe what happened in the story?*	Red finally had to fight the wolf, but she needed help. Grandma had to use her ninja skills to beat the wolf.	✓
Analyzes main character and discusses change over time in actions or motives	• *Can you think of some words to describe…?* ⊙ *Describe how…changed over time. What was he/she like at the beginning, middle and end of the story?* • *What event/s caused the character/s to think and act a certain way?* • *How did the change affect the outcome in the story?* • *How do you feel about… change?*	At first, the wolf was bad. After he lost the fight with Grandma, he turned into a peaceful wolf.	✓
Asks questions; e.g., unfamiliar vocabulary or word meanings, complex sentences or phrases, and/or puzzling parts of the text	⊙ *Was there any vocabulary that the author used that you didn't understand?* ⊙ *Were there any sentences or parts of the text the author crafted that you didn't understand?* ⊙ *Do you have any other questions or thoughts that you would like to share?*	The student responded "NO" to each of the three prompts.	

Figure 3.7   Comprehension Checklist for Fiction Text for a Transitional Reader

reading. If a student experiences difficulty, the teacher asks specific questions to probe for understanding. This measure is used to assess the student's literal understanding of an expository text, based on the following behaviors:

- States the main idea from the text; includes key ideas to support the main idea.
- Uses some content-specific vocabulary from the text.
- Uses text features/aids to support understanding.
- Identifies new learning; compares previous understandings to new learning.
- Asks questions about content, vocabulary, etc.

The comprehension checklist and reading behavior checklist are analyzed for evidence of the student's reading strategies for problem-solving and comprehending an instructional-level text. This information is used for monitoring the student's progress in response to the intervention method.

Oral Reading Fluency Scale. The fluency scale from the National Assessment of Educational Progress (NAEP) is a useful measure for assessing change over time in fluent reading (Pinnell et al. 1995). The NAEP scale measures fluency at three language levels: (1) grouping or phrasing of words as revealed through intonation, stressing, and pausing; (2) using author's syntax for representing the message; and (3) expressiveness. A student's fluency is measured on a scale of 1 to 4.

- Level 1: Reads primarily word by word. Occasional two-word or three-word phrases may occur, but these are infrequent and/or they do not preserve meaningful syntax.
- Level 2: Reads primarily in two-word phrases with some three- or four-word phrases. Some word-by-word reading may be present. Word groupings may seem awkward and unrelated to larger context of sentence or passage.
- Level 3: Reads primarily in three- or four-word phrases. Some smaller groupings may be present. Some larger groupings may be present. The majority of the phrasing seems appropriate and preserves the syntax of the author. Little or no expressive interpretation is present.
- Level 4: Reads primarily in large, meaningful phrase groups. Although some regressions, repetitions, and deviations from text may be present, they do not detract from the overall structure of the story. The story is read with expressive interpretation.

The fluency scale is used for students who are reading at a Late Early Level (approximately text level 12 or F on most leveling systems). For students who are reading at emergent and beginning early levels, teachers record notes about fluency.

Writing About Reading Checklist. This written measure is used to provide evidence of a student's understanding of a text through a special prompt. This assessment, which aligns with the Phase II component of the GRP intervention (see Chapter 4), includes rubrics at the emergent, early, and transitional reading levels. (See Figure 3.8 for examples of student writing samples and checklists; see Resource C.6a, b, c, and d, Writing About Reading Checklists for Emergent to Transitional Readers, for reproducible forms.) Each rubric is designed to measure how well the student is integrating multiple sources of information through writing about their reading. The charts are based on a continuum of literacy behaviors in five areas:

- Writing behaviors that document the student's knowledge of spelling strategies for problem-solving on unknown words and the ability to transcribe known words with accuracy and fluency.
- Composing strategies that indicate the student's knowledge of rehearsal techniques for holding ideas in memory, use of a practice page for planning and organizing the message, and rereading strategies for monitoring the production of a meaningful message.
- Comprehension strategies that indicate the student's ability to read for specific information, including utilizing the vocabulary and ideas from the text while responding in writing to an oral prompt.

- Language behaviors that document the student's increasing control of written language as evidenced by more complex sentence structures and language patterns.
- Knowledge of print conventions, including punctuation, capitalization, and grammar functions.

Figure 3.8 Writing Samples and Writing About Reading Checklists at Emergent, Late Early, and Beginning Transitional Levels

Student:												

Writing About Reading for Late Early Intervention
(Levels 9-12/F-G)
Check all behaviors observed without support.

Writing Behavior (Spelling Strategies and Writing Fluency)	Writes more complex high-frequency words fluently. (**there, where, when**)	—	—	—									
	Uses a practice page to think strategically about spelling unknown words.	X	X	X									
	Says words slowly, hears and records beginning, ending, and middle consonants including blends, clusters, and diagraphs; spells most words using visual analysis (**bike, stripe**).	X	X	X									
	Uses familiar words and word parts to spell unknown words; spells word endings (**s, ing, ed, es**) correctly; uses complex rime patterns (phonogram patterns) to spell unknown words (**down**-**crown**).	—	X	X									
	Demonstrates movement from **phonetic** to the **transitional** stage of spelling development.	—	X	X									
Composing	Uses the rereading strategy (**phrases, words, word**) as needed to help with writing a meaningful response.	X	X	X									
	Response is longer and more complex; reflects fluency of thinking, fluency of encoding, and an increase in language control.	X	X	—									
Comprehension	Response reflects understanding of the text and prompt.	X	X	X									
	Incorporates a writing vocabulary that reflects attention to reading; uses vocabulary appropriate for topic.	X	X	X									
Language Structure	Demonstrates use of language structures that reflects increasing complexity in conventional language patterns, i.e., • composes simple sentences (**noun + verb**) • uses prepositional phrases (**on the floor, in the bag**) • uses conjunctions (**and, but**) • uses modifiers (**red dress**)	—	X	—									
Conventions	Rereads writing and thinks about punctuation and capitalization, i.e., • uses ending punctuation appropriately (**periods, exclamation marks, question marks**) • capitalizes sentence beginnings and proper names	X	X	—									
	Progress Monitoring Date	4/19	4/29	5/12									
	Total Number of Observed Behaviors	7	10	7									

Figure 3.8   *(Continued)*

~~the Hung ry Giant he~~

The Giant wos meah he
~~tod the pepol to get hem~~
~~p ood~~

The giant was   mean he told   the people
to get him food

IS your Pail Full?
littol Ber   trid   to Feed   the
berds but   thet   A Floow
a.wat.

Little bear tried to feed   the   birds
but they flew away.

Figure 3.8   (*Continued*)

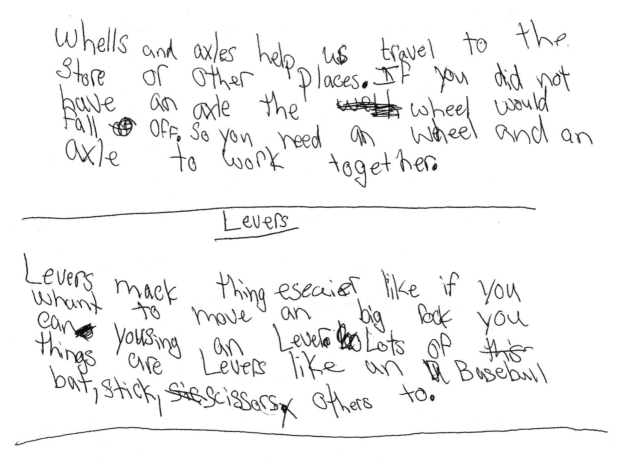

Wheel & axle

Simple Machines
Describe how one kind of simple machine makes work easier.

Whells and axles help us travel to the Store or other places. If you did not have an axle the ~~well~~ wheel would fall off. So you need an wheel and an axle to work together.

Levers

Levers mack thing eseaier like if you whant to move an big Rock you can yousing an Lever ~~lots~~ Lots of ~~this~~ things are Levers like an ~~a~~ Baseball bat, stick, ~~siss~~scissors~~x~~ others to.

Figure 3.8   (*Continued*)

Writing Behaviors Checklist. The Writing Behaviors Checklist identifies critical writing behaviors that indicate encoding strategies and writing fluency at the emergent and early levels. Here are the writing behaviors at the emergent level:

● Writes known words with correct formation.
● Uses spaces between words.
● Recognizes the link between sounds and letters.
● Uses ABC chart as a resource.
● Writes a few high-frequency words.

Student:

Writing About Reading for Transitional Intervention
(Level H-M)
Check all behaviors observed without support.

Writing Behavior (Spelling Strategies and Writing Fluency)	Writes more complex high-frequency words fluently. (**because, once, knew**)	–	–	–	–	X	X					
	Uses complex rime patterns (phonogram patterns) to spell unknown words (d**own**-cr**own**).	–	–	–	–	–	X					
	Breaks multi-syllabic words into parts and records new words in parts.	–	–	–	X	X	X					
	Uses **transitional** and/or **conventional** spelling for most words.	–	–	–	–	X	X					
Composing	Plans response (**notes, outline, chart, web**) on the planning page to organize thinking.	–	–	–	–	X	X					
	Uses the rereading strategy (**phrases, words, word**) as needed to help with writing a meaningful response.	X	X	X	X	X	X					
Comprehension	Response reflects understanding of the text and prompt.	X	X	X	–	X	X					
	Incorporates a writing vocabulary that reflects attention to reading; uses vocabulary appropriate for topic.	–	X	X	X	X	X					
Language Structure	Demonstrates use of language structures that reflects increasing complexity in conventional language patterns. • Uses modifiers (**red dress**) • Uses two phrases linked by a relative pronoun (who, that, what, which) • Uses two phrases linked by an adverb (when, where, how, however, whenever, wherever)	X	–	–	X	X	X					
Conventions	Rereads writing and thinks about punctuation. • Uses ending punctuation appropriately (**periods, exclamation marks, question marks**) • Uses additional forms of punctuation appropriately (**quotation marks, apostrophes in contractions or possessives, commas to identify a series, ellipses to show pause**) • Capitalizes sentence beginnings and proper names.	–	–	–	X	–	–					
	Progress Monitoring Date	10/1	10/23	11/24	12/14	3/1	5/18					
	Total Number of Observed Behaviors	4	4	4	6	8	9					

Figure 3.8 (*Continued*)

As students progress to the transitional level, the writing behaviors focus on understanding how to write narrative and expository texts. (See Resource C.7a, b, c, and d, Writing Behavior Checklists for Emergent, Beginning Early, Late Early, and Transitional Writers.)

Informal Reading Inventories. An informal reading inventory (IRI) can provide teachers with valuable information for placing students in intervention groups. The IRI consists of two major components: graded word lists and graded passages. Once teachers become familiar with the administration and interpretation, the IRI can provide insight into word analysis, comprehension strategies, background information, word habits, and interests. Numerous commercial inventories are available; teachers should review the grades, skill areas, and other features to determine the best IRI for their needs. (See Gunning 2018 for a review of commercial IRIs.)

Adapted Miscue Analysis. It is important for teachers to analyze the reader's miscues for patterns of responding to unknown words. Based on the running record or IRI, teachers can categorize the reader's miscues according to semantic similarity, structural similarity, or graphic similarity. Under graphic similarity, the teacher can analyze the student's response according to degree of graphic similarity (beginning, middle, ending), then determine whether the miscue was self-corrected or not (Gunning 2018). For a deeper analysis of growth over time, teachers can use an electronic AIM line for plotting a student's miscues and charting change over time in the student's literacy processing system. Specifically, teachers can chart behaviors that indicate faster decoding, improved cognitive flexibility (ability to simultaneously integrate multiple sources of information), higher accuracy rate (indicating the reader is monitoring the problem prior to making the error), and reading to learn from the author's message (pausing when the text is not making sense, questioning the author, reacting to the message, etc.). An electronic AIM line can provide the teacher with valuable data for identifying the best intervention to meet the student's needs, including the proportion of time devoted to targeted instruction on specific tasks with the intervention. (See Figure 3.9.)

District Assessments. This category includes district or state assessments, such as the Stanford Achievement Test or the State Benchmark Examination. The student's performance on these measures is aggregated with other assessments in the literacy diagnostic.

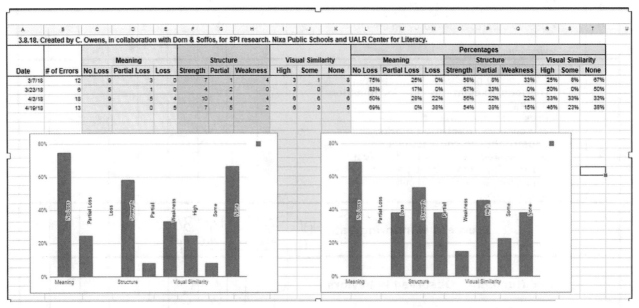

Figure 3.9   Electronic AIM Line for Analyzing Reading Miscues and Charting Change over Time in Literacy Processing

Selected Work Samples. This measure reflects the student's performance on authentic curriculum-based tasks. The teacher selects three or four work samples to include in the literacy diagnostic. These samples are assessed with classroom writing rubrics and scoring guides.

Classroom Rubrics, Checklists, and Writing Scoring Guides. These assessments are curriculum-based measures that directly reflect how well the students are performing on specific literacy tasks. These assessments can be teacher-made or published rubrics.

Guided Reading Plus Word Study Form. The recording sheet for the GRP Word Study intervention provides teachers with a record of words and patterns that have been taught during the word study component. The first column includes high-frequency words that are processed fluently and have been added to the student's word dictionary, and the second column includes rime patterns that have been taught and have been recorded on spelling charts. This record of word learning is a useful tool for planning effective word study that is based on students' strengths and needs. (See Figure 3.10; see also Resource C.8, Recording Sheet for Guided Reading Plus Word Study, for reproducible form.)

Guided Reading Teacher Conference Form. This form provides teachers with a framework for documenting students' reading behaviors and degrees of teacher scaffolding during one-to-one reading conferences. The form includes sections for recording strategies used and neglected on particular pages and the teacher's language for scaffolding a successful problem-solving action. Teachers can use this form to self-assess the precision of their prompts for empowering students to apply flexible strategies with greater independence and efficiency. (See Figure 3.11; see also Resource C.9, Conference Form for Recording Notes During Reading Conferences of Guided Reading Plus Intervention, for reproducible form.)

Writing Portfolio District Checklist. Most districts have expectations for types of writing that students should control in kindergarten to third grade. These expectations generally align with state writing standards. The writing portfolio checklist is a record that documents students' writing in the expected genres and modes.

Anecdotal Notes. An assessment system would not be complete without the teacher's anecdotal notes, including observation notes of children's literacy behaviors during guided reading, independent reading, writing conferences, word study activities, and other authentic events (Afflerbach and Klein 2020).

Teacher CIM Assessment Notebook. The assessment notebook includes a table of contents with dividers for organizing all assessment data for students in the interventions (see Video 3.1). These record-keeping forms provide an accounting of each student's progress over time, while informing the teacher of instructional decisions within the intervention framework for accelerating the student's learning.

 Video 3.1   The teacher explains how she organizes her CIM assessment notebook for students in the small-group interventions.

Observation Protocols. Each intervention in the CIM portfolio includes an observation protocol for ensuring that the intervention is implemented with integrity. (See Resource C.10a, b, c, d, e and f, Observation Protocols for Comprehension Focus Group, Guided Reading Plus, Interactive Writing, Writing Aloud, Language Phase, and the Strategic Processing Interventions.) Each observation protocol, which is aligned with the CIM planners and Guide Sheets, provides a valid tool not only for assessing implementation integrity but also for identifying areas where instruction (or lack of instruction) is affecting student learning. If a student is not making expected progress from participating in a particular intervention, the team needs to determine whether the intervention has been implemented as designed before changing interventions. We recommend that a CIM coach or colleague observe the intervention lesson using the specific protocol and provide feedback on lesson integrity. Since all interventions within the portfolio include similar components, if a student is not progressing at the anticipated rate in a particular area, the CIM specialist may elect to mix interventions to address the areas of need.

Group Members

High-Frequency Words				Rime Patterns			
✓ Can read and write fluently				✓ Taught and have been recorded on students' independent chart			
a*		at*		an		at	
am*		an*		am		ap	
and *		all		and		ash	
are		ask		ack		ank	
asked		after		all		ake	
away		be		ale		ame	
big		but		ain		ate	
by		back		ar		ay	
can*		car		aw			
come		did					
do*		day		et		ed	
for		from		est		ell	
go*		going		eat			
get		gets					
he*		had		in		ip	
has		have		ill		ick	
him		his		ink		ing	
here		her		ine		ice	
how		I*		ide		ight	
I'm		if		ir			
in*		into					
is*		it*		op		ock	
just		like*		oke		or	
look		little		ore			

Figure 3.10   Recording Sheet for Guided Reading Plus Word Study

High-Frequency Words			Rime Patterns			
✓ Can read and write fluently			✓ Taught and have been recorded on students' independent chart			
me*		man				
my*		make	ug		uck	
mom		no*	ump		unk	
not*		now				
on		or				
of		one				
out		our				
over		put				
play		so*				
see*		she*				
saw		said				
to*		too				
the*		them				
than		that				
then		this				
their		there				
up*		us				
very		we*				
will		with				
went		was				
were		when				
what		where				
who		you				
your		zoo				

Figure 3.10   *(Continued)*

	Guided Reading Teacher Conference Form for Noting Reading Behaviors and Degrees of Assistance	
Student's Name: _____ Date: _____		
Name of Text/Genre: _____ Text Level: _____		
Reading Behaviors Noted and Teacher Prompts to Facilitate Strategic Activity		
Page #'s	Strategies Used – Demonstrates Efficient Processing/Comprehension	
	Strategies Neglected and Prompts Used – Demonstrates Need for Assistance	Degrees of Assistance ☐ L ☐ M ☐ H
Page #'s	Strategies Used – Demonstrates Efficient Processing/Comprehension	
	Strategies Neglected and Prompts Used – Demonstrates Need for Assistance	Degrees of Assistance ☐ L ☐ M ☐ H
Page #'s	Strategies Used – Demonstrates Efficient Processing/Comprehension	
	Strategies Neglected and Prompts Used – Demonstrates Need for Assistance	Degrees of Assistance ☐ L ☐ M ☐ H
Summary of Behavioral Data and Goals:		

Figure 3.11   Conference Form for Recording Notes During Reading Conferences of Guided Reading Plus Intervention

Response to Intervention Planner. In Chapter 2, we introduced the RTI planner as a decision-making tool for selecting the best interventions for low-performing students. During this collaborative meeting, the classroom teacher and intervention specialists look across all data sources to identify each student's strengths and needs and align instructional support across classroom and intervention settings. (See Video Link 3.2.)

 Video 3.2   Classroom and intervention teachers analyze student data for strengths and needs and plan intervention services using the RTI Planner.

CLOSING THOUGHTS

Assessments should never be viewed in isolation, as this could lead to a narrow or deficit interpretation. Instead, multiple assessments should be analyzed for evidence of the student's knowledge, thinking, and problem-solving, including observations of the student's learning during routine classroom instruction, as well as consultation with educators who have worked with the student.

The Comprehensive Intervention Model is a diagnostic model that uses assessment and intervention as reciprocal and generative processes. Therefore, assessment must include a balance of measures that reflect the student's learning at two developmental levels. The actual level of development is determined through summative assessments that indicate the student's level of independent performance. This level is identified through pre- and post-assessments and through progress monitoring materials that are administered in formalized contexts. It is important for the teacher to know the student's independent level; however, it is even more important to understand the student's proximal (or potential) level of development. In other words, where is the zone in which a student can learn from instruction, that is, the zone in which teaching leads development? (See Vygotsky 1978.) As an RTI method, intervention can be effective only if it promotes acceleration; and acceleration occurs when the student is able to access new information through instruction.

The Comprehensive Literacy Diagnostic represents a balanced and multifaceted method that helps to ensure a more accurate identification of students at risk of reading failure. During the intervention, the teacher uses a variety of formative assessments, including dynamic assessment, to monitor the student's responsiveness to instruction. This interactive process provides the teacher with ongoing data for planning and evaluating how well the intervention is meeting the needs of the particular student. At designated intervals during the intervention, the teacher monitors the student's reading development on unseen texts and compares his actual growth with where he needs to be in order to catch up with average-performing peers.

Chapter 4

TEACHING FOR ALIGNMENT, CONGRUENCY, AND TRANSFER

The classroom literacy program is the first line of defense against illiteracy. In Chapter 2, we proposed that if more than 15 to 20 percent of students in a school are struggling in literacy, the classroom program might be the problem. Interventions are designed to supplement (not replace or supplant) high-quality classroom instruction; therefore, any discussion about interventions must begin with a discussion about the classroom curriculum. Here are a few questions to consider:

- Is the curriculum differentiated to meet the needs of all students?
- Does the curriculum include evidence-based practices?
- How much time is devoted to reading and writing?
- How is assessment used to monitor student learning?
- Do supplemental interventions align with the curriculum?

Creating a literate environment that is conducive to reading is a necessary step in developing motivated learners who read for pleasure and purpose. The environment should be designed to guarantee every child's success in reading. To achieve this goal, teachers need to differentiate their instruction in order to meet the diverse needs of all students. The reading curriculum should include a blend of whole-group, small-group, and individual instruction, as well as opportunities for students to read independently. Differentiated teaching also applies to the degree of assistance provided to the learner for accomplishing a particular task. A workshop approach allows for differentiation, providing a supportive context that enables teachers to meet the literacy needs of all students (Dorn and Jones 2012, Dorn and Soffos 2005). If all these pieces are in place and a student is still not responding to high-quality differentiated classroom instruction, the student should be assessed for intervention.

The CIM provides a portfolio of interventions to meet the needs of individual learners. The portfolio builds on four principles:

- Teachers select the most appropriate intervention to meet student needs.
- The intervention aligns with high-quality classroom instruction.
- Student progress is closely monitored across interventions and classroom instruction.
- Intervention teams collaborate on student learning and make data-based decisions for continued improvement.

Within this theory, classroom instruction and interventions are viewed as reciprocal and generative processes involving collaboration among teachers. This collaboration ensures that students have opportunities to transfer their knowledge across multiple settings. In this way, the CIM guards against the danger of student learning becoming environmentally contingent (i.e., dependent on a particular learning context).

In this chapter, we discuss how classroom instruction and interventions are intentionally aligned within a layered design (see Chapter 2). Specifically, we illustrate how an integrated workshop framework in the classroom provides a scaffold for differentiating instruction for all students, thus balancing rigor and support. We also describe how interventions (classroom and supplemental) are positioned within this framework to enable low-progress readers to experience success on grade-level tasks. Then we focus on the language workshop as the foundation for reading and writing workshops, and we share how the language workshop aligns with the language phase in all small-group interventions. Next we take a closer look at reading and writing workshops. We explore ways that classroom teachers can design high-impact minilessons that emphasize evidence-based strategies for all students. These minilessons are followed by opportunities for students to apply these strategies independently and in small groups, with varying degrees of teacher assistance, including Targeted Intervention for low-progress learners. Finally, we discuss the role of assessment in the writing process, with an explanation of how writing develops along a writing continuum.

An Integrated Workshop in the Classroom

The goal of an integrated workshop is to align and coordinate instructional objectives across varied settings. The integrated framework allows teachers to develop grade-level content in a whole-group setting, to follow up with differentiated instruction in a small-group or one-to-one setting, to conclude with a debriefing session and teacher assessment, and finally to create opportunities for students to transfer their learning to varied contexts. Instead of simply covering the curriculum, the integrated workshop focuses on cultivating students' capacity to generalize their knowledge of critical concepts across multiple content areas. With transfer in mind, the integrated workshop includes four interrelated settings: language workshop, reading workshop, writing workshop, and content workshop. Each workshop is characterized by seven common features:

- Rigorous curriculum with differentiated instruction and targeted interventions.
- Meaningful and motivating text experiences.
- Explicit teaching to build background knowledge.
- Guided participation with adjustable and self-destructing scaffolds.
- Comprehension and problem-solving strategies on complex texts.
- Predictable structures to nurture self-regulation and independence.
- Integration of language, reading, and writing systems.

The goal of an integrated curriculum is for students to notice relationships among common concepts and apply flexible strategies for transferring this information to diverse settings. For example, during reading workshop, teachers could introduce nonfiction texts that relate to the content workshop; and during writing workshop, teachers could provide minilessons that focus on the reading-writing connection, including an analysis of how writers craft texts to support readers' comprehension (Dorn and Jones 2012; Dorn and Soffos 2005).

The workshop framework is based on a recurring cycle that begins with a minilesson and ends with a sharing component (Figure 4.1). The framework provides a differentiated structure with varying degrees of support for meeting students' needs. Students who require additional assistance are provided with targeted interventions that align with the literacy curriculum. Each workshop has five components:

- **Minilessons:** The minilesson is based on grade-level standards. It is an explicit teaching demonstration that focuses on strategies, skills, and procedures for learning a process. For students who are not responding to the whole-group lesson, the teacher might provide an additional small-group lesson in a targeted area.
- **Small-group instruction:** During small groups, the teacher provides focused instruction to students with similar needs. The teacher selects the most appropriate materials and prompts students to use their existing knowledge to accomplish new learning goals. The teacher meets with average or above-average readers at least three times during the week, but meets with the lowest-achieving students daily, providing targeted interventions to meet their literacy needs (e.g., word study and/or Writing About Reading interventions).
- **One-to-one or small-group conferences:** The conference serves two essential goals for differentiating instruction: (a) it allows the teacher to collect personal data on how well the student is responding to instruction, and (b) it provides the student with tailored support for achieving the learning goal. The

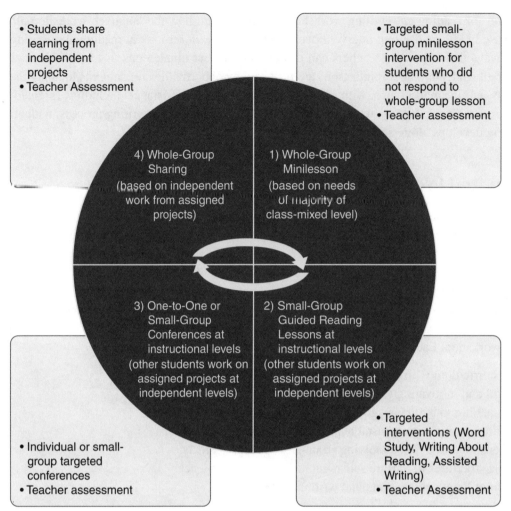

Figure 4.1   A workshop cycle includes predictable components, beginning with explicit teaching and guided practice during a whole-group minilesson, followed by small, leveled reading groups and individualized conferences, and concluding with whole-group sharing with evidence of student learning from independent activities. Assessment and intervention are embedded within the workshop framework.

teacher provides individual conferences (generally three to five minutes in duration) with approximately five students daily. For the struggling learner, the teacher conducts an intervention conference, providing more intensity in three areas: duration (number of minutes), frequency (number of times per week), and precision (expertise of teacher).

- **Independent practice:** Independent practice is an essential component of self-regulation. The teacher creates opportunities for students to transfer their knowledge and strategies to an unassisted situation. For instance, during a minilesson, the teacher might model how to use text features to aid reading comprehension; during independent practice, students would locate text features in a text and describe in their reading log how this information increased their understanding.

- **Reflection time:** This component is designed to bring closure to the workshop cycle through revisiting the content from the minilesson. The teacher calls on several students to share their learning from independent practice, including evidence from books, response logs, and other literacy artifacts. The workshop cycle enables students to understand the relationship between the minilesson, guided practice, and their independent work.

BUILDING BACKGROUND KNOWLEDGE DURING LANGUAGE WORKSHOP

The language workshop serves as the foundation for building students' content knowledge of complex topics. It incorporates students' structural knowledge about how writers organize texts to support readers, along with their strategic knowledge about which approaches work best in particular situations. Ideally, students use all these knowledge sources in synchrony to construct meaning from the text experience. Language workshop is intentionally designed to build students' listening and speaking competencies when dealing with more complex structures and topics, thus providing them with a rich data base for learning about written language.

Using specialized procedures, teachers engage students in interactive read-aloud experiences and language investigations around themed units of study. Their instructional tools include mentor texts, text maps, anchor charts, and reading response logs. Teachers use these tools to teach the functions of the language system, including grammatical structures, text conventions, vocabulary, and crafting techniques. Teachers revisit mentor texts to highlight ten essential language-based strategies (listed below) that authors use to enhance readers' comprehension of complex ideas. To promote transfer across classroom and intervention settings, the CIM teacher uses common instructional tools to awaken students' knowledge of the ten language strategies, while providing opportunities for students to transfer these strategies to guided and independent practice during the Comprehension Focus Group intervention. Here are the ten language strategies; we'll revisit them in Chapter 8, within the setting of the CFG framework.

- Manipulate forms of speech for expressing meaning.
- Make good word choices that communicate clear messages.
- Use nouns as well as pronouns to identify key people, places, and objects in a text.
- Use punctuation to clarify meanings and regulate fluency.
- Combine simple sentence structures into more complex sentence structures.
- Organize related ideas into paragraphs, chapters, and text genre.
- Use dialogue to carry and extend meanings.
- Use figurative language to symbolize meanings.
- Build vocabulary knowledge through relationships with other words.
- Use transitional words and phrases to connect ideas.

Within the language workshop framework, teachers engage students in an interactive read-aloud for developing their background knowledge in four critical areas:

1. Content or topical knowledge.
2. Comprehension strategies.
3. Text organization, features, and language structures.
4. Vocabulary knowledge.

Deeper readings allow the students to critically analyze the information gained from the text and integrate these sources within and across texts, including charting relationships for bigger concepts and ideas. The framework for interactive read-aloud includes the following components:

- Introduce the text and set a purpose for listening.
- Read the entire text for meaning.
  - Model the think-aloud process at strategic places in the text.
  - Discuss priority vocabulary before and/or within the context of reading.
  - Create situations for students to engage in oral discussions of important ideas from the text.
  - Revisit particular passages within the text for a closer analysis.
  - Co-construct charts for important vocabulary, ideas, and structures within and across texts.
  - Provide opportunities for students to respond to the text through writing about their reading.

To illustrate, we share a classroom teacher's lesson planner for the interactive read-aloud component based on the theme of Overcoming Obstacles (see Figure 4.2); then, we share the CIM teacher's anchor chart, which highlights the changes in the characters' actions at three points in time (see Figure 4.3). To promote students' comprehension of important ideas, the classroom teacher and the CIM teacher implement the unit of study across universal and intervention settings. As discussed previously, this intentional practice fosters the capacity of low-progress readers to transfer their knowledge, skills, and strategies across multiple contexts.

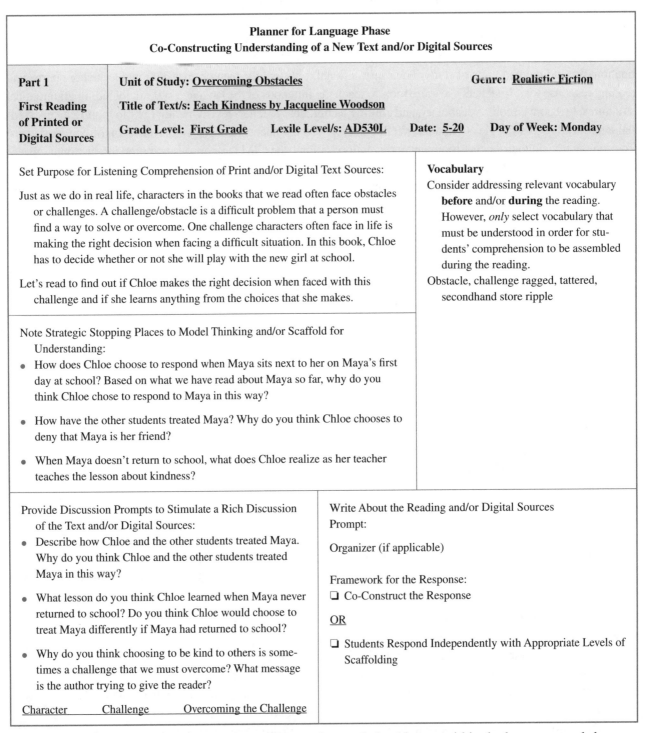

Planner for Language Phase
Co-Constructing Understanding of a New Text and/or Digital Sources

| Part 1 — First Reading of Printed or Digital Sources | Unit of Study: <u>Overcoming Obstacles</u>   Genre: <u>Realistic Fiction</u> Title of Text/s: <u>Each Kindness by Jacqueline Woodson</u> Grade Level: <u>First Grade</u>   Lexile Level/s: <u>AD530L</u>   Date: <u>5-20</u>   Day of Week: Monday |

Set Purpose for Listening Comprehension of Print and/or Digital Text Sources:

Just as we do in real life, characters in the books that we read often face obstacles or challenges. A challenge/obstacle is a difficult problem that a person must find a way to solve or overcome. One challenge characters often face in life is making the right decision when facing a difficult situation. In this book, Chloe has to decide whether or not she will play with the new girl at school.

Let's read to find out if Chloe makes the right decision when faced with this challenge and if she learns anything from the choices that she makes.

Vocabulary
Consider addressing relevant vocabulary **before** and/or **during** the reading. However, *only* select vocabulary that must be understood in order for students' comprehension to be assembled during the reading.
Obstacle, challenge ragged, tattered, secondhand store ripple

Note Strategic Stopping Places to Model Thinking and/or Scaffold for Understanding:
- How does Chloe choose to respond when Maya sits next to her on Maya's first day at school? Based on what we have read about Maya so far, why do you think Chloe chose to respond to Maya in this way?
- How have the other students treated Maya? Why do you think Chloe chooses to deny that Maya is her friend?
- When Maya doesn't return to school, what does Chloe realize as her teacher teaches the lesson about kindness?

Provide Discussion Prompts to Stimulate a Rich Discussion of the Text and/or Digital Sources:
- Describe how Chloe and the other students treated Maya. Why do you think Chloe and the other students treated Maya in this way?
- What lesson do you think Chloe learned when Maya never returned to school? Do you think Chloe would choose to treat Maya differently if Maya had returned to school?
- Why do you think choosing to be kind to others is sometimes a challenge that we must overcome? What message is the author trying to give the reader?

<u>Character</u>   <u>Challenge</u>   <u>Overcoming the Challenge</u>

Write About the Reading and/or Digital Sources
Prompt:

Organizer (if applicable)

Framework for the Response:
❏ Co-Construct the Response

OR

❏ Students Respond Independently with Appropriate Levels of Scaffolding

Figure 4.2 The classroom teacher designs an interactive read-aloud lesson within the language workshop; the intervention teacher builds on this theme during the language phase of the CFG.

Language Phase: Revisiting Text/s **Nurturing Close Listening and Reading: Analyzing and Marinating on Critical Aspects of Text/s**			
Part 2 **Revisit Printed or Digital Text for Further Study and Investigation**	**Unit of Study:** <u>Overcoming Obstacles</u> **Genre:** <u>RF</u> **Title of Text/s:** <u>Each Kindness</u> **Grade Level:** <u>1st Grade</u> **Lexile Level/s:** <u>AD530L</u> **Date:** _____ **Day of Week:** _____	**Part 2** **Revisit Printed or Digital Text for Further Study and Investigation**	**Unit of Study:** <u>Overcoming Obstacles</u> **Genre:** <u>RF</u> **Title of Text/s:** <u>Each Kindness</u> **Grade Level:** <u>1st Grade</u> **Lexile Level/s:** <u>AD530L</u> **Date:** _____ **Day of Week:** _____

Set Purpose for Analysis: Today, we want to think about the important events in a story and how they are related to each other. This will help us to understand the author's message. Let's reread the important parts of the story to discover what we think the author is trying to convey to the reader.	Set Purpose for Analysis: Today, we want to think about how authors choose certain words to help the reader better understand the characters in a story. Let's reread part of the story to see what words the authors uses to describe Maya.
Record Pages and/or Section/s to be Revisited for Closer Analysis: • **Modeled Practice:** Read page ____. What important event(s) happens here at the beginning of the story? How do you think Maya is acting or feeling? What evidence can we find in the text? What message do you think the author is trying to give us? • **Guided Practice:** Read page ____. What important event(s) happens here at the middle of the story? How do you think Maya is acting or feeling? What evidence can we find in the text? What message do you think the author is trying to give us? • **Independent Practice:** Read page ____. What important event(s) happens here at the end of the story? How do you think Maya is acting or feeling? What evidence can we find in the text? What message do you think the author is trying to give us? • Why do you think the author chose these words to describe Maya? How did this help us better understand why the other kids treated Maya differently? Co-Construct Chart: | **Key Event**	**Character's Actions/Feelings**	**Evidence From the Text**	**Author's Message**
---|---|---|---|	Record Pages and/or Section/s to be Revisited for Closer Analysis: • **Modeled Practice:** Read page ____. What specific words did the author use to describe Maya? Circle/underline the words. What did we learn about Maya? • **Guided Practice:** Read page ____. What specific words did the author use to describe Maya? Circle/underline the words. What did we learn about Maya? • **Independent Practice:** Read page ____. What specific words did the author use to describe Maya? Circle/underline the words. What did we learn about Maya? • Why do you think the author chose these words to describe Maya? How did this help us better understand why the other kids treated Maya differently? Co-Construct Chart: | **How does Maya look/act?**	**What did we learn?**
Beginning	
Middle	
End		
Write about the Learning Prompt: What did we learn today that will help us better understand the stories that we read? Framework for the Response: ❏ Co-Construct the Response: Students are in the **acquisition stage** with writing about the learning. ❏ Students Respond Independently with Appropriate Levels of Scaffolding	Write about the Learning Prompt: What did we learn today about author's craft? Framework for the Response: ❏ Co-Construct the Response: Students are in the acquisition stage with writing about the learning. ❏ Students Respond Independently with Appropriate Levels of Scaffolding

Figure 4.2 (*Continued*)

| Title: Each Kindness   Author: Jacqueline Woodson | | | |
Key Event	Character's Actions or Feelings	Evidence from the Text	Author's Message
Maya arrives for her first day of school.	Maya is scared and shy.	She looks down and whispers, "Hello."	Being the new kid at school can be scary. Doing something new in life can be scary.
Chloe moves her chair and books farther away from Maya when Maya sits next to her.	Chloe doesn't want to be friends with Maya	Every day, Chloe refuses to speak to or look at Maya.	People are sometimes unkind to others who are different from them.
Every day, Maya tries to get the other kids to play with her at school.	Maya wants to make friends with the other kids and wants to be accepted.	Maya brings jacks and other toys to school and tries to play with Chloe and the other kids.	People want to feel accepted so they don't feel lonely or left out.
Maya wears new clothes to school.	Maya thinks that wearing new clothes will make the other kids want to be friends with her.	Maya wears a pretty dress and fancy shoes to school one day. The outfit came from a secondhand store.	People want to feel accepted so they don't feel lonely or left out.
• Maya doesn't come to school one day. • The teacher teaches a lesson about kindness.	• Maya moves away because the students were unkind to her. • The teacher chooses this lesson because the kids were unkind to Maya.	• Maya's seat is empty. • The teacher's lesson is about how kindness spreads to others. She drops a stone into water and compares it to spreading kindness.	How we treat one another has consequences, good or bad.
Chloe learns a lesson about kindness.	Chloe feels sorry for the way she treated Maya and wishes she could fix things.	Chloe thinks about all the kind things she could have done for Maya when she throws a stone into the water.	Sometimes we can't fix our mistakes, but we can learn from them.

Central Message
- We shouldn't judge a person by appearance, how much money they have, etc.
- We should always treat others with kindness.
- Our choices have consequences that we might not be able to fix.

Figure 4.3   During the language phase of the CIM intervention, the CIM teacher and students collaborate on creating an anchor chart for examining changes in the characters' actions at three points in time.

ALIGNING THE CIM LANGUAGE PHASE TO LANGUAGE WORKSHOP IN THE CLASSROOM

To support the goal of building background knowledge, all small-group interventions in the CIM portfolio include a language phase (phase one). This intervention phase mirrors the language workshop in the classroom integrated workshop. To promote transfer, the intervention teacher designs units of study that align with the classroom curriculum and may also revisit some of the same texts for a closer read. As with language workshop in the classroom, the CIM language phase is intentionally designed to build students' listening and speaking comprehension at higher levels, thus providing a solid foundation for increasing the text rigor during the reading and writing phases of the intervention.

In the next section, we present the components of the language phase, and in subsequent chapters, we return to this phase as an essential feature for accelerating the reading and writing development of low-progress readers. Also, to further support teachers in planning instructional activities, we provide the blank lesson planner (Resource D.1, Lesson Planner for Language Phase of Interventions) along with the Guide Sheet (Resource D.2, Guide Sheet for Language Phase).

Phase One: The Language Phase. During the language phase, the teacher engages students in structured activities for increasing their listening, speaking, and reading comprehension through interactive read-aloud, text-based conversations, vocabulary enrichment, and Writing About Reading. The teacher carefully selects a complex text that is worthy of multiple readings, with opportunities for children to explore the forms and functions of language within meaningful print. During rereadings of specific sections within the text, the teacher models how to examine important passages for a closer analysis, scaffolds students' learning as they apply these strategies to a different passage within the text, and promotes their metacognition of useful strategies as they write about their learning in their reading logs. Generally, the interactive read-aloud text is several levels above the students' independent reading level, thus exposing them to richer language and inferred meanings. The language phase occurs over a two- or three-day sequence of predictable steps, as outlined below:

- **Before the First Reading:** The teacher provides an orientation to the read-aloud text, including important vocabulary, and sets a purpose for students' listening comprehension.
- **During the First Reading:** The teacher pauses at two or three strategic places to engage students in talking about key concepts, vocabulary, and text meaning. Depending on the students' needs, the teacher might model his/her thinking and use textual evidence to support the students' listening comprehension.
- **After the First Reading:** The teacher engages students in a rich discussion of the text, while scaffolding them to use vocabulary and language structures from the text in their oral discussions.
- **Writing About Text:** The teacher and students co-construct a written response to the text on a large chart or board. Other opportunities might focus on having students record important vocabulary words or phrases from the text in their reading logs or write about the text in response to an oral prompt.
- **Revisiting Sections Within the Text:** The teacher models close reading strategies with memorable passages that enable students to reflect more deeply about the text meaning. For example, the teacher may direct students' attention to how words, phrases, and sentences are used to communicate inferred meanings. When appropriate, the teacher makes a photocopy of particular pages from the text and guides students to highlight specific language (see video link 4.1).
- **Writing About Learning:** The teacher prompts students to write about particular strategies they used to problem-solve during text reading.

Video 4.1   During the language phase, the intervention teacher and students revisit the text for a closer analysis of the book *Each Kindness*, by Jacqueline Woodson.

READING WORKSHOP IN THE CLASSROOM

During reading workshop, classroom teachers meet with students in small reading groups. In the early grades (generally kindergarten through second grade), the teacher selects texts that match students' instructional needs and prompts for successful strategies during a guided reading lesson (see Dorn and Jones 2012, Fountas and

Pinnell 1996). During these highly-tailored situations, the children read orally as the teacher observes their processing behaviors and provides the least amount of scaffolding to foster the students' independence. For students who are not progressing at the expected rate, the teacher analyzes the students' reading data for problem areas. For instance, if the students' data reveals a weakness in the area of decoding, the teacher might add a targeted intervention in word-solving and Writing About Reading to the traditional guided reading lesson. These additions mirror the supplemental Guided Reading Plus Intervention (see Chapter 6) that is delivered by the intervention specialist.

Once students have moved into silent reading (generally by the beginning or middle of second grade), the teacher transitions students into literature discussion groups. During literature discussion groups, the students read and discuss texts that are clustered around units of study. The format includes strategy-based minilessons, previewing and surveying strategies, silent reading, book discussions, and Writing About Reading (see Henderson and Dorn 2011; Dorn and Soffos 2005). During reading workshop, teachers plan explicit minilessons based on ten high-impact reading strategies (listed below) and provide students with opportunities to apply the strategies during guided and independent practice. These same ten strategies are carried over to the CFG intervention, as discussed in Chapter 8:

- Apply previewing strategies to gather information about the text and anticipate meanings.
- Ask questions before, during, and after reading to continually clarify and extend meaning.
- Reread the text for a closer analysis to refine and enhance meanings.
- Apply flexible strategies, including visualizing, predicting, summarizing, inferring, and monitoring, to construct meaning for the text.
- Activate prior knowledge (world experiences and specific academic knowledge) to make sense of the text.
- Use knowledge of text structures, language conventions, and genres to predict main and subordinate ideas.
- Highlight and annotate the text to remember content, ask questions, and make connections.
- Use context and word parts to infer meaning.
- Reflect on text meanings through Writing About Reading.
- Engage in focused, high-quality discussions on the meaning of the text.

Themed units provide students with a bridge for building relationships across genre, vocabulary, and story elements, thus fostering their capacity to comprehend bigger ideas, build fluency, and activate strategies for making meaning. Within the themed unit, the teacher selects one or more complex texts and uses the following structure for engaging students in reading for deeper comprehension.

- Teacher provides a brief overview of the text meaning, including important vocabulary, and students preview and survey the text independently.
- Teacher guides students to set a purpose for reading and encourages students to use comprehension strategies.
- Students read silently and highlight areas in text where they have questions, make connections, or want to discuss with others.
- Teacher and students engage in one-to-one teacher conferences about the text meaning.
- Students respond to text in their reading logs.
- Students engage in book discussion with teacher mediation at critical points.

ADDITIONAL SUPPORT FOR LOW-PROGRESS READERS

For students who are experiencing difficulty with reading complex texts, the teacher should provide additional experiences with the text. After analyzing the student's reading data to determine the problem areas, the teacher should design a Tier 1 classroom intervention, for example, providing the student with one-to-one reading conferences in the targeted area or preparing an audiotape of the text for the student's repeated reading. If the student is experiencing significant difficulties with reading complex texts, they could receive supplemental instruction (Tier 2 or 3, depending on intensity) in the CFG intervention. The CFG intervention includes the literature discussion group component and is designed to align with text types or units in the classroom. In Table 4.1, we distinguish between the instructional goals for guided reading groups and literature discussion groups based on the students' reading competencies. Then, in Figure 4.4, we illustrate the complementary features of small-group reading instruction across classroom and intervention settings.

Table 4.1.   Instructional Goals for Guided Reading Groups and Literature Discussion Groups

Guided Reading Group (Emergent to Transitional)	Literature Discussion Group (Transitional and Beyond)
• To build foundational skills, apply cognitive strategies, and develop fluency while reading for meaning on texts that gradually increase in difficulty. • To respond to instruction and prompts that focus on integrating multiple sources of text information in order to construct and confirm the author's meaning. • To gain proficiency with leveled texts that gradually increase in difficulty and complexity. • To read independently with teacher support after hearing a book orientation. • To teach for strategic activity, including word-solving strategies. • To move from oral reading to partial silent reading at transitional level.	• To use knowledge of text structure, vocabulary, author's craft, and close reading strategies to understand complex ideas and themes within and across texts. • To engage in teacher-mediated book discussions using conversational moves among peers to facilitate and sustain discourse around big ideas and themes within complex texts. • To gain proficiency with trade books with more complex themes, vocabulary, and inferred meanings. • To employ strategies for previewing texts and/or self-selecting texts in a preplanned unit. • To make use of close reading strategies and deep comprehension. • To engage in silent reading, with oral reading of specific passages to provide evidence or clarify thinking.

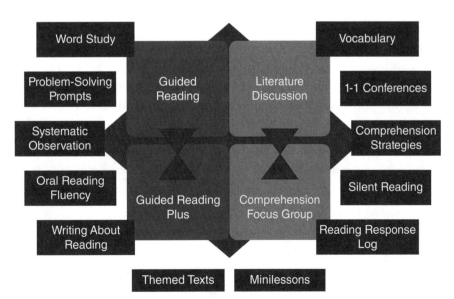

Figure 4.4   Complementary Features of Small-Group Reading Instruction Across Classroom and Intervention Programs

WRITING WORKSHOP IN THE CLASSROOM

Writing workshop is a differentiated framework in which students learn the processes of how to write. The teacher structures the time to ensure that students have an opportunity to plan, organize, and carry out writing projects. During writing workshop, students learn how to select their own topics, write in response to class topics, and develop these topics through revising and editing processes (see Dorn and Soffos 2002; Fletcher and Portalupi 2001).

The writing act is associated with four interrelated phases: planning, drafting, revising, and editing. These phases are not static, because writing is much too complex to organize in a strict sequence. Instead, good writers engage in simultaneous processes; for example, during drafting, the writer might revise on the spot or edit a spelling error when it is noticed. Good writers understand that the goal of writing is the creation of the message; therefore, any mechanical diversions during the drafting phase are carried out with minimal interruption. The four phases provide the writer with a flexible framework for developing a piece of writing with varying degrees of teacher scaffolding.

- **Planning:** The first step in writing is planning. Talking about a topic is one of the best ways to develop an idea for writing. During writing workshop, the teacher encourages students to share ideas for writing with one another. Additionally, the teacher uses minilessons to demonstrate how students can employ planning tools (e.g., writing guides, text maps, notes) to organize their thoughts for writing.
- **Drafting:** Once the topic is determined, the writer begins drafting the message on paper. For beginning writers, the greatest challenge occurs with transcribing thoughts while holding the ideas in working memory. At this level, the stories are short enough to be held in memory as students deal with the mechanical issues of getting the message on paper. As students acquire more skill with print, their transcribing process becomes smoother and more automatic. As a result, they write longer and more coherent texts, and they might have multiple drafts in process at one time. In Figure 4.5, a student reviews several drafts in his writing portfolio and selects a piece to work on.
- **Revising:** The revision process is regulated by the desire to express a clear and comprehensible message. Good writers revise at two development levels. The first level occurs during the composing process: the writer self-monitors the message for clarity and revises it when the meaning is threatened. This behavior is a natural part of the meaning-making process. The next level occurs after the writing is completed: the writer applies revising and crafting techniques to improve the clarity of the message. This behavior is the result of specialized knowledge that the writer has acquired through reading and writing experiences.
- **Editing:** The editing process involves monitoring the writing for mechanical errors: punctuation, grammar, and spelling. As with the revision process, good writers apply editing processes at two developmental levels. During the composing process, the writer notices an error when it occurs and makes a quick correction at that point. After the piece is completed, the writer searches for mechanical errors and uses editing tools to self-correct.

During writing workshop, teachers plan explicit minilessons based on ten essential writing strategies and provide students with opportunities to apply these strategies during writing conferences and independent writing experiences. In Chapter 8, we apply these same strategies to the Comprehension Focus Groups:

- Apply prewriting strategies (e.g., brainstorming, notetaking, outlining).
- Utilize various resources (e.g., graphic organizers, checklists, rubrics, internet, texts, media, interviews) to gather, organize, and check information throughout the writing process.
- Revise message for word choice and clarity of meaning.
- Apply editing and self-correcting strategies, including technological tools.
- Use sentence combining to organize short, choppy sentences into longer, more effective sentences.
- Vary sentence structures (length and complexity) to promote fluency, rhythm, and effect.
- Use transitional words and phrases to connect ideas and increase readability.

Figure 4.5   A third-grade student keeps multiple drafts of his writing in a writing portfolio. He selects a draft of an expository text that he started in content workshop to work on today.

- Use varied punctuation to communicate meaning.
- Use descriptive language and sensory details to create mind images (show, not tell).
- Use appropriate language conventions and text structures to communicate a clear and cohesive message for a particular audience and purpose.

WRITING CONFERENCES

The writing conference provides the student with the highest degree of differentiation. The tailored nature of the writing conference enables the teacher to respond at the student's instructional level. This occurs within the student's zone of proximal development—that is, the point at which a student is able to acquire new understandings with teacher assistance. The teacher's prompting is central to the student's performance; therefore, the teacher should ask three important questions:

- How might my prompting help the writer?
- How might my prompting hinder the writer?
- Am I promoting behaviors of dependence or independence in the writer?

The instructional goal is to engage the students in the problem-solving process while keeping the focus on constructing a clear and meaningful message. Here are some prompts for encouraging students to expand and elaborate on their message:

- What do you mean by that?
- Can you say more?

- Can you explain this to me?
- Can you help me understand this part?
- Can you say this another way to help your reader understand it better?

ADDITIONAL SUPPORT FOR LOW-PROGRESS WRITERS

If a student is not responding to differentiated instruction during writing workshop, the student should be assessed for a Tier 1 Writing Process (WP) intervention. The assessment begins with the systematic observation of the student's unassisted activity during the independent writing block. The intervention teacher records the number of minutes the student is able to work without help. If a student is unable to sustain attention during the independent writing block, they might be assessed for a WP intervention. The goal of the WP intervention is to provide tailored support within the classroom for a small group of students who are at risk of failure in writing.

For the intervention to be most effective, the classroom teacher and intervention teacher must collaborate on meeting the students' needs. The WP intervention is aligned with the classroom writing workshop, beginning with the classroom minilesson. If students are not responding to the minilesson, the intervention teacher provides a small-group minilesson (approximately five to seven minutes) to support their needs, followed by independent writing and conferences. During independent writing, the students use their writing journals or portfolios from the classroom workshop. They might develop a new piece or continue to work on a piece that was started during writing workshop. The WP intervention is typically twenty minutes long, and it is designed to provide struggling writers with "just right" support, while also ensuring they will have time to work independently within the classroom writing program.

In assessing students for a WP intervention, teachers follow a five-step cyclic process (see Figure 4.6):

- Provide a high-quality differentiated writing program to all students. Analyze student performance according to benchmark writing behaviors.
- Use data to determine if students will need a writing intervention.
- For students who are nearing proficiency, the classroom teacher provides some additional support, such as a tailored small-group minilesson or a tailored writing conference.
- For students who need significant help, the intervention teacher comes into the classroom and provides a twenty- to thirty-minute WP intervention.
- Students' progress is monitored at designated intervals using benchmark writing guides.

ASSESSING WRITING DEVELOPMENT

During writing instruction, teachers must understand the complexity of the task and strive to create a balance between the composing and transcribing processes. If teaching becomes unbalanced, the students' view of the writing process will reflect this bias. When teachers analyze students' writing, they can design their writing program based on what students already know and what they need to know to move their writing forward (Dorn and Soffos 2002).

The success of a WP intervention is based on two types of knowledge: the teacher's knowledge of the writer and the teacher's knowledge of the writing process. This means that the teacher will respond differently to an early writer than to a fluent writer. The teacher will gauge the level of scaffolding according to the writer's ability to accomplish the task.

USING A WRITING CONTINUUM

A writing continuum can be a valuable tool for assessing the link between instruction and learning. A continuum serves three purposes in a writing program:

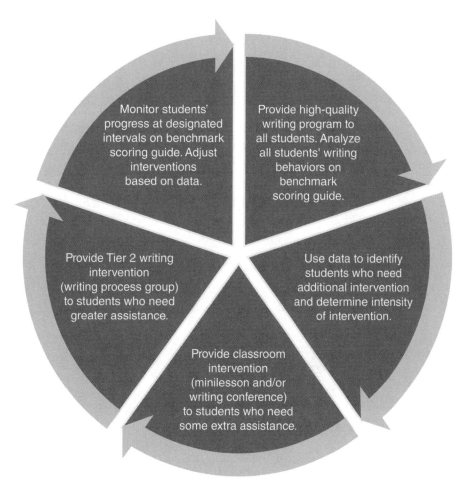

Figure 4.6   Cyclic Process for Using Data and Interventions to Meet the Needs of Struggling Writers During Writing Workshop

- It describes writing behaviors in clear and positive language.
- It aligns with national and state standards.
- It provides teachers with a practical and manageable system for assessing the links between curriculum, teaching, and student learning.

However, in order for writing continuums to be effective, teachers must be able to do the following:

- Recognize and understand the behavioral changes that occur as writing moves along a developmental continuum of simple to more complex.
- Understand the role of responsive instruction for accelerating writing growth.

In Table 4.2, we present typical behaviors for students along a writing continuum that spans the stages of emergent to transitional and beyond. The behaviors are classified under the phases of the writing process (planning, drafting, revising, and editing). For example, in the planning phase, the typical kindergarten writer is able to plan ideas by drawing a picture; at the transitional level, the typical third-grade writer uses a writing guide related to text structure for planning ideas. In the drafting phase, the typical kindergarten writer uses a practice page to experiment with spellings; at the transitional level, the third-grade writer uses a planning page for word choices. As students make gains along the revising and editing continuum, they acquire more skills, strategies, and knowledge for improving their writing. In Resource D.3a, b, c, and d, we provide scoring guides for assessing change over time in kindergarten to third-grade writing behaviors along a writing continuum.

Table 4.2.   Change over Time in Planning, Drafting, Revising, and Editing Behaviors of Writers

	Emergent Planning Behaviors Kindergarten	Beginning Early Planning Behaviors First Grade	Late Early Planning Behaviors Second Grade	Transitional Planning Behaviors Third Grade
Planning	• Generates topics or ideas for writing across genres with teacher assistance • Organizes ideas prior to drafting; uses planning ideas to compose message ○ Plans writing by drawing a picture/s or symbols in journal or on writing paper that represent an event or several loosely linked events ○ Plans informational/explanatory writing by drawing a picture/s or symbols to represent some information ○ Plans persuasive piece by drawing a picture/s that represents their opinion about a book or topic • Rehearses message orally (conferences ideas) with teacher	• Generates topics or ideas across genres with or without teacher assistance; begins to demonstrate some understanding of author's purpose and its relationship to text structure • Organizes ideas prior to drafting; draws picture/s of key ideas on writing paper organized to support text structure ○ Plans simple recount by drawing picture/s to represent events or key ideas ○ Plans informational/explanatory writing by drawing picture/s to represent information about topic and topic details ○ Plans persuasive piece by drawing and discussing their opinion on an idea or topic; uses language to support opinion and reasons • Rehearses message orally (conferences ideas) with teacher or peers	• Generates topics or ideas for writing across genres; demonstrates an understanding of author's purpose and its relationship to text structure • Organizes ideas prior to drafting; narrows focus on a topic • Uses writing guide related to text structure or creates outline ○ Plans recount by using words or phrases to support event sequence and details ○ Plans informational/explanatory writing by gathering information pertinent to a specific topic or to answer a question/s using a variety of provided text sources; sorts information into major categories ○ Plans persuasive piece by taking a stance on an idea or topic; uses words and/or phrases to provide opinions and reasons • Rehearses message orally (conferences ideas) with teacher or peers as needed	• Generates topics or ideas for writing across genres; demonstrates an understanding of author's purpose and its relationship to text structure • Organizes ideas prior to drafting; narrows focus on a topic • Uses writing guide related to text structure or creates outline ○ Plans story by recording words and/or phrases to develop event sequence and actions of characters ○ Plans informational/explanatory writing by researching and gathering information pertinent to a specific topic or to answer questions using a variety of text sources; sorts information into major categories ○ Plans persuasive piece by taking a stance on an idea or topic; uses words and/or phrases to provide opinion and reasons • Rehearses message orally (conferences ideas) with teacher or peers as needed

Drafting			
• Establishes a relationship between print and pictures • Writes left to right across several lines of text; uses spaces between words with greater accuracy • Holds simple sentences in memory while encoding message; rereads to remember next word • Writes most alphabet letters fluently and with correct formation • Analyzes unknown words using slow articulation; records letters in word sequence • Uses parts of known words to help spell parts of unknown words (analogy)	• Holds simple ideas in memory while encoding message • Rereads to remember next word or phrase; begins to reflect on meaning, sentence structures, and word choice when prompted • Writes alphabet letters fluently and with correct formation • Analyzes unknown words using slow articulation; records letters in word sequence; spells grade level words conventionally, e.g., words composed of short vowel patterns • Breaks unknown words into onset and rime or at meaningful and logical units; uses common spelling patterns to spell words conventionally • Uses known words as a base for adding simple inflectional endings, e.g., s, ing, ed	• Holds ideas in memory while encoding message • Rereads to remember next idea; reflects on meaning, sentence structures, and word choice • Analyzes unknown words on the run; thinks visually about how words look; spells grade level words conventionally, e.g., words composed of long vowel patterns • Breaks unknown words into syllables, onset, and rime or at meaningful and logical units; uses common spelling patterns to spell words conventionally • Uses known words as a base for adding inflectional endings, e.g., s, es, ing, ed • Writes grade level high-frequency words fluently and accurately • Uses practice page to try out word spellings less often; analyzes unknown words on the run	• Holds more complex ideas in memory while encoding message • Rereads to remember next idea; reflects on meaning, sentence structures, and word choice • Analyzes unknown words on the run; spells grade level words conventionally, e.g., words composed of r-vowels, other vowels, and some irregular vowels • Breaks unknown words into syllables, syllables into onset and rime or at meaningful and logical units; uses common and irregular spelling pattern knowledge to spell words conventionally • Uses known words as a base for adding inflectional endings, e.g., s, es, ing, ed • Uses word meanings to spell words conventionally, e.g., prefixes, suffixes, and homophones

(Continued)

Table 4.2. *(Continued)*

	Emergent Drafting Behaviors Kindergarten	Beginning Early Drafting Behaviors First Grade	Late Early Drafting Behaviors Second Grade	Transitional Drafting Behaviors Third Grade
Drafting	• Spells most unknown words phonetically drawing on phonemic awareness and sound-letter relationships • Uses a practice page to try out letters or word spellings • Uses resources for sound-letter link, e.g., ABC chart, name chart, and/or letter books • Writes easy grade level high-frequency words fluently and accurately • Uses syntax of oral language; may include some book language and content-specific vocabulary • Experiments with simple punctuation, e.g., uses punctuation as markers between words or to designate the end of each line or page	• Writes grade level high-frequency words fluently and accurately • Uses a practice page to try out letters or word spellings • Uses resources less often for sound-letter link, e.g., ABC chart, name chart, and/or letter books • Includes some words that reflect attention to vocabulary and word meanings from reading • Applies grade level standard English grammar and language usage appropriately • Applies grade level conventions of standard English, e.g., capitalization and punctuation appropriately	• Begins to use practice page for trying out word choice; begins to consider words and phrases from reading to support craft • Includes words that reflect attention to vocabulary and word meanings from reading • Applies grade level standard English grammar and language usage appropriately • Applies grade level conventions of standard English, e.g., capitalization and punctuation appropriately	• Writes grade level high-frequency words fluently and accurately • Writing includes words that reflect attention to vocabulary and word meanings from reading • Uses practice page to try out crafting techniques (word choice, leads, endings etc.) • Applies grade level standard English grammar and language usage appropriately • Applies grade level conventions of standard English; e.g., capitalization and punctuation appropriately

• Rereads message and reflects on meaning when prompted	• Uses a simple writing checklist to check on writing process • Rereads message and reflects on meaning and sentence structures when prompted • X-out unwanted words; revises language for more appropriate word choice to stimulate imagery when prompted • Eliminates some redundant and unnecessary information when prompted • Circles a few words that do not look right; uses a simple dictionary to look up words and self-correct spelling • Revises conventions of standard English, e.g., capitalization and punctuation when prompted and supported • Revises standard English grammar and language usage when prompted and supported	• Uses a simple writing checklists to check on writing process • Rereads message and reflects on meaning and sentence structures more independently • X-out unwanted words; revises language for more appropriate word choice to stimulate imagery when prompted more independently • Eliminates redundant and unnecessary information when prompted • Circles words that do not look right; uses a dictionary to look up words and self-correct spelling • Revises conventions of standard English, e.g., capitalization and punctuation more independently • Revises standard English grammar and language usage more independently	• Uses a writing checklist to check on writing process • Rereads message and reflects on meaning and sentence structures • Eliminates redundant and unnecessary information • Revises and groups ideas by rearranging words, sentences, or phrases; uses cut-and-paste, circles, and lines to group ideas • Revises language to stimulate imagery; uses a thesaurus to support craft as needed • Circles words that do not look right; uses a dictionary to self-correct spelling and to check on word meanings • Revises conventions of standard English, e.g., capitalization and punctuation independently • Revises standard English grammar and language usage independently

A QUICK LOOK AT SPELLING INSTRUCTION

As we conclude this chapter, we acknowledge the importance of systematic spelling instruction within a language workshop framework, including opportunities for students to transfer their phonological and orthographic knowledge to reading and writing tasks. The theory of transfer implies that knowledge has become more integrated and generalizable and is therefore more useful for learning new information. Through successful repeated practice, students' literacy behaviors become more refined, accurate, and automatic. In the process, particular behaviors become unconscious responses to stimuli, thus freeing the reader's attention to focus on more important aspects of the reading process.

In Chapter 1, we discussed how students use multisensory information, including motor movements and language descriptors, to perceive and organize phonological and orthographic sources into associative networks. To develop cognitive flexibility, low-progress readers need opportunities to sort their knowledge according to decoding and semantic categories simultaneously. For sure, word knowledge is essential in learning to read, but not to the exclusion of meaning. The ultimate goal of teaching is for students to become self-regulated and independent learners with the capacity to initiate plans, monitor results, maintain persistence toward a successful solution, and utilize their knowledge, skills, and strategies for learning from experience. Learning to comprehend, organize, and respond to verbal information is a complex process. To deal with this level of complexity, teachers must be knowledgeable about learning theory and skillful at using observational data to select interventions that promote reading development.

CLOSING THOUGHTS

As stated before, the first line of literacy defense occurs at the classroom level. All students must be provided with high-quality, evidence-based, differentiated classroom instruction. An integrated workshop provides the design for balancing rigor and support through whole-group, small-group, and one-to-one experiences. In the workshop, students engage in challenging and motivating work, while teachers provide varying degrees of scaffolding to ensure a successful experience. The instructional goal is achieved when students are able to transfer their knowledge and strategies to new situations for varied purposes. However, if a student needs additional support beyond the classroom, the classroom and intervention teachers should meet to align instructional goals. All interventions within the CIM portfolio feature evidence-based practices that are also part of the integrated workshop, thus creating situations that promote transfer.

Chapter 5

ASSISTED WRITING FOR INCREASING READING POWER

Reading and writing are language processes that involve many of the same strategies to communicate meaning. Writing is a powerful intervention for increasing reading achievement, but only if reading and writing are taught as reciprocal processes. The physical act of writing slows down the reading process, which allows the learner to focus on word-solving strategies and concepts of print while composing a message. If the writing is meaningful, it promotes the integration of three language systems: (a) comprehension of ideas (semantic system), (b) expression of ideas (syntactic system), and (c) facility with mechanics (orthographic and phonological systems). The links between reading and writing are established as students use their written messages as reading materials.

Learning to write is both a cognitive and a social process. Young students are apprenticed into writing through meaningful interactions with a more knowledgeable person. As an intervention, the physical act of transcribing language, while keeping the message up front, is a complex neurological activity. It engages higher-level psychological functions, such as conscious awareness (actively paying attention, working memory (holding important information in place while acting upon it), integration (pulling related sources together), and problem-solving (using strategies to deal with barriers). When students write, they acquire cognitive strategies for attending, monitoring, searching, evaluating, and self-correcting their actions. These invisible processes are made more visible through the overt actions of transcribing a message.

Clay (2015) presents a strong case for the power of early writing in orchestrating brain activity. A young writer must be able to utilize information (background knowledge) from the semantic, syntactic, phonological, and orthographic systems—along with a set of useful strategies (intentional actions)—for achieving a purposeful goal. As Healy (2004) explains, to construct a writing system, the writer must coordinate a number of complex cognitive tasks:

- Assemble background information for expressing ideas (semantic system).
- Formulate an original statement that represents the message to be communicated (semantic and syntactic systems).
- Find the right words to express the ideas in a clear and precise way (semantic and syntactic systems).
- Place the words in the correct order to communicate meaning (semantic and syntactic systems).
- Hold the ideas in working memory long enough to transcribe the message on paper (semantic, syntactic, phonological, and orthographic systems (Healy, 2004).

In this chapter, we'll describe how a writing intervention is used to increase the achievement of struggling readers at the emergent, early, and transitional levels. We will describe two types of Assisted Writing and the specialized procedures for implementing each intervention.

ASSISTED WRITING INTERVENTION

Assisted Writing is an umbrella term for classifying two types of writing: Interactive Writing (IW) and Writing Aloud (WA). At the emergent to beginning early levels, the IW intervention provides a language context for enabling students to take the following critical steps:

- Compose simple messages.
- Acquire foundational concepts about print.
- Understand that writing is about communicating a message.
- Apply rereading strategies to predict and monitor the reading.
- Articulate words slowly and hear and record letters in words.
- Use simple resources as self-help tools (ABC chart, personal dictionary, writing checklist).
- Write letters fluently and with correct letter formation.
- Build a core of high-frequency words.

The WA intervention is used with writers who have knowledge of foundational writing concepts (see above) but are struggling with the writing process. The goal of Writing Aloud is to help students build on these foundational concepts in the following ways:

- Develop an understanding of the writing process and apply problem-solving strategies for organizing, composing, editing, and revising a meaningful message.
- Understand how to use resources for planning, monitoring, and regulating the writing process.

In Table 5.1, we describe the differences and similarities between the IW and the WA interventions. To select the best intervention, the teacher must understand three learning theories:

- Theory of the student: what the student knows about writing and how this knowledge can be used to acquire new information.
- Theory of the intervention procedure: why and when a specific procedure is implemented.
- Theory of contingent scaffolding: how to adjust scaffolding based on what the student needs in order to accomplish the learning goal.

For kindergarten and first-grade students with low concepts about print, the teacher might use the IW intervention for several weeks prior to the Guided Reading intervention (Owens 2015). Also, the teacher might choose to layer the two interventions (e.g., GRP on Monday through Thursday and IW on Friday). Teachers can use the following questions to determine the most appropriate intervention based on a student's knowledge about print:

- Can the student distinguish between text and illustration?
- Does the student have some understanding of directionality?
- Does the student have some knowledge of one-to-one matching?
- Does the student know the difference between letters and words?
- Does the student know the letters of the alphabet and a few frequently encountered words (e.g., *I*, *the*, *a*)?
- Does the student actively participate in shared reading by predicting events and language structures that show an awareness of comprehension, rhythm, and rhyme? (See Dorn and Jones 2012.)

Table 5.1.   Comparison of Interactive Writing and Writing Aloud Interventions

Interactive Writing	Writing Aloud
A short story read aloud, a story told by the teacher, or a personal experience may be the basis of the group composition. The text is negotiated. The final story is decided upon by the group and rehearsed before writing.	A short story read aloud, a story told by the teacher, or a personal experience may be the basis of the group composition. The text is negotiated, and the teacher thinks aloud about the story's development.
The students and the teacher share the role of scribe. The students actively contribute by writing known letters and/or words from the text on individual dry erase boards. The teacher transcribes the text on the class chart, while inviting individual students to record a few known words on the class chart.	The teacher is the primary scribe, who guides the students in composing a meaningful and interesting message. The teacher selects two or three examples from the text and invites the students to apply problem-solving strategies to the words.
The teacher models early reading and writing strategies while engaging the students in creating the text.	The teacher thinks aloud while writing and involves the students in constructive dialogue about the story and the writing process.
The goal of writing is to develop an awareness of print concepts within the context of a meaningful language composition. Students learn how to use resources for planning and monitoring their thinking. The writing is used as a text for teaching important reading and writing concepts.	The goal of writing is to develop an understanding of the writing process and to apply problem-solving strategies for organizing, composing, editing, and revising a meaningful message. Students learn how to use resources for planning and monitoring their thinking.
The finished text ranges from one to five sentences in length and is read as a shared experience with the teacher. The finished text is accurate.	The finished text is well developed and may be organized according to text conventions. The teacher and students read the text together several times during the writing process. The finished text may include many revisions and editing techniques.
The writing of a single text is completed in one setting. The writing is displayed in the room and might be used for shared or familiar reading.	The writing of the text may occur over several days. A final version might or might not be published, since the focus is on the process. The revised version is not generally used for rereading.

INTERVENTION FRAMEWORK FOR INTERACTIVE WRITING

The lesson framework for Interactive Writing occurs in three phases (language phase, writing phase, and reading phase), with thirty minutes of instruction each day. Each phase includes specialized procedures for building students' knowledge of reading and writing as language-based processes. It is essential for students to have daily instruction as they strive to build connections between past and future learning. With struggling readers, familiarity and recency are the cornerstones of accelerated learning.

Phase One: Language Phase. During the language phase, the students enhance their listening and speaking comprehension through shared and interactive reading experiences. At the same time, they acquire knowledge about book concepts, text structures, literary language, and specialized vocabulary as they begin to anticipate particular language structures that occur within written language with additional targeted support for English Acquisition Learners (EALs). This knowledge gives them a personal foundation for making meaningful predictions as they read stories on their own. The interactive read-aloud component is designed to meet five instructional goals:

- Provide a good model of fluent and expressive reading.
- Provide opportunities for writing.
- Provide opportunities for retelling.
- Increase students' concept and vocabulary knowledge.
- Promote an enjoyable and engaging experience with books.

Phase Two: The Writing Phase. In both the writing and reading phases, the first component uses activities to develop the students' knowledge of sounds, letters, and words (see Chapter 7). One procedure focuses on the shared reading of an enlarged alphabet chart. The purpose is to help the students acquire letter–sound connections they can use when they are reading and writing. Each child has a reduced version of the chart, which is also used during independent writing.

During the shared reading, the teacher leads the students in saying the name of each upper- and lowercase letter and pointing to a drawing of an item beginning with that letter. The letters are read fluently, and the teacher pauses occasionally to allow the students to say the letters or the name of the picture symbol.

Another phase two activity involves the students' personal word dictionary. In this activity, the students record their known words in alphabetical order under a familiar picture cue. Then they read the words to promote fast visual recognition. The teacher can then use the students' newly acquired word knowledge as a resource for learning new words. The personal word dictionary is particularly supportive for EALs to have a visual record of their expanding vocabulary.

In the writing phase, the teacher designs instruction with specialized procedures for linking the reading and writing processes. The writing phase begins with Interactive Writing—a collaborative experience in which the teacher and students co-construct a meaningful message. Language development is embedded in all aspects of the IW intervention. Therefore, teachers need to consider two language-based principles:

- Students must have adequate time to engage in a meaningful discussion around a common event.
- Students must be fully invested in the words and ideas they will work with in their message.

These principles imply that the teacher cannot decide in advance exactly what the message will be; however, the teacher can plan for a shared experience that will engage the students in a meaningful and interesting discussion.

Validating & Activating Knowledge

Teacher praises child for correct responses as he/she
places a light check over the correct responses.

√   √ √   √ √   √ √   √ √   √   √ √

I lk mi dge he s ns.

Teacher writes story at the bottom of page. The teacher
models saying words slowly as he/she writes the child's
story.

I like my dog. He is nice.

Figure 5.1   Validating and Activating the Student's Phonological and Orthographic Knowledge

The IW component provides a context for helping students acquire early reading and writing behaviors. The teacher uses specialized language to activate the students' problem-solving strategies (planning, monitoring, searching, confirming, and self-correcting actions). Here are some examples of instructional prompts:

- Reread and make sure your message makes sense and sounds right.
- Say the word slowly to help you spell the word.
- What do you hear first? Next? Last?
- Can you think of another word that could help you write this word?
- Use your ABC chart to help you start that word.
- What two letters would you need to make the word look right?

Following Interactive Writing, the students are ready to write on their own, and the teacher conducts individual writing conferences. Each writing conference includes specialized procedures for validating and activating the student's knowledge.

- The teacher prompts the student to read the message; if the student struggles on a word, the teacher joins the reading, keeping the focus on fluency and comprehension. At the end of the reading, the teacher validates the student's writing by responding to the message as the goal of reading.
- The teacher validates the student's phonological and orthographic knowledge by going through each letter in a left-to-right sequence and placing a light checkmark above the correct letter-to-sound match, including whole words that are spelled correctly (see Figure 5.1).
- The teacher writes the student's message at the bottom of the page, explaining, "I'll write it the way it looks in a book." Then the teacher prompts the student to point to the words and read the message. The goal of the interaction is to validate the student's work while simultaneously modeling how written language looks in a book.

Phase Three: Reading Phase. This component uses the same letter, sound, and word activities as discussed above in the Writing Phase (see Chapter 7). In the following component of the reading phase, the teacher provides a book orientation to a simple text that contains familiar letters and words, with opportunities for students to develop early monitoring and cross-checking strategies. As the students read, the teacher observes their behaviors and prompts them to match visual and sound cues with syntactic and semantic sources as they read for meaning. During the final component, the students engage in the discussion of text, and share examples of the strategies they used when problem-solving on challenging words.

MATERIALS FOR INTERACTIVE WRITING

Interactive Writing is designed to increase students' reading development through a writing intervention. The intervention includes a predictable framework, established routines, and clear procedures. It is critical that the teacher is well organized, with all materials easily accessible. The teacher's materials include large poetry charts, big books, books for read-aloud, large chart tablet, black marker and eraser, large alphabet chart and name chart, language and strategy charts, and large writing checklist. The students' materials include small ABC chart, small dry erase board, black marker and eraser, magnetic letters and small bowl for holding letters, letter–sound books, personal word dictionary, and unlined writing journal with practice page at the top.

PLANNING FOR INSTRUCTION

Planning is a critical component of a successful IW intervention. Prior to instruction, the teacher selects the appropriate materials and plans specific activities to meet the instructional goals. We have included two resources to assist teachers with effective planning: the lesson planner and the Guide Sheet. The lesson planner provides a decision-making framework for responsive teaching based on students' strengths and needs and in alignment with the literacy continuum (see Resource E.1, Lesson Planner for Interactive Writing Intervention).

The Guide Sheet provides procedural steps for implementing the IW group with consistency. (See Figure 5.2; see also Resource E.2, Guide Sheet for Interactive Writing Intervention, for the reproducible form.) Additionally, we have provided video links to specific lesson components discussed in the Guide Sheet.

Guide Sheet for Interactive Writing Intervention	
Section on Planner	**Phase Two: Writing** *Fluent Writing, Phonological Awareness,* *Letter and Word Learning, Record of Learning, Reflection and Goal Setting*
Part 1	**Fluent Writing:** The goal is for students to write all letters and a small core of high-frequency words fluently. The teacher supports students in the following ways: • Selects one or two partially known letters for the students to bring to fluency through fluent practice. • Selects one or two partially known high-frequency words for the students to bring to fluency through fluent practice. **Reading of ABC Chart:** The goal is for students to read all letters of the alphabet with speed and accuracy. The teacher and students practice the following activities: • Read the name of each upper- and lowercase letter fluently and point to the adjacent picture that begins with that letter. • Read the ABC chart in a variety of ways (e.g., read all the vowels, read all the consonants) to develop print knowledge.

Figure 5.2   Guide Sheet for Interactive Writing Intervention

Figure 5.3   Teacher and students engage in choral reading of the ABC chart. Student reads small version of chart while teacher reads from the large chart.

Phonological and Phonemic Awareness: The goal is for students to hear and manipulate both larger and smaller units of sound within the sound structure of spoken words: word boundaries, syllables, rhyming (onset and rime), and individual phonemes within words. The teacher supports students in the following ways:

- Provides explicit instruction in hearing and identifying individual words within spoken language.
- Provides explicit instruction in hearing and identifying syllables within a spoken word.
- Provides explicit instruction in hearing, identifying, generating, and manipulating onset and rime in spoken words.
- Provides explicit instruction in hearing, segmenting, blending, deleting, substituting, and adding individual phonemes within words.

Letter and/or Word Learning: The goal is for students to become fluent with identifying letters, mapping letter and word patterns to sounds, blending letter sounds, identifying syllable types, and using morphological units to enhance word learning.

Letter Learning: The goal is for students to become fluent with identifying and naming all letters in the alphabet and to distinguish between consonants and vowels. The teacher supports students in the following ways:

- Provides explicit instruction in letter learning and opportunities for fluent practice.
- Provides explicit instruction in letter learning by supporting students in learning how to notice the features of letters and to understand how the features come together in a specific order to give the letter its name.
- Provides kinesthetic experiences (salt, sandpaper, shaving cream) to help the students learn the directionality principle of the features of the letters.
- Directs students' attention to the features of letters by providing them with an opportunity to trace over letters, describe the path of movement, and name the letters.
- Provides students with an opportunity to sort letters by letter features, similarities and differences, uppercase and lowercase, letter sounds, and letter name.
- Provides an opportunity for students to read and write letters fluently.

Figure 5.2   (*Continued*)

Word Learning: The goal is for students to use their phonological and orthographic knowledge to develop a system for learning how words work along a continuum and to transfer their knowledge across reading and writing events. The teacher supports students in the following ways:

- Provides explicit and systematic phonics instruction to help children learn how words work along a continuum from simple to more complex.
- Uses a gradual release model to make decisions about explicit instruction of the phonetic principle being addressed.
- Provides explicit instruction in letter–sound mapping, including segmenting and blending.
- Provides opportunities for fluent decoding and reading practice using decodable sentences or text.
- Provides explicit and systematic instruction in building words that include the targeted phonetic principle being addressed and plans opportunities for fluent reading of words.
- Provides explicit instruction in identifying the difference between consonants and vowels.
- Provides explicit and systematic instruction in how to use known words and word parts to build, read, and write unknown words.
- Provides explicit instruction in building a core of high-frequency words.

Decodable Sentences or Text (optional): The goal is for students to practice reading decodable sentences or text fluently, with attention to both decoding and comprehension. The teacher supports students in the following ways:

- Provides an opportunity for students to read decodable texts that include phonics skills that have been previously taught in the phonics scope and sequence continuum.
- Provides an opportunity for students to read decodable texts to build fluency and automaticity.

Personal Dictionary (optional): The goal is for students to have a resource for organizing and storing partially known high-frequency words. The teacher supports students in the following ways:

- Uses prior word-learning experiences that focus on building high-frequency words and other words along the word-learning continuum.
- Provides an opportunity for students to record partially known high-frequency words in their personal dictionaries.
- Provides students with an opportunity to read their recorded words from a few pages in their dictionaries for fluency practice.

Reflection and Goal Setting: The goal is for students to become metacognitive about their learning and to transfer their knowledge across reading and writing events. The teacher supports students in the following ways:

- Encourages students to reflect on the prior word-learning principle and provide examples.
- Provides students with an opportunity to set new goals for transferring the phonetic principle to problem-solving on unknown words when reading and writing.

Section on Planner	*Co-Construction of Group Message*
Part 2	**Co-Construction of Group Message:** The goal is for the students to acquire strategies for writing across different genres.

Before Co-Construction of Message:

The teacher prepares students in the following ways:

- Holds a genuine conversation with the students around a common experience, a story or poem read aloud in the Language Phase, or a simple text that they have read previously to capture a message for writing.
- Records quickly the group message on the lesson planner while the students rehearse the message.
- Makes a quick decision based on the students' spelling development about which letters and/or words to take to fluency, which words to use as a tool for assisting the students in learning how to map sounds to letters, and which letters or words need to be written by teacher.

Video 5.1a   The teacher and students generate a group message during interactive writing intervention.

Figure 5.2   (*Continued*)

During Co-Construction of Message:

The teacher supports students in the following ways:

- Engages students in sharing the responsibility of transcribing the message.
- Models and encourages students to use their dry erase boards to write letters and high-frequency words for fluency and to participate in the spelling process of selected words.
- Prompts students to apply writing and spelling strategies while encoding a message and scaffolds the process as needed.
- Rereads message with students to check for meaning, language, and spelling accuracy.

Video 5.1b   The teacher guides students in composing, and transcribing a group message.

Figure 5.4   Teacher scaffolds student to use ABC chart as special cue in solving a new word.

After Co-Construction of Message:

The teacher supports students in the following way:

- Engages students in using a simple writing checklist to reflect on the problem-solving processes used while writing the group message and to promote transfer to independent writing.

Section on Planner	*Independent Writing* *Reflection and Goal Setting*
Part 3	**Independent Writing:** The goal is for students to transfer writing strategies to their own writing and to provide the teacher with an opportunity to observe how students are transferring their skills and strategies independently. The teacher supports students in the following ways: • Prompts and appropriately scaffolds students to apply rereading strategies to prepare for next move and to think about meaning and language. • Prompts and appropriately scaffolds students to use spelling strategies to conventionally spell words with simple word patterns. • Provides students with an ABC chart and an individual writing checklist as tools for prompting transfer and strategic problem-solving actions.

Figure 5.2   (*Continued*)

- Provides an opportunity for students to write their message using unlined paper and also provides a blank practice page for applying problem-solving strategies while writing.
- Prompts students to use their personal dictionaries to look up word spellings after writing if needed to confirm or edit spelling.

Figure 5.5   Student uses ABC chart as a self-help tool during independent writing.

Writing Checklist

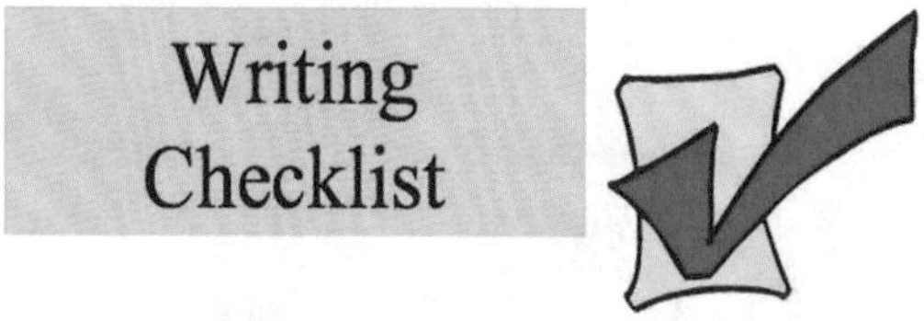

➤ Did you start in the right place ___?

➤ Did you leave spaces between words to make it easier to read ___?

➤ Did you say the words slowly and write the letters that make those sounds ___?

➤ Did you use the alphabet chart to help you with letters and sounds ___?

➤ Did you reread to help you know the next word to write ___?

➤ Did you use your practice page to help you work on the hard parts ___?

➤ Did your story make sense ___?

➤ Did you use an ? or ! or . at the end of each sentence ___?

Figure 5.6   The writing checklist is first introduced as a shared reading experience, then students use a personal copy of the checklist to help themselves during independent writing and teacher conferences.

Figure 5.2   (*Continued*)

Video 5.2   The teacher conducts individual conferences with students while prompting them to use personal resources to solve problems within text. At the end of the conference component, the teacher engages the students in reviewing the strategies they used.

Reflection and Goal Setting: The goal is for students to reflect on their writing and to set goals for transferring their knowledge across other writing events. The teacher supports students in the following ways:

- Provides an opportunity for students to reflect on writing strategies employed, using a writing checklist, and to present an example from their writing to demonstrate the strategy shared.
- Provides an opportunity for students to set goals for transferring successful planning and writing strategies to other writing events.

Section on Planner	**Phase Three: Reading** *Fluent Writing, Phonological Awareness,* *Letter and Word Learning, Record of Learning, Reflection and Goal Setting*
Part 1	**Fluent Writing:** The goal is for the students to write fluently all letters and a small core of high-frequency words. The teacher supports students in the following ways: - Selects one or two partially known letters for the students to bring to fluency through fluent practice. - Selects one or two partially known high-frequency words for the students to bring to fluency through fluent practice. **Shared Reading of ABC Chart:** The goal is for students to read all letters of the alphabet with speed and accuracy. The teacher and students practice the following activities: - Read the name of each upper- and lowercase letter fluently and point to the adjacent picture that begins with that letter. - Read the ABC chart in a variety of ways (e.g., read all the vowels, read all the consonants) to develop print knowledge. **Phonological and Phonemic Awareness:** The goal is for the students to hear and manipulate both larger and smaller units of sound within the sound structure of spoken words: word boundaries, syllables, rhyming (onset and rime), and individual phonemes within words. The teacher supports students in the following ways: - Provides explicit instruction in hearing and identifying individual words within spoken language. - Provides explicit instruction in hearing and identifying syllables within a spoken word. - Provides explicit instruction in hearing, identifying, generating, and manipulating onset and rime in spoken words. - Provides explicit instruction in hearing, segmenting, blending, deleting, substituting, and adding individual phonemes within words. Video 5.3 Teacher guides students in shared reading of a poem and the ABC chart. **Letter and/or Word Learning:** The goal is for the students to become fluent with identifying letters, mapping letters and word patterns to sounds, blending letter sounds, identifying syllable types, and using morphological units to enhance word learning. **Letter Learning:** The goal is for students to become fluent with identifying and naming all letters in the alphabet and to distinguish between consonants and vowels. The teacher supports students in the following ways: - Provides explicit instruction in letter learning and opportunities for fluent practice.

Figure 5.2   (*Continued*)

- Provides explicit instruction in letter learning by supporting students in learning how to notice the features of letters and to understand how the features come together in a specific order to give the letter its name.
- Provides kinesthetic experiences (salt, sandpaper, shaving cream) to help the students learn the directionality principle of the features of the letters.
- Directs students' attention to the features of letters by providing them with an opportunity to trace over letters, describe the path of movement, and name the letters.
- Provides students with an opportunity to sort letters by letter features, similarities and differences, uppercase and lowercase, letter sounds, and letter name.
- Provides an opportunity for students to read and write letters fluently.

Word Learning: The goal is for students to use their phonological and orthographic knowledge to develop a system for learning how words work along a continuum and to transfer their knowledge across reading and writing events. The teacher supports students in the following ways:

- Provides explicit and systematic phonics instruction to help children learn how words work along a continuum from simple to more complex.
- Uses a gradual release model to make decisions about explicit instruction of the phonetic principle being addressed.
- Provides explicit instruction in letter–sound mapping, including segmenting and blending, and provides opportunities for fluent decoding and reading practice.
- Provides explicit and systematic instruction in building words that include the targeted phonetic principle being addressed and plans opportunities for fluent reading of words.
- Provides explicit instruction in identifying the difference between consonants and vowels.
- Provides explicit instruction in identifying the syllable type and how it aligns with the phonetic principle being addressed.
- Provides explicit and systematic instruction in how to use known words and word parts to build, read, and write unknown words.
- Provides an opportunity for students to transfer their word knowledge to reading and writing unknown words.
- Provides explicit instruction in building a core of high-frequency words.

Personal Dictionary (optional): The goal is to provide students with a resource for organizing and storing known high-frequency words. The teacher uses prior word-learning experiences that focus on building high-frequency words to provide the students with an opportunity to record words in their dictionary. The teacher supports students in the following ways:

- Provides an opportunity for students to record partially known high-frequency words in their personal dictionaries.
- Provides students with an opportunity to read their recorded words from a few pages in their dictionaries for fluency practice.

Video 5.4   Teacher guides students in learning about letters and words.

Reflection and Goal Setting: The goal is for students to become metacognitive about their learning and to transfer their knowledge across reading and writing events. The teacher supports students in the following ways:

- Encourages students to reflect on the prior word-learning principle and provide examples.
- Provides students with an opportunity to set new goals for transferring the phonetic principle to problem-solving on unknown words when reading and writing.

Figure 5.2   (*Continued*)

Section on Planner	Guided Reading *Orientation to Text—Set Purpose for Reading, Independent Reading*
Part 2	**Guided Reading:** The goal is for students to set a meaningful purpose for reading and use flexible comprehension and word-solving strategies as needed to comprehend the text. **Before Reading—Orientation to New Text:** The goal is for students to apply their background knowledge of topic, text genre, text structure, language, and word-solving strategies to prepare for the reading. The teacher supports students in the following ways: ● Provides an overview of the text and scaffolds students to apply their background knowledge of the topic and to use previewing strategies to build a meaningful framework for reading. ● Uses specific language structures that will enable the students to predict the language during reading. ● Points out important features within the text (e.g., illustrations, text structure, and text features to support comprehension). ● Discusses relevant or new vocabulary that will help the students read the text with understanding. ● Guides the students to locate known and/or unknown words using their knowledge of letters, sounds, words, and word patterns. **During Independent Reading:** The goal is for students to use meaning, language structures, and decoding and visual searching strategies in an orchestrated way to read fluently and for comprehension. The teacher supports students in the following ways: ● Holds one-to-one conferences, listens as students read orally, notes their reading fluency and problem-solving strategies, and checks on comprehension through a brief discussion. ● Prompts students to initiate decoding, blending, and searching strategies when needed and provides appropriate levels of scaffolding.
Section on Planner	Discussion of Text *Reflection and Goal Setting*
Part 3	**Discussion of Text:** The goal is to enhance students' comprehension through engaging them in a meaningful discussion about the text and to lift strategy use through precise teaching. The teacher supports students in the following ways: ● Engages students in a discussion of the text at the meaning level. ● Encourages students to reflect on the problem-solving strategies they used or neglected. ● Identifies a common problem-solving strategy neglected by students and explicitly teaches how to use that strategy to support comprehension. **Reflection and Goal Setting:** The goal is for students to become metacognitive about their strategy use or neglect while reading and to set goals for transferring their knowledge across reading and writing events. The teacher supports students in the following ways: ● Prompts students to reflect on comprehension and problem-solving strategies used and/or neglected and to provide examples. ● Provides students with an opportunity to discuss their reflection and examples. ● Provides students with an opportunity to set new goals for transferring successful strategic work to other texts and across reading events.

Figure 5.2   (*Continued*)

MOVING INTO WRITING ALOUD

The WA intervention is designed for students who are reading at higher levels but experiencing difficulty with the writing process. Teachers can determine if a student is ready for Writing Aloud by observing behaviors that indicate knowledge of early writing. The following questions can guide the teacher's observations and decision-making process.

- Does the student understand concepts of letter, word, and punctuation?
- Does the student reread to predict the next word and/or to confirm the text thus far?
- Does the student recognize basic high-frequency words during reading?
- Does the student spell correctly some basic high-frequency words (e.g., *I, a, like, am, come, can, he, me, my*)?
- Does the student say words slowly when writing?
- Does the student hear and record dominant consonant sounds and some vowels?
- Does the student apply simple analogies to problem-solve on unknown words?
- Does the student compose simple messages of three to five sentences?

If the teacher answers yes to most of these questions, yet the student is having difficulty with the writing process, the WA intervention might be a good choice for the struggling writer. The goal of the WA intervention is to assist students in understanding that writing is a process of generating ideas, drafting a message, revising, editing, and preparing a piece for a particular audience. The WA intervention uses clear demonstrations, explicit teaching, guided practice, and scaffolding techniques to enable writers to acquire knowledge of the writing process. The intervention includes five essential components:

- Word Learning
- Group composition around a common event or Writing Strategies Minilesson
- Independent writing
- Teacher-student conferences
- Reflections on learning

INTERVENTION FRAMEWORK FOR WRITING ALOUD

The WA intervention focuses on assisting students to learn how to compose longer messages; problem-solve on more complex words (including vocabulary); and apply revising, editing, and crafting strategies. An additional focus is to assist students to learn how to use literacy resources for planning their writing, monitoring their thinking, correcting their spelling, and selecting good word choices. The intervention is organized into two phases: language phase (see Chapter 4) and writing phase. Each thirty-minute phase spans several days and includes authentic experiences, predictable routines, explicit teaching, and scaffolding techniques.

The language phase follows the predictable structure of interactive read-aloud activities to build students' background knowledge in the four areas we discussed in previous chapters. The reading experience provides the raw material for the writing experience, as the teacher provides opportunities for students to examine how authors use particular structures and crafting devices to support the readers' deeper comprehension.

The writing phase provides an apprenticeship framework for learning about the writing process. Over several days, the teacher and students interact around a jointly constructed piece of writing, followed by opportunities for the students to apply their knowledge to an independent piece of writing. The process consists of the following steps:

- The teacher models the thinking process for composing, revising, editing, and crafting a message.
- The teacher writes the message on a large chart tablet and engages the students in contributing to the writing process.
- The teacher stops at strategic points to problem-solve on particular aspects of the writing process.
- The teacher uses clear demonstrations, explicit teaching, and guided participation to keep the students actively involved in the learning.
- Students apply their knowledge from the co-constructed experiences to the various stages of the writing process as they independently produce a unique message.
- The teacher conducts one-to-one writing conferences to scaffold students in the writing process.

MATERIALS FOR WRITING ALOUD

The efficiency of any intervention is largely dependent on the teacher's ability to engage the students' attention, promote their concentration, and facilitate good responses. The teacher assembles the following materials for the WA intervention: large chart tablet for writing the group text, dry erase board for demonstrating problem-solving strategies, large laminated writing checklist, variety of large laminated writing guides, and dictionary and thesaurus (see Resource K.2 and Figure 5.7). During the intervention, the teacher and students create word pattern charts based on the word learning lessons. Most of the students' materials are smaller versions of the teacher's tools, including writing guides and a writing checklist, which are used during independent writing; these models are helpful for EALs as a reference across the grades. Early writers use a writing journal with a practice page at the top (as in Interactive Writing), but as the students acquire more knowledge of the writing process, they write on lined paper or an electronic device and file their writing pieces in a writing portfolio.

Figure 5.7   Teacher models how to use a large writing guide during Writing Aloud Intervention and engages students in co-constructing the message.

PLANNING FOR INSTRUCTION

The focal point of Writing Aloud is the shared message: a co-constructed event that enables the teacher to demonstrate important writing concepts while engaging the students in the process. This component requires careful planning on the teacher's part. First, the teacher must create a common message that will involve the students. Then the teacher must select an appropriate writing guide for planning the message. The message can be related to a shared book, a mentor text, a particular type of writing, or a field experience. Finally, the writing guide is used to organize the content into a conventional language structure. Prior to the demonstration, the teacher creates the message, selects the appropriate writing guide, and identifies critical places where he/she can involve the students in specific learning, for example, applying word-solving strategies, revising the message for better word choices, and using a writing checklist to reflect on the quality of the message. The teacher uses two resources for planning instruction in the WA intervention. The intervention planner provides a tool for planning lessons within the WA framework (see Resource E.3, Lesson Planner for Writing Aloud Intervention), and the Guide Sheet for Writing Aloud Intervention (Figure 5.8 and Resource E.4) provides specialized procedures for implementing the intervention.

Guide Sheet for Writing Aloud Intervention	
Section on Planner	**Phase Two: Writing** *Fluent Writing, Word Learning, Reflection and Goal Setting*
Part 1	**Fluent Writing:** The goal is for students to write a large core of high-frequency words fluently. The teacher supports students in the following ways: ● Selects one or two partially known high-frequency words for the students to bring to fluency through fluent practice. **Reading of Word Pattern Chart: (Optional)** The goal is for students to read the word pattern charts fluently. The teacher supports students in the following ways: ● Provides students with an opportunity to practice reading the word pattern chart fluently. **Word Learning:** The goal is for students to become fluent with mapping letters and word patterns to sounds, recording sounds for letters and word patterns, and using morphological units to expand word knowledge. The teacher supports the learning in the following ways: ● Provides an opportunity for students to build and spell unknown one-syllable words conventionally using word pattern knowledge. ● Provides an opportunity for students to break multisyllabic words apart at meaningful and logical units and use pattern knowledge to spell words conventionally. ● Provides an opportunity for students to develop knowledge of the different syllable types. ● Provides explicit instruction to help students develop their knowledge of morphological units and derivational relationships for students to build and spell words conventionally. ● Records the word-learning process on a chart or log to be referred to as students write and in future lessons. ● Provides students with an opportunity to apply the skill strategically to their writing or to a co-constructed text. Video 5.5 Teacher guides students to apply knowledge of spelling pattern to a new word. **Reflection and Goal Setting** The goal is for students to become metacognitive about their learning and to transfer their knowledge across other writing events. The teacher supports students in the following ways: ● Prompts students to discuss the word learning and spelling strategy principle and provide examples to signal and demonstrate understanding. ● Affords students an opportunity to set a goal for transferring the learning across writing events. ● Provides students with an opportunity to chart their goal with an example on a sticky note or in a log.
Part 2	**Co-Construction of Text:** The goal is for students to acquire knowledge of the writing process through a supportive and engaging context. *The composing of the collaborative group mentor text may span several days.* The teacher supports students in the following ways: ● Provides an opportunity for the teacher and students to collaboratively consider author's purpose and genre for the writing and plan accordingly. ● Provides an opportunity for the teacher and students to co-construct a group text map or outline to support comprehension of the collaborative mentor text.

Figure 5.8   Guide Sheet for Writing Aloud Intervention

- Provides an opportunity for the teacher and students to co-construct the group mentor text by engaging and participating in the composing, spelling, revising, and editing processes.
- Provides an opportunity for the students to independently or collaboratively puzzle out word spellings and crafting techniques in their log or on a white board.
- Provides an opportunity for the teacher and students to revisit the text map or outline before beginning the group writing for that particular writing event.
- Provides an opportunity for the teacher and students to continue to co-construct the group mentor text by engaging and participating in the composing, spelling, revising, and editing processes.

Video 5.6   The teacher and students apply writing strategies to a group composition over several days.

OR

Writing Strategies Minilesson: The goal is for students to use their knowledge of author's purpose, text genre, text structure, and the writing process to independently compose a meaningful piece of writing. The teacher supports students in the following ways:

- Presents a writing minilesson that focuses on a writing strategy or strategies that students need to think more about during their own writing.
- Uses mentor texts, co-constructed texts, teacher's writing, or student's writing to teach or draw students' attention to the strategy or strategies under investigation.
- Provides students with an opportunity to apply the strategy or strategies to their writing or to a co-constructed text and scaffold as needed.

Reflection and Goal Setting: The goal is for students to reflect on the writing strategies discussed and investigated and set goals for transferring the knowledge across other writing events. The teacher supports students in the following ways:

- Provides an opportunity for students to reflect on the writing strategies used during the co-construction of group text or minilesson and provides examples to demonstrate understanding.
- Provides an opportunity for the students to set goals for transferring successful writing strategies to their independent writing and across other writing events.

| Part 3 | **Independent Writing:** The goal is for students to use their knowledge of author's purpose aligned with text structure and the writing process to complete their own piece of writing. The teacher supports students in the following ways:

- Conducts individual conferences; teacher records students' problem-solving processes and use of craft; teacher records prompts given to support the writer.

Reflection and Goal Setting: The goal is for students to reflect on their writing and to highlight some successful writing strategies they used during independent writing.

- Teacher provides writing strategies checklist aligned with the strategies discussed and learned during prior lessons.
- Students identify and discuss strategies used and provide evidence to support their thinking.
- Students set writing goals for transferring efficient and effective writing strategies across other writing events.

Video 5.7   The teacher conducts individual conferences with students while prompting them to use personal resources to plan and improve their writing. At the end of the conference component, the teacher engages students in reviewing the strategies they used.

Figure 5.8   (*Continued*)

CLOSING THOUGHTS

As an intervention, writing is a powerful way to lift reading achievement. Teaching reading and writing as reciprocal processes enables students to build pathways among multiple systems (visual, auditory, motor, language) and to use strategies to monitor and regulate a meaningful production. The Assisted Writing interventions reflect a continuum of writing development, and they can be implemented by intervention teachers or classroom teachers. One of the advantages of the Comprehensive Intervention Model is that different interventions can be mixed or layered to address the students' strengths and needs. The RTI team should look at student data and determine the best interventions to meet the unique needs of struggling learners. In the next chapter, we'll describe how teachers can use the Guided Reading Plus Intervention to support struggling readers at the emergent to transitional levels.

Chapter 6

GUIDED READING PLUS FOR ASSEMBLING A PROCESSING SYSTEM

Reading is a complex thinking process that requires the use of efficient strategies for dealing with problems as they arise within texts. The reader must keep the focus on meaning at all times, while simultaneously developing a toolbox of visual searching strategies for solving words with speed and efficiency. Through the act of reading, the reader learns to integrate multiple sources of information, access background knowledge, apply monitoring strategies, use content skills, and regulate attention and pacing in order to gain the deepest understanding from the reading experience. Certainly, reading is more than visual information; however, without visual information, reading cannot occur.

Can a reading intervention promote the use of effective visual strategies while also keeping the focus on comprehension? Can writing be used as an intervention to accelerate reading achievement? We know that writing can work wonders for helping readers develop fast and efficient visual processing strategies. Also, a well-designed word study can help readers acquire orthographic and phonological knowledge for decoding and spelling words. If these two components were added to a guided reading lesson, what would the intervention look like? More importantly, would it affect the reading achievement of struggling readers?

In this chapter, we'll discuss Guided Reading Plus (GRP) as a diagnostic intervention for struggling readers at the emergent to early transitional levels. We'll describe the three phases of the GRP intervention, along with specialized procedures for implementing the intervention as a component of the CIM design.

INTERVENTION FRAMEWORK FOR GUIDED READING PLUS

The GRP intervention is designed for students who are functioning at the emergent to transitional level of reading and writing, but are lagging behind their classmates in reading abilities. The goal is to build students' listening and speaking comprehension through interactive read-aloud experiences with complex texts, while providing them with tailored opportunities to acquire decoding skills and flexible strategies for reading increasingly complex instructional texts. Writing plays a special role in lifting reading achievement, as writing slows down the reading process and increases the reader's orthographic and phonological knowledge through motor production. The addition of writing, word study, and read-aloud to the traditional guided reading group is especially important for struggling readers. Below, we discuss the three phases of the GRP intervention.

Phase One: The Language Phase. As discussed in Chapter 4, all interventions begin with Phase 1, the language phase, which focuses on building the students' listening and speaking comprehension through an interactive read-aloud with a complex text that has been organized from simple to more complex using a complexity rubric. Additionally, the language phase provides students with multiple opportunities to revisit the text for a closer analysis of vocabulary, inferred meanings, text structures, language principles, and author's craft. During this phase, the teacher engages students in the creation of large anchor charts that highlight important elements of texts, including comparing common features across multiple texts, with subsequent opportunities for students to transfer this knowledge to small-group and independent literacy activities. The language phase also includes time for students to respond to the read-aloud text through two types of writing experiences: (1) writing about the text, and (2) writing about the strategies used to understand the text.

Phase Two: Reading Phase. During Phase Two, the reading phase, the teacher engages students in a pre-planned word-learning activity, an orientation to the new book, an independent reading with teacher observations and tailored support, and follow-up teaching points, including discussion of the message. The teacher carefully selects texts that enable students to integrate multiple sources of information and orchestrate flexible strategies in order to build background knowledge for learning from texts. Here, the independent reading is not about teaching, but rather an opportunity for students to apply strategic activity while reading for meaning.

Phase Three: Writing Phase. During Phase Three, the writing phase, the teacher begins with taking a running record on two students while the other students read easy or familiar texts. Then the focus shifts to the writing component, which includes four distinct parts: (1) the teacher provides a prompt that requires students to think more analytically about the previous day's guided reading text; (2) students verbally respond to the prompt, and the teacher scaffolds their responses; (3) students write messages independently; and (4) students participate in one-to-one writing conferences with the teacher.

In sum, the GRP intervention empowers low-progress readers to read for understanding, think critically about their reading, practice efficient decoding strategies, and use what they know about reading to assist with their writing and vice versa. The GRP is based on four theoretical explanations for increasing reading achievement.

- **Matching Texts to Readers.** Teachers need a theory of literacy processing to explain the shifts in processing that are likely to occur with scaffolding and to select texts that require readers to deal with more complex problems (Clay 2019). Beginning readers are constructing literacy processing systems that change over time in response to texts. Teachers can observe these behavioral changes and select texts that not only draw upon the processing systems already in place, but also challenge these systems to change. Texts that gradually increase in difficulty and complexity provide readers with opportunities for strategic reading work that lifts their decision-making power to higher levels. For example, early chapter books and series books introduce new complexities to transitional readers, and when students read several books in a series, their comprehension increases.

- **Flexible Working Systems for Efficient Problem-Solving.** Low-progress readers have developed inappropriate or guessing behaviors in response to instruction; over time, these reactions have become habituated. Teachers should observe literacy behaviors that indicate a breakdown in the processing system and provide tailored opportunities for readers to monitor their thinking before reacting to a problem. As the reader becomes more efficient at assembling the most relevant information for solving the problem, the teacher creates text-based situations for fostering the reader's flexibility and transfer. Ultimately, with successful practice on varied texts, the reader will develop greater efficiency and accuracy, which can be applied to more complex texts. As described in Singer's (1994) theory of working systems and Clay's (2019) account of literacy processing theory, the reader assembles different processing systems of the brain to solve particular problems; in this way, the reader becomes flexible with utilizing the most reasonable information to solve a problem with speed and efficiency.

- **Writing About Reading to Foster Literate Language.** When students write about the books they are reading, they are more likely to use the structures and vocabulary associated with these texts. This experience shapes their knowledge of how written text is organized. In the process, they learn to consolidate their spontaneous (everyday) language with literate (academic) language, which forms the basis of good writing. This is especially important for English Acquisition Learners; writing about reading supports language mentoring with the very texts used for instruction (Briceño and Klein 2019). Additionally, when students write about

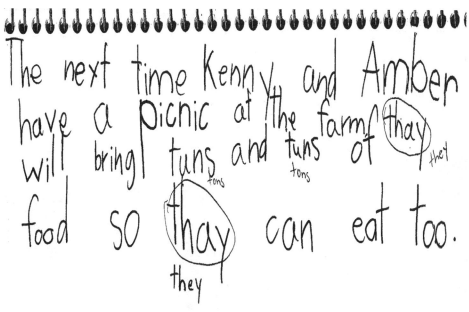

Figure 6.1   Writing Sample of an Early Reader's Response to a Guided Reading Text

their reading, this literary response affects their reading comprehension. In Figure 6.1, we analyze the writing sample of an early reader from a GRP intervention. The sample indicates that reading, writing, and spelling are language processes that work together to communicate clear and precise messages. And in Figure 6.2, we share one student's response to the book he had read the day before.

The next time Kenny and Amber have a picnic at the farm, they will bring tons and tons of food so they can eat too.

Knowledge of Meaning Making (Comprehension)

Responds to the reading prompt, "Based on evidence from the text, what do you think Kenny and Amber will do the next time they have a picnic?" Makes a logical inference for characters' future action (they will bring tons of food) and establishes a cause-effect relationship (so they can eat too). Uses characters' names and other details (farm, picnic) to express clear message. Uses descriptive language (tons and tons) to enhance meaning.

Knowledge of Syntax (Language)

Uses complex sentence structures to communicate the message. Uses "next time" to indicate when the event will occur, and adds the word "too" at the end to indicate other people will be at the picnic. Uses correct subject-verb match. Integrates meaning and structure to communicate a clear and precise message.

Knowledge of Orthographic Information (Spelling)

Spells 21 out of 24 words correctly.

Knowledge of the Writing Process (Revising and Editing)

Composes and records the message with fluency, as evidenced by the focus on meaning. Monitors by circling misspelled word "they." During writing conference, teacher wrote correct spellings under that word, also under "tons."

- **Personal Resources Promote Independence.** It is important for low-progress readers to have a record of what they know and be able to use this knowledge for learning new information. For example, students can use their personal dictionary as a resource for recording known words, then use those known words as tools

Figure 6.2   During the Writing About Reading component, the student makes an inference in his written response to the text.

to learn new words. In a similar way, the word pattern charts provide students with a visual tool for organizing and classifying word knowledge according to conventional patterns, which can then be accessed during independent work. Additional resources include writing checklists, reading logs, and anchor charts.

ASSESSMENTS

The GRP intervention is formatted to provide opportunities for teachers to collect ongoing assessments throughout the intervention. In Chapter 3, we discussed the GRP assessment process as an important feature of an RTI approach.

In Phase Three, during the one-to-one reading conference, the teacher takes a running record of the student's independent reading of the previous day's guided reading book. This assessment occurs at least once a week and is used by the teacher to study how well the student is responding to the GRP intervention. Also, during the one-to-one writing conference, the teacher observes the student's ability to respond to a writing prompt based on the previous day's guided reading book. Here, the teacher notes the student's writing behaviors and uses this information to plan instruction.

To determine the student's optimal level for responding to instruction, the teacher administers a dynamic assessment (DA) task in a particular area (e.g., comprehension strategies, spelling principles). This assessment highlights the student's ability to transfer item knowledge, along with strategic knowledge, to a challenging task with varying degrees of teacher assistance. If the student is able to perform the task with minimal scaffolding, the teacher uses this information to plan instruction at a higher level on the processing continuum. The DA procedure is embedded into the instructional components and can occur at any time during the intervention.

Additionally, at progress monitoring intervals (generally every four weeks), the teacher takes a running record of each student's ability to read a new text with a standard introduction. The highest level is plotted on the Text Reading AIM line and compared with the benchmark level for evidence that the GRP intervention is narrowing the reading gap. Also, the teacher prompts the student to respond in writing to the book and scores the writing sample with the Writing About Reading checklist. Additional progress monitoring assessments might include a word test or a phonological measure.

Collectively, these assessments provide teachers with reliable data for diagnosing the students' strengths and needs in literacy areas, while keeping the focus on their ability to transfer knowledge and strategies to new situations. These data are used during RTI meetings to determine the effectiveness of the GRP intervention on the student's rate of learning.

SCAFFOLDING FOR INDEPENDENCE DURING BOOK ORIENTATIONS

In guided reading, the teacher's role is to predict the type and amount of support the students will need to be able to read and understand the author's message. The teacher prompts students to apply reading strategies and intervenes only when one of the students is unlikely to problem-solve independently, is frustrated, or is in jeopardy of losing meaning. The teacher intervenes by asking questions that relate to the reading process.

The level of support in the text orientation decreases as the students move toward self-regulated reading. During the emergent reading stage, the teacher provides a rich introduction with active discussions around the pictures, the sentence patterns, and the text sequence. As the students move into the early stages, the introduction may be reduced to a summary statement, a few selective questions, and a purpose for reading. By the transitional and beyond levels, the students have acquired strategies for orienting themselves to the text, as they apply previewing techniques for surveying the text and constructing meaning. In Table 6.1, we highlight three levels

Table 6.1. Levels of Teacher Support During Book Orientation

High Teacher Support	Moderate Teacher Support	Low Teacher Support
• Introduces text and sets purpose for reading. • Guides students to discuss pictures/text features to support meaning-making while reading. • Encourages students to ask questions and make predictions. • Draws students' attention to unfamiliar language structures to support language anticipation during reading. • Draws students' attention to a decoding strategy to use when encountering an unknown word during reading. • Draws students' attention to the process of figuring out the meaning of unknown words during reading.	• Scaffolds students to set purpose for reading. • Scaffolds students to look at pictures/text features to support meaning-making during reading. Later on, teacher reads aloud a part of the text, allowing students to set their own purpose for reading. • Encourages students to ask questions and make predictions. • Draws students' attention to unfamiliar language structures to support language anticipation during reading. • Draws students' attention to a decoding strategy to use when encountering an unknown word during reading. • Draws students' attention to the process of figuring out the meaning of unknown words during reading.	• Invites students to use knowledge of genre, text structure, author, topic, etc. to set purpose for reading. • Allows students to preview and read parts of the text to set purpose for reading. • Invites students to ask questions and make predictions. • Draws student's attention to unfamiliar language structures and vocabulary to support anticipation during reading. • Draws students' attention to decoding strategy, then later on, allows students to use an example from previous readings to demonstrate how they will use this process when needed. • Draws students' attention to the process of figuring out the meaning of unknown words during reading.

of teacher support during book orientations and illustrate these techniques through video examples from guided reading groups.

Video 6.1   The teacher provides a high level of support during book orientation for emergent readers.

Video 6.2   The teacher provides a moderate level of support during book orientation for late early readers.

Video 6.3   The teacher provides a low level of support during book orientation for readers beyond the transitional level.

SCAFFOLDING FOR INDEPENDENCE DURING WORD-LEARNING ACTIVITIES

Scaffolding is a complex interactive process in which the teacher regulates levels of support according to how well the student understands the task at hand. The degree of teacher support will depend on how much the student brings to the task. In order to promote self-monitoring behavior, the teacher should consider two questions:

- What source of information does the child need to attend to?
- What is the least amount of support I can give to ensure the child will accomplish the task? (See Dorn and Jones 2012.)

In Figure 6.3, we apply Wood's five levels of contingent scaffolding to the strategy of visually searching into an unknown word.

INTERVENTION FRAMEWORK

The GRP intervention consists of three phases that are implemented over several days:

- **Phase One: Language Phase.** The goal is for students to build background knowledge for understanding the content, text structures, and vocabulary associated with more complex texts.
- **Phase Two: Reading Phase.** The goal is for students to read an instructional text that includes opportunities to develop efficient decoding and comprehension strategies for reading with fluency and understanding.
- **Phase Three: Writing Phase.** The goal is for students to respond to the guided reading text through writing about the text.

Daily instruction is critical, because the struggling reader is attempting to build connections across events, and lapses in time can present extra challenges. Each phase includes specialized procedures that are structured within a predictable, thirty-minute framework.

PROCEDURAL STEPS FOR PHASE ONE: LANGUAGE PHASE

- For the interactive read-aloud experience, the teacher selects a meaningful text with an appropriate degree of complexity for maintaining the students' interest over several readings.
- Before the first reading of the text, the teacher provides or scaffolds students in setting a purpose for listening to the text. This is a key support for students, particularly English Acquisition Learners.

	Level	Description	Meta-Cognition
Low	1 General Verbal	*Provide general assistance.* • What can you do to help yourself? • You know how to help yourself; try something and check to see if it works there.	NA
	2 Specific Verbal	*Direct student's attention to the strategy that needs to be mobilized.* • Can you run your finger under the word? • Can you move your eyes through the word and blend the parts together?	
Moderate	3 Specific Verbal Prompt plus Nonverbal Indicators	*Direct student's attention to the searching process that needs to be mobilized and provides a nonverbal clue to support the student's understanding of the strategy.* Teacher moves pencil across the word or uses a sliding card to provide a clue to the strategy that needs to be initiated.	Student explains the strategy used and provides an example.
High	4 Prepare for Next Action	*Supply specific information and ask the student to confirm or disconfirm.* Could that word be *play*? Does it look like *play*?	The teacher draws student's attention to the part of the text where a strategy was demonstrated or highly supported. The teacher records the strategy and the student draws a picture on a card, sticky note, or chart to be used later as a reminder of productive work.
	5 Demonstrates Next Action	*Teacher models the thinking and action needed to solve the problem.* • I'm going to write the word in parts on the wipe board and blend the parts together to help me read the word. • Teacher models confirming that the word read looks right.	

Based on the work of Wood, D. 2002. "The Why? What? When? And How? of Tutoring: The Development of Helping and Tutoring Skills in Children."

Figure 6.3   Wood's Five Levels of Contingent Scaffolding Applied to Visual Searching Strategy

• During the first reading, the teacher reads the entire text, stopping at strategic points to model, prompt, or engage students in understanding the author's message.
• During subsequent readings, the teacher guides the students in a closer analysis of memorable passages within the text for evidence of writer's craft, language structures, vocabulary, and other important text features.
• After analysis, the teacher guides the students in a group response to the text, or the students respond to the written prompt independently.

PROCEDURAL STEPS FOR PHASE TWO: READING PHASE

- The teacher conducts a word study lesson for the group, providing tailored support for students within the group who need extra assistance. Students record known words in their personal word dictionary, and/or the teacher creates a word pattern chart as a visual resource.
- The teacher provides a group orientation to the guided reading text, and students engage in constructing meaning for the text.
- The students read the text independently while the teacher conducts one-to-one reading conferences with each student.
- The teacher convenes the group for a follow-up discussion that includes one or two teaching points.

PROCEDURAL STEPS FOR PHASE THREE: WRITING PHASE

- The teacher takes a running record on two students while the other students read independently.
- The teacher provides a group prompt for responding to the previous day's guided reading text.
- Each student composes orally a personal response to the teacher's prompt.
- Each student writes a response in a writing journal, and the teacher conducts one-to-one writing conferences with each student.

GUIDED READING PLUS INTERVENTION LESSON PLANNER

Planning for the GRP intervention takes time. The teacher must read the guided reading book, plan the book orientation, design the writing prompt, select the word study activities, and analyze the students' running records and writing journals. The lesson planner provides teachers with a tool for planning and structuring these activities. In Resource F.1, Lesson Planner for Guided Reading Plus Intervention, we've included a reproducible blank intervention planner. For further guidance on lesson planning, teachers should use the Figure 6.4/Resource F.2, Guide Sheet for Guided Reading Plus Intervention, as a decision-making tool.

Section on Planner	Phase Two: Reading *Fluent Writing, Phonological Awareness, Letter and Word Learning,* *Reading the Record of Prior Learning, Reflection, and Goal Setting*
Part 1	**Fluent Writing:** The goal is for students to write all letters and a large core of high-frequency words with fluency. The teacher supports students in the following ways: • Selects one or two partially known letters for the students to bring to fluency through fluent practice. • Selects one or two partially known high-frequency words for the students to bring to fluency through fluent practice. **Phonological Awareness:** The goal is for students to hear and manipulate both larger and smaller units of sound within the sound structure of spoken words: word boundaries, syllables, rhyming (onset and rime), and individual phonemes within words. The teacher supports students in the following ways: • Provides explicit instruction in hearing and identifying individual words within spoken language. • Provides explicit instruction in hearing and identifying syllables within a spoken word. • Provides explicit instruction in hearing, identifying, generating, and manipulating onset and rime in spoken words. • Provides explicit instruction in hearing, segmenting, blending, deleting, substituting, and adding individual phonemes within words.

Figure 6.4   Guide Sheet for Guided Reading Plus Intervention

Letter and/or Word Learning (Phonics): The goal is for the students to become fluent with identifying letters, mapping letters and word patterns to sounds, blending letter sounds, identifying syllable types, and using morphological units to enhance word learning.

Letter Learning: The goal is for students to become fluent with identifying and naming all letters in the alphabet and distinguishing between consonants and vowels. The teacher supports students in the following ways:

- Provides explicit instruction in letter learning and opportunities for fluent practice.
- Provides explicit instruction in letter learning by supporting students in learning how to notice the features of letters and to understand how the features come together in a specific order to give the letter its name.
- Provides kinesthetic experiences (salt, sandpaper, shaving cream) to help students learn the directionality principle of the features of the letters.
- Directs students' attention to the features of letters by providing them with an opportunity to trace over letters, describe the path of movement, and name the letters.
- Provides students with an opportunity to sort letters by letter features, similarities and differences, uppercase and lowercase, letter sounds, and letter name.
- Provides an opportunity for students to read and write letters with fluency.

Word Learning (Phonics): The goal is for students to build a core of high-frequency words to be read fluently and to use their word-solving strategies fluently and flexibly when problem-solving within continuous text. The teacher supports students in the following ways:

- Provides explicit and systematic phonics instruction to help children learn how words work along a continuum from simple to more complex.
- Uses a gradual release model to make decisions about explicit instruction of the phonetic principle being addressed.
- Provides explicit instruction in letter–sound mapping, including segmenting and blending, and provides opportunities for fluent decoding and reading practice.
- Provides explicit and systematic instruction in building words that include the targeted phonetic principle being addressed and plans opportunities for fluent reading of words.
- Provides explicit instruction in identifying the difference between consonants and vowels.
- Provides explicit instruction in identifying the syllable type and how it aligns with the phonetic principle being addressed.
- Provides explicit and systematic instruction in how to use known words and word parts to build, read, and write unknown words.
- Provides an opportunity for the students to transfer their word knowledge to building, decoding, and reading unknown words.
- Provides explicit instruction in building a core of high-frequency words.

Video 6.4   The teacher provides a word study lesson in the Guided Reading Plus Intervention.

Decodable Sentences or Text (optional): The goal is for students to practice reading decodable text fluently, with attention to both decoding and comprehension. The teacher supports students in the following ways:

- Provides an opportunity for students to read decodable text that includes phonics skills that have been previously taught up to that point in the phonics scope and sequence continuum.
- Provides an opportunity for students to reread the decodable text to build fluency and automaticity.

Figure 6.4   (*Continued*)

	Adding Words to Personal Dictionary: The goal is to provide the students with a resource for organizing and storing known high-frequency words. The teacher uses prior word study experiences that focus on building high-frequency words to provide students with an opportunity to record the words in their dictionaries. The teacher supports students in the following ways: • Provides an opportunity for students to record known high-frequency words in their personal dictionaries. • Provides students with an opportunity to read their recorded words from a few pages in their dictionaries for word fluency practice. **OR** **Adding Word Patterns to Chart:** The goal is to provide students with a resource for organizing and storing words that contain targeted word patterns. The teacher supports students in the following ways: • Provides an opportunity for students to record and categorize, on a chart, partially known words that include a targeted pattern; students write the words on their individual charts and read the words for fluency practice. **Reflection and Goal Setting:** The goal is for students to become metacognitive about their learning and to transfer their knowledge across reading events. The teacher supports students in the following ways: • Prompts students to reflect on the prior word-learning principle and provide examples. • Provides students with an opportunity to set new goals for transferring the phonetic principle to problem-solving on unknown words while reading texts across multiple contexts.
Section on Planner	*Guided Reading* *Orientation to Text—Set Purpose for Reading, Independent Reading*
Part 2	**Guided Reading:** The goal is for students to set a meaningful purpose for reading and to use flexible comprehension and word-solving strategies as needed to comprehend the text. **Before Reading—Orientation to New Book:** The goal is for students to apply their background knowledge of topic, text genre, text structure, language, and word-solving strategies to prepare for the reading. The teacher supports students in the following ways: • Provides an overview of the text or scaffolds students to apply their background knowledge of the topic and use previewing strategies to build a meaningful framework for reading. • Uses specific language structures that will enable the students to predict the language during reading. • Points out important features within the text (e.g., illustrations, text structure, and text features) to support comprehension. • Discusses relevant or new vocabulary that will help students read the text with understanding. • Guides students to locate known and/or unknown words using their knowledge of letters, sounds, words, and word patterns. Video 6.5 The teacher provides a moderate level of support during the orientation to the text features of a nonfiction book. **During Reading of New Book:** The goal is for students to use meaning, language structures, and decoding and visual searching strategies in an orchestrated way to read fluently and for comprehension. The teacher supports students in the following ways: • Holds one-to-one conferences, listens as students read orally, notes their reading fluency and problem-solving strategies, and checks on comprehension through a brief discussion. • Prompts students to initiate decoding, blending, and searching strategies when needed and provides appropriate levels of scaffolding. • Prompts students to use morphological units to support word meaning and comprehension of text.

Figure 6.4   (*Continued*)

Figure 6.5   A sliding card is used to direct the student's eyes to search through a word and blend the sounds to produce the word. The teacher slides the card across the word, uncovering parts as she prompts the student to read the word in parts. A small dry erase board can also be used to promote visual searching. The unknown word is written in parts and the student reads the parts as the word is constructed.

Section on Planner	Discussion of Text *Reflection and Goal Setting*
Part 3	**After Reading New Book—Discussion of Text and Strategy Reflection:** The goal is to enhance students' comprehension through engaging them in a meaningful discussion about the text and to lift strategy use through precise teaching and reflection. The teacher supports students in the following ways: • Engages students in a discussion about the text at the meaning level. • Encourages students to reflect on the problem-solving strategies they used or neglected. Identifies a common problem-solving strategy neglected by students and explicitly teaches how to use that strategy to support comprehension **Video 6.6** The teacher and students engage in a book discussion following the independent reading. **Reflection and Goal Setting:** The goal is for students to become more metacognitive about efficient strategy use by reflecting on their problem-solving while reading. The teacher supports students in the following ways: • Prompts students to reflect on their comprehension and/or word-solving strategies and provide an example on a sticky note. • Provides students with an opportunity to discuss their reflection and example. • Provides an opportunity for students to set new goals for transferring their learning to other texts and across reading events.

Figure 6.4   (*Continued*)

Section on Planner	Phase Three: Assessment and Writing About Reading *Assessment, Writing About Reading Prompt, Reading and Writing Analysis*
Part 1	**Assessment:** The goal is for the teacher to code, score, and analyze students' reading behaviors and to use the collected data to plan for instruction. The teacher collects data in the following ways: • Takes a running record on two or more students reading the text, article, or passage from the previous day's session. • Analyzes the behaviors used and/or neglected during reading. • Uses language to validate and/or activate strategic processing behaviors while reading.
Part 2	**Writing About Reading Prompt:** The goal is for students to deepen their comprehension by writing about their reading and providing textual evidence to support their thinking. The teacher supports students in the following way: • Provides appropriate levels of support to ensure students understand the goal of the writing task and the planning, encoding, revising, and editing processes involved in completing the response. **Writing About Reading Lesson—High to Moderate Level of Scaffolding:** The teacher scaffolds students in the following ways: • Models and/or scaffolds the planning process by using language and a practice page or planner to prepare for Writing About Reading. • Co-constructs the response with the students and scaffolds the thinking as needed (e.g., composing strategies, specific vocabulary, spelling strategies, language principles, and revising and editing techniques). • Engages students at appropriate times in the problem-solving process on their individual dry erase boards. • Provides an opportunity for students to reflect on writing by using a Writing About Reading rubric or checklist and makes revisions if need. **OR** **Independent Writing About Reading—Moderate to Low Level of Scaffolding:** The teacher scaffolds students in the following ways: • Provides students with a comprehension prompt that stimulates deeper thinking. • Prompts students to use a practice page or planner to prepare for writing about their reading. • Prompts students to use composing strategies, specific vocabulary, spelling strategies, language principles, and revising and editing techniques while writing. Video 6.7 The teacher introduces the graphic organizer for procedural writing to support the students' writing about the reading. Video 6.8 The teacher conducts an individual conference with a student about writing. **Reflection and Goal Setting:** The goal is for students to reflect on their writing about reading and to set goals for transferring their knowledge across other Writing About Reading events. The teacher supports students in the following ways: • Provides an opportunity for students to reflect on writing strategies used and to offer examples to demonstrate their learning. • Provides an opportunity for students to set goals for transferring successful planning and writing strategies to other Writing About Reading events.
Part 3	**Reading and Writing Analysis:** The goal is to use students' data across reading and writing episodes to plan future lessons (Phases Two and Three). The teacher: • Reflects on focus across lessons. • Uses reading and writing data to validate progress. • Uses reading and writing data to prepare for a new focus and writes predictions of progress.

Figure 6.4   (*Continued*)

CHANGES OVER TIME IN READING INSTRUCTION

For emergent and early readers, the intervention includes two additional components for promoting fast and fluent control of visual information. The first component focuses on acquiring a core of high-frequency words, approximately 150 by the end of the early level. The teacher selects one or two partially known words for the students to write fluently. This fast motor production of common words promotes automaticity and leads to the fast retrieval of words during the reading and writing of whole texts. After the words are written, the teacher instructs the students to find the correct pages in their personal dictionaries and record the new words. The second component focuses on learning about words and how they work along a processing continuum. The students build letter–sound relationships and spelling pattern knowledge as well as gain knowledge about word meanings. The students can transfer their learning when reading and writing continuous text (see Chapter 7).

Transitional readers have acquired successful decoding skills, along with flexible strategies, for reading grade-level texts. Typically, the transitional level begins at second grade, as students are expected to read silently. When students move into transitional levels, the GRP intervention is organized around themed sets that expose readers to a range of text types.

During the language phase, the teacher and students co-construct anchor charts that highlight text structures and language features from the read-aloud text. Then, during the reading and writing phases, the anchor charts become valuable resources. For example, during the reading phase, students apply their knowledge of character traits to a narrative text; and during the writing component, students use a text map of character traits to help them plan their written responses to the text.

CHANGES OVER TIME IN WRITING INSTRUCTION

At the emergent level, the Writing About Reading component is designed to promote the students' attention to concepts of print (directionality, spacing, letter formation, letter–sound matching, etc.) while they transcribe a simple message. When the students are ready for the next level, the teacher introduces the writing prompt. The goal of the writing prompt is to stimulate the reader's ability to think beyond the text and construct a meaningful response to an author's message.

The writing tools are adjusted to reflect changes in writing development. At the emergent and early levels, the students use a writing journal that is bound across the top: the top part of the journal is used as a practice page and the bottom part is used for recording the message. The practice page provides students with a place to try out letters and words and to fluently write high-frequency words. At the late early to transitional levels, the writing journal is replaced with a writing log: the left side of the log is used as a planning page, and the right side is used for recording the message. The planning page provides students with a place to organize their thinking, experiment with word choices and language phrases, and apply crafting techniques. In Figures 6.6, 6.7, and 6.8, we illustrate the differences between early and transitional writing samples.

WRITING ABOUT READING AT THE EMERGENT LEVEL

Emergent writers are constructing knowledge of the print system, including an understanding of left-to-right order in sentences and words. At this level, the students are reading simple, patterned texts in their guided reading group. In their writing group, they are writing simple sentences (generally one or two). Writing prompts are carefully chosen. They reflect the teacher's knowledge of the students' reading behaviors and the teacher's understanding of how the writing can increase reading knowledge, and vice versa.

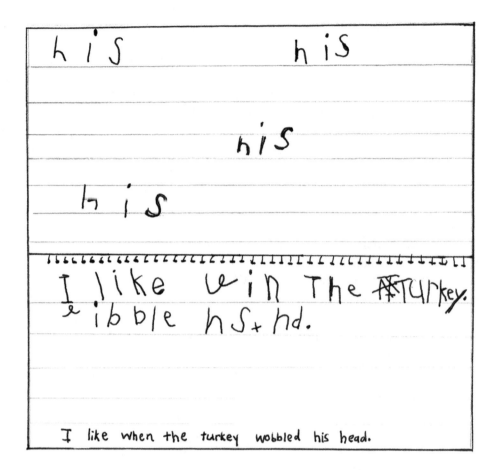

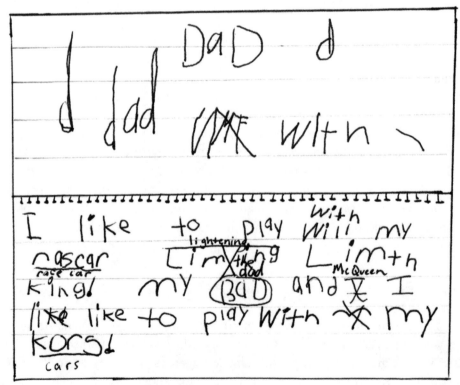

Figure 6.6   Examples of Emergent Writing Journal with Practice Page. The student records the message on the top page to practice letter formation and spelling strategies.

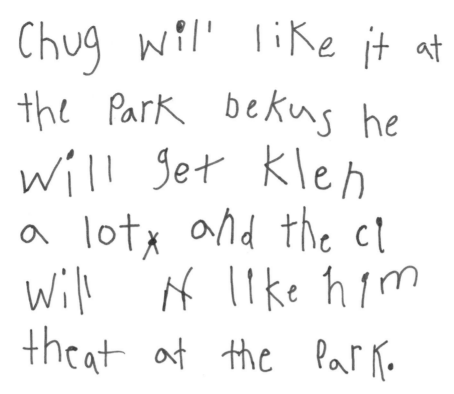

Figure 6.7 Example of an Early Writing Journal. An early writer composes a response to the book she read during the guided reading lesson.

During the writing conference, the teacher provides tailored feedback to meet the needs of the individual writer. Each writing conference includes specialized procedures for validating and activating the student's knowledge. Here are the procedures for writing conferences at the emergent level:

- The teacher prompts the student to read the message; if the student struggles on a word, the teacher joins the reading, keeping the focus on fluency and comprehension. At the end of the reading, the teacher validates the student's writing by responding to the message as the goal of reading.
- The teacher validates the student's phonological and orthographic knowledge by going through each letter in a left-to-right sequence and placing a light checkmark above the correct letter-to-sound match, including whole words that are spelled correctly.
- The teacher writes the student's message at the bottom of the page, explaining, "I'll write it the way it looks in a book." Then the teacher prompts the student to point to the words and read the message. The goal of the interaction is to validate the student's work while simultaneously modeling how written language looks in a book.

USING WRITING PROMPTS TO RESPOND TO READING

As students become more competent readers, the teacher adjusts the writing instruction to accommodate their strengths and needs. Through the reading of higher-level texts, students increase their problem-solving efficiency, as well as their knowledge of new vocabulary, content information, and more complex print conventions (text structures, genre conventions). When students write in response to their reading, they are more likely to borrow the language of the text, thus incorporating more complex language structures and academic vocabulary into their compositions.

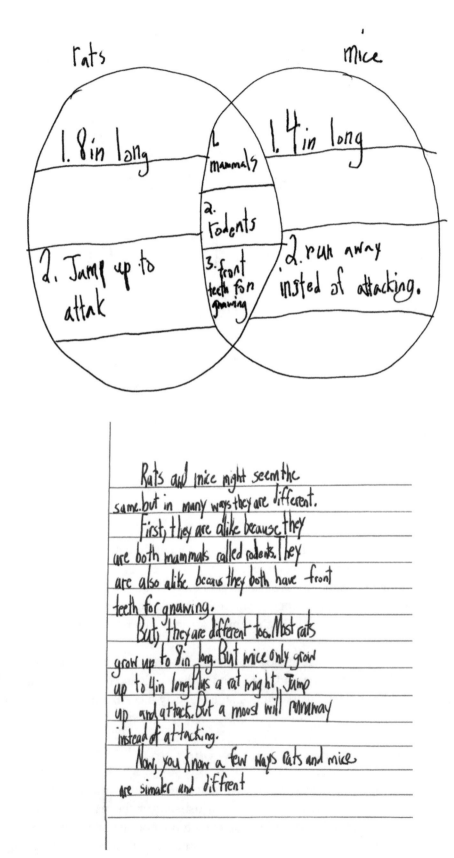

Figure 6.8 Example of Early Transitional Reading Log. The student records the message on the right side and uses the left side to plan the writing.

The success of the writing intervention will be influenced by the teacher's ability to create good writing prompts. The prompts should provide opportunities for students to assemble their knowledge from language experiences and apply their strategies to deal with the goals of the writing task. To create effective writing prompts, the teacher must have three types of knowledge:

- **Knowledge of the book**, including the author's purpose, the theme of the book and its underlying meanings, important information presented and to be learned, and the genre, text structures, and features of the book.
- **Knowledge of comprehension strategies**, including higher-level comprehension strategies for understanding relationships (e.g., inferring, predicting, connecting, and analyzing).
- **Knowledge of student's processing behaviors**, including formative assessments (running records, writing samples) for analyzing reading and writing behaviors.

To illustrate, let's look at an example of a writing prompt for early readers and at the students' written responses. The story, *Greedy Cat Is Hungry*, by Joy Cowley, is about a persistent but lovable cat that is always begging for food. Consequently, he is much too fat. He appeals to members of the family, but they refuse to feed him. He finally achieves success by appealing to Katie, the youngest member. The goal of the writing prompt is to encourage the students to think beyond the text and offer a logical solution to Greedy Cat's problem (i.e., begging for food, which has led to his being overweight). The teacher asks the prompt, "Katie did not help Greedy Cat learn a lesson. What should Katie do the next time Greedy Cat wants everything for himself?" The writing journal responses of two students indicate their ability to use the prompt to stimulate logical thinking.

- Student One: Katie should teach Greedy Cat to share his food.
- Student Two: Katie should give him a little bit of the food and milk.

As the students move into the transitional level, the teacher introduces text maps and incorporates these organizers into the writing component. In the list, we describe ways that students can respond to different types of texts.

Informational/Explanatory Writing in Response to Informational Texts

- Responds personally to the text (e.g., gives an opinion of the text and/or responds to the learning from the text).
- Writes some interesting facts learned from text and uses text features to support information (e.g., diagrams, labels).
- Writes a simple report and uses text features to support the information. Here are some examples:
  - Uses headings to introduce information to follow.
  - List facts from text supported by illustrations.
  - Writes a prediction based on information from text.
  - Writes directions to show a process or a sequence of steps, for example, a life cycle, a set of instructions, a recipe (see Figure 6.9).
  - Writes questions from reading.
  - Takes notes during reading and summarizes learning after reading.
  - Writes a letter to someone explaining their learning from text.
  - Compares and contrasts information from texts.
  - Critiques the text.

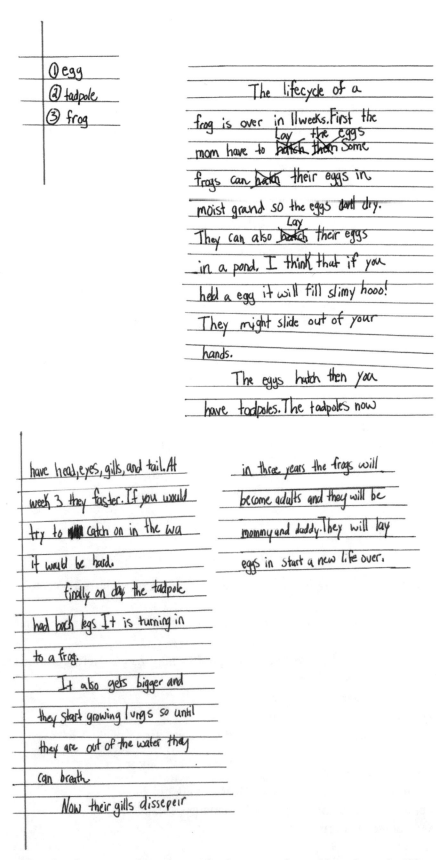

Figure 6.9   A transitional writer responds to the teacher's prompt for writing about the life cycle of a frog using evidence from the text.

Narrative Writing in Response to Narrative Texts

- Responds personally to the text; that is, gives an opinion of the text, characters, problem, solution, and/or theme.
- Retells story using a sequence of events.
- Writes simple statements to summarize the text.
- Writes about a favorite part and explains why.
- Writes about specific story elements (e.g., setting, problem, solution) or analyzes characters.
- Draws inferences (e.g., "What can you infer about _____ from reading this story?"); identifies the theme or message gleaned from reading story.
- Makes personal connections to text ideas, characters, situations, theme, and/or setting (e.g., "I can add information about _____" or "I can understand _____ because _____."). (See Figure 6.9)
- Makes predictions (e.g., "I think _____ because _____.").
- Compares and contrasts different aspects of text.
- Writes a book review.
- Critiques the text.
- Writes questions.

CLOSING THOUGHTS

The Guided Reading Plus Intervention can be an effective intervention for preventing reading difficulties with struggling readers at the emergent to early transitional levels. The GRP is based on the following principles:

- Specialized procedures and predictable routines free the reader's attention to focus on problem-solving.
- Strategy-based prompts during reading and writing promote self-monitoring, searching, and self-correcting behaviors within whole texts.
- Writing about reading is an effective way to increase reading achievement.
- Progress monitoring provides systematic data for studying change over time in each student's learning and for informing teaching decisions.
- One-to-one conferences during independent reading and writing events enable teachers to tailor instruction to meet the strengths and needs of the learner.
- Instruction is continually adjusted to accommodate the shifts in each student's learning.

Chapter 7

LEARNING ABOUT LETTERS, SOUNDS, AND WORDS

The primary purpose of reading and writing is to share information and ideas. There is little value in being able to decode words or write letters in a sentence if the meaning of those sentences is not accessed.

In order to access the meaning of a written message, students must first master the mechanics of reading and writing. Acquiring this competency with written language is an integrated process that develops along a word-solving continuum that moves from simple to more complex.

A literacy processing system can be defined as a network of interrelated cognitive processes that work together to construct meaning for a given event (Clay 2015). The system is shaped as children apply their knowledge and problem-solving strategies on literacy tasks that increase in difficulty. When the student's learning is new, the literacy behaviors are more deliberate and intentional. As the student acquires more opportunities to apply flexible strategies in connected texts, the once-observable behaviors become skilled actions. As this development occurs, the teacher is able to observe the changes in the student's learning as the behaviors move from overt to covert. The goal of a word study intervention is to increase students' phonological and orthographic knowledge while simultaneously fostering their word-solving strategies as they read for meaning.

In previous chapters, we presented numerous examples of how teachers use word study activities during the Assisted Writing and Guided Reading Plus Interventions. For instance, students use ABC charts, magnetic letters, sliding cards, and practice boards to learn about letters, sounds, spelling patterns, and words. During independent writing, students analyze the sequence of sounds within words and apply strategies for noting relationships between spelling patterns; and during one-to-one conferences, the teacher provides tailored scaffolding for enhancing the student's word-solving skills. As part of the text reading phase, the teacher sets a purpose for solving words within text. For instance, if the word study lesson focuses on onset and rime patterns within words, the teacher prompts the students to apply this strategy when encountering an unknown word in text. In the process of reading and writing, children learn how to transfer their knowledge about letters, sounds, spelling patterns, and words across varied and changing circumstances.

In this chapter, we describe specific behaviors that indicate the changes that occur over time in the development of the phonological and orthographic systems. To illustrate, we share principles along with specific examples for teaching students about letters, sounds, and words based on a continuum of complexity. Teachers should use students' data from reading and writing, along with the resources in this chapter, to plan effective letter and word study activities for the small-group interventions.

IMPORTANT TERMS FOR INSTRUCTION

Each intervention in the CIM portfolio includes systematic instruction for learning about letters, sounds, and words. In planning for instruction, teachers should understand the terms associated with these phonological and orthographic systems.

- **Phoneme:** The smallest unit of language, a speech sound with no inherent meaning.
- **Phonemic Awareness:** The ability to hear and manipulate the sounds in spoken words, and the understanding that spoken words and syllables are made up of sequences of speech sounds.

- **Phonological Awareness:** An umbrella term that involves working with the sounds of language at the word, syllable, and phoneme level.
- **Phonics:** The use of sound-symbol relationships to recognize words.
- **Continuous Sound:** A sound that can be stretched out without distortion.
- **Onset-Rime:** The onset is the part of the word before the vowel. The rime is the part of the word including the vowel and the part that follows it.
- **Segmentation:** The separation of words into phonemes.

PHONOLOGICAL SYSTEMS

Understanding the typical development of phonological awareness, including phonemic awareness, is essential for teachers who work with children at risk of reading difficulties (Blevins 2016, 2017, 2021; Ehri 1998; Perfetti et al. 1987). Phonological awareness generally emerges in a developmental sequence from awareness of larger units, such as syllables and onset-rimes, to awareness of individual phonemes in words (Goswami and Bryant 1990). Phonemic awareness is the ability to hear sounds in words and to be able to identify those sounds. Phonemic awareness continues to develop as children acquire greater control over these processes. Table 7.1 and Resource G.1, Change over Time in the Early Development of Phonological and Phonemic Systems, display typical changes in the development of the phonological and phonemic systems of beginning readers (emergent to late early). The cognitive tasks described in this chapter grow in complexity from identification to manipulation, from identifying words that begin with the same sound to substituting initial sounds.

Learning about letters, sounds, and words is an integral part of all interventions in the CIM portfolio. To illustrate, we've embedded examples of word-learning activities throughout the text (e.g., see Videos 7.4 and 7.5 in Chapter 5; Video 6.4 in Chapter 6; and Videos 9.4 to 9.6 in Chapter 9). In all situations, intervention is intentionally designed to mediate change over time in students' control of phonological and phonemic systems, as evidenced by their ability to transfer this knowledge to reading and writing within continuous texts. In Videos 7.1, 7.2, and 7.3, we illustrate explicit procedures from the GRP intervention that enable young readers to acquire knowledge of letters, sounds, and words along a processing continuum; and in Videos 7.4 and 7.5, the teachers prompt students to apply their strategic knowledge for solving unknown words within texts.

Video 7.1 Emergent readers practice fluency with a known word, listen and distinguish the beginning sounds in common words, and build a new high-frequency word with magnetic letters.

Video 7.2 Beginning early readers learn how to build a word in serial order.

Video 7.3 Transitional readers learn flexible ways to solve multisyllabic words in reading and writing.

Video 7.4 The teacher prompts a student to solve unknown words within text by writing the letter parts in sequence, then blending the parts together to form the word.

Video 7.5 The teacher prompts a student to solve unknown words within text by writing the letter parts in sequence, then blending the parts together to form the word.

Table 7.1.   Change over Time in the Early Development of Phonological and Phonemic Systems

Becoming Aware—Developing and Extending Control of the System

Emergent	Beginning Early	Late Early
Phonological Awareness • Counts and identifies individual words in spoken phrases or sentences (*I · like · my · dog*) • Hears and identifies syllables in one- to three-syllable words (1: *dog*, 2: *apple*, 3: *elephant*) • Generates rhyming words (*dog, log*; *cat, mat*) • Segments and manipulates onset (consonant) and rimes of spoken words (*S-am*, *h-am*; *s-and*, *h-and*)	*Phonological Awareness* • Hears and identifies syllables in three- to four-syllable words (*ba-na-na, wa-ter-me-lon*) • Develops fluency and ease in generating rhyming words (*fun, run*; *sit, split*) • Develops fluency and ease in segmenting and manipulating onset (consonant) and rimes of spoken words (*am, Sam, ham; and, sand, hand*) • Hears and identifies long and short vowel sounds in words (*make, mad*)	*Phonological Awareness* • Develops speed, fluency, and ease in identifying syllables in words • Develops speed, fluency, and ease in hearing, saying, and generating rhyming words (*play, stray, stay*; *meat, heat*) • Develops speed, fluency, and ease in hearing, segmenting, and manipulating onset (consonant) and rimes, including consonant blends (*sp-ike, l-ike, str-ike*) • Develops speed, fluency, and ease in hearing and identifying long and short vowel sounds in words (*make, mad; heat, hat*)
Phonemic Awareness • Segments two- and three-letter words (CVC) into complete sequences of individual phonemes (*c-a-t*) • Blends two to three phonemes in words (*c-a-t, cat*; *s-u-p, sup*) • Adds or substitutes individual phonemes in simple, one-syllable words to make new words (*at, sat, mat*; *mat, map*) • Hears and recognizes the same and different sounds in words in beginning, middle, and ending positions (*ball, boat*; *fat, fit*; *lip, lit*)	*Phonemic Awareness* • Segments one-syllable words into complete sequences of individual phonemes, including consonant blends (*c-a-p*; *f-l-i-p*) • Blends individual phonemes to form one-syllable words, including words with consonant blends (*c-u-p, cup*; *p-i-g, pig*; *b-l-a-ck, black*; *s-l-i-p, slip*) • Adds or substitutes individual phonemes in simple, one-syllable words to make new words (*at, sat, mat*; *mat, map*) • Hears and recognizes the same and different sounds in words in beginning, middle, and ending positions (*ball, boat*; *fat, fit*; *lip, lit*)	*Phonemic Awareness* • Develops speed, fluency, and ease in segmenting words into sequences of individual phonemes, including consonant blends (*s-ea-t, cl-a-m, ch-i-p, t-ar-p*) • Develops fluency and ease in blending one-syllable phonemes to form words, including words with blends (*c-u-p, cup*; *p-i-g, pig*; *b-l-a-ck, black*; *s-l-a-p, slap*) • Develops fluency and ease in adding or substituting individual phonemes in simple, one-syllable words to make new words (*at, sat, mat*; *mat, map*) • Develops fluency and ease in hearing and recognizing the same and different sounds in words in beginning, middle, and ending positions (*ball, boat*; *fat, fit*; *lip, lit*)

MATCHING INSTRUCTION TO STUDENT NEEDS

Learning About Sounds. Interventions should include explicit instruction in how words work, along with opportunities to transfer this knowledge to other reading and writing events (Scammacca et al. 2007). Teachers can promote children's phonological and phonemic knowledge within texts in the following ways:

- Draw children's attention to how words have more than one syllable by clapping the parts in multisyllabic words.
- Draw children's attention to rhyming words and how to segment onset from rime.
- Draw children's attention to words that begin or end the same.
- Draw children's attention to words that sound the same or different at the beginning, middle, or end of the word (phoneme manipulation and deletion).
- Draw children's attention to the sounds within words by saying words slowly and hearing and identifying the individual phonemes in the words.

ORTHOGRAPHIC SYSTEMS

Letter knowledge has been shown to be a strong predictor of later reading ability (Adams 1990; Caravolas, Hulme, and Snowling 2001). However, traditional activities, such as copying letters off the board or tracing letters on worksheets, are not productive learning tasks. Instead, learning about letters should be taught as a strategic process, involving the ability to notice similarities and differences among letters, to understand spatial and sequential aspects of letter knowledge, to recognize letters within words, and to produce well-formed letters with fluency while composing meaningful messages (Dorn and Jones 2012).

Learning About Letters. When children learn how to analyze the features of letters, they notice the finer distinctions that occur between the letter shapes. This perceptual process can be accelerated when teachers use language prompts (see Figure 7.1 and Resource G.2, Language for Describing the Path of Movement for Learning Letters) that emphasize spatial orientation and motor sequences. For instance, when demonstrating how to form the letter *a*, the teacher would direct the child's attention to the starting point, then describe the path of movement for constructing the letter form in a conventional sequence: "over, around, up, and down." When children learn the appropriate path of movement, they can generalize this knowledge to other letters with the same starting point and initial sequence (*s, c, q, d, o, g*).

As children attend to letters, they need opportunities to develop automaticity and flexibility (see Figure 7.2 for examples). This can be accomplished through the fast reading of letters and patterns on small charts (see Resource K.1 for reproducible copies of charts). Children need opportunities to perceive letters on different planes: on a dry erase board directly in front of them, on a vertical easel, or in a pocket chart. Here are some common letter-learning experiences:

- Using magnetic letters or sandpaper letters to draw attention to the directionality and distinctive features of letters.
- Using an ABC chart as a reference tool for writing letters and key words that begin with the letters on the chart.
- Noticing and locating known letters in big books, pocket chart stories, poems, letter books, and Interactive Writing texts.
- Writing letters in the sand, salt, and on a dry erase board.
- Using magnetic letters to construct simple words in left-to-right order.

Specifically, teachers should draw children's attention to the features of letters through sorting activities, such as sorting by letter features, by upper- and lowercase letters, or by alphabetical order. In

A slant down, slant down, across	a over, around and down
B down, up around, around	b dow . . . n, up and around
C over, around and open	c over, around and open
D down, up, around	d over, around u . . . p and down
E down, across, across, across	e across, over, around and open
F down, across, across	f over, dow . . . n, across
G over, around, across	g over, around, dow . . . n and curve
H down, down, across	h dow . . . n, up and over
I down, across, across	i down, dot
J down, curve	j down, curve, dot
K down, slant in, slant out	k dow . . . n, slant in, slant out
L down, across	l dow . . . n
M down, slant down, slant up, down	m down, up, over, up, over
N down, slant down, up	n down, up, over
O over, around, close	o over, around, close
P down, up, around	p dow . . . n, up, around
Q over, around, close, slant out	q over, around, down
R down, up, around, slant out	r down, up, curve
S over, around, curve	s over, around and curve
T down, across	t down, across
U down, curve up	u down, curve up, down
V slant down, slant up	v slant down, slant up
W slant down, slant up, slant down, slant up	w slant down, slant up, slant down, slant up
X slant down, slant across	x slant down, slant across
Y slant down, slant up, down	y slant down, slant dow . . . n
Z across, slant down, across	z across, slant down, across

Figure 7.1   Language for Describing the Path of Movement for Learning Letters

Figure 7.2 Teachers provide students with varied opportunities to learn about letters, including fast reading of alphabet and pattern charts and sorting activities

Figure 7.3, we provide examples of sorting activities for calling students' attention to distinctive features of letters:

- Sort by features (e.g., down part, curved part, around part, slant part, tall down part, short down part, short slants, long slants, over part, circle part, circles, and no circles).
- Sort by uppercase and lowercase.
- Sort by letter groups (e.g., put all the *a*'s in the circle).
- Sort by consonants and vowels.
- Sort by alphabetical order.

Learning About Words. Letter learning progresses through a perceptual continuum, beginning with a primitive classification of similarities, moving to an analytical comparison of differences, and resulting in the automatic, unconscious recognition of letters (Dorn and Jones 2012). As children work with letters and words, they build letter knowledge, letter–sound relationships, spelling patterns, high-frequency words, and word meanings. Then, during reading and writing, they apply visual information from known words to solve unknown words within texts.

Teachers can help students to understand how words work by focusing on three learning principles:

- Always work left to right when teaching, building, writing, or checking a word. It will enable children to look across the letters in sequence.
- Use language to help the children understand you are talking about a word and not a letter. For example, run your finger under the word, left to right, as you say the word.
- Present words in different contexts (word study, reading, and writing) many times so that they become known.

The Assisted Writing and Guided Reading Plus Interventions include explicit instruction in word study. For instance, during the AW Intervention, the teacher might guide students to sort words that end with *ing* in a pocket chart, or to sort words with a particular short-vowel rime pattern. During the word study component of the GRP intervention, the teacher might create a word chart of known patterns, and students could use this resource as a spelling tool during the writing component of GRP. Here are some ways to sort words:

- Sort by beginning, middle, and ending letters and sounds (*can, come*; *can, fin*).
- Sort by simple short-vowel rime patterns and sounds (*hat, mat*).
- Sort by beginning and ending letter clusters and sounds (*stop, stump*; *best, fist*).
- Sort by beginning and ending digraphs and sounds (*the, thin*; *bath, tooth*).
- Sort by long-vowel rime patterns and sounds (*ea——— seat, ai——— rain*).
- Sort words by r-vowel patterns and sounds (*car, shirt*) and other vowel patterns and sounds (*boy, boil*; *book, cool*).
- Sort words by infrequent vowel patterns (*enough, tough*).
- Sort words by meaningful parts (*do, undo*; *care, careless*).

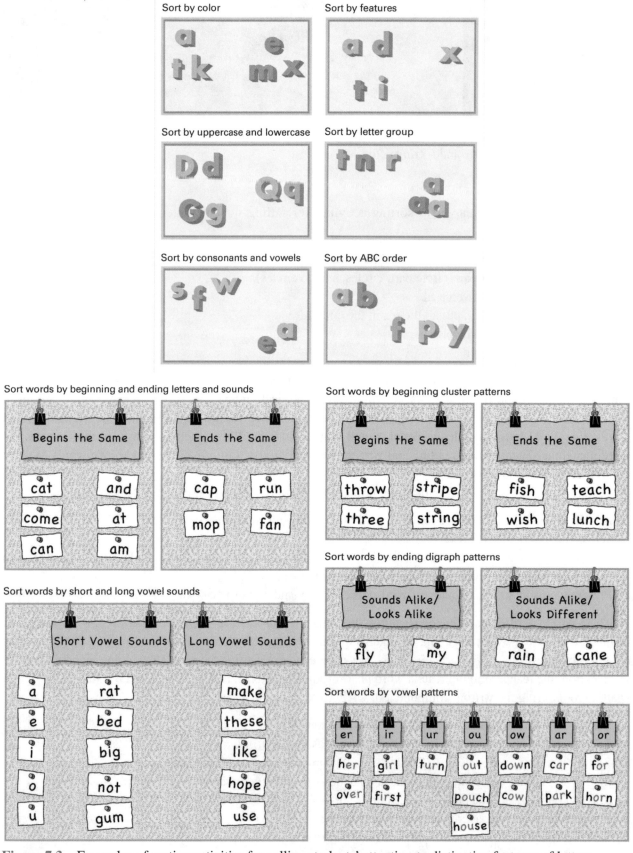

Figure 7.3   Examples of sorting activities for calling students' attention to distinctive features of letters.

As children become more automatic with their letter knowledge, they begin to notice how letters come together in left-to-right sequence to represent whole words. In the process, they learn that many words contain predictable and recurring spelling patterns. They attend to larger chunks within words (blends, clusters, inflectional endings, word families, prefixes, suffixes, root words), and they note relationships between chunks of letters and clusters of sound. Teachers should examine students' reading and writing for evidence of how they solve unknown words in connected text; then teachers should use this information along with the word study continuum to plan constructive word study activities. A word study intervention would enable students to acquire knowledge for breaking words apart in flexible ways. Here are typical ways that good readers operate on unknown words:

- Letters (*c-a-n*)
- Single consonant onsets and rime (*s-it*)
- Letter cluster onsets and rimes (*str-eet*)
- Inflectional endings (*look-ing*)
- Meaningful and logical units (*str-ee-t*)
- Syllables (*hap-py*)
- Prefixes (*un-do*)
- Suffixes (*week-ly*)

Making connections between words is a powerful way for children to analyze words and to understand how to use known information to assist with unknown words. Children must recognize word parts and understand the concept of substituting, adding, and deleting letters to generalize the process. The following steps provide an example of an instructional framework for learning this process.

- Have children build a known word.
- Have children break the word into parts (break word using single consonant or consonant cluster onset and rime, or at meaningful and logical units).
- Have children blend the parts back together to say the word.
- Have children generate other words that sound the same. Record the words on a large chart or on cards.
- Have the children sort the words using sound-alike/look-alike or sound-alike categories, and knowledge of word parts and spelling patterns.
- Draw children's attention to how known words can provide readers and writers with tools for solving unknown words within continuous texts (see Figure 7.4).

In the word study continuum of sound-symbol relationships, the following sequence is widely accepted (Blevins 2016; see Dorn and Jones 2012).

- **Start with consonants and short vowels** so that many CVC (consonant-vowel-consonant) words can be generated, such as *hat, hit, sit, cat*
- **Build to more advanced phonetic elements.** After consonants and short vowels are known, instruction should then move to more complex patterns. Here are some examples:
  - Blends (*r* family blends, *s* family blends, *l* family blends)
  - Digraphs (*ch, sh, th, wh*)
  - Final *e* (*a_e, e_e, i_e, o_e, u_e*)
  - Long vowels with multiple spelling patterns (*ai, ay, ea, ee, oa, ow*, etc.)
  - Variant vowels (*oo, au, aw*)
  - Diphthongs (*ou, ow, oi, oy*)
  - Structural analysis (contractions, compound words)
  - Silent letters (*kn*)
  - Inflectional endings (*-ed, -s, -ing*)
  - Prefixes and suffixes

Figure 7.4   During word learning, the student applies spelling principles to learn a new word. During writing, the student uses the practice page to solve unknown words. During reading, the student uses her finger to break apart an unknown word in text.

- **Extend to multisyllabic words.** At this stage, word analysis and synthesis are addressed. In addition, more advanced structural analysis is covered, such as more complex compound words, affixes, and so on.

A WORD STUDY CONTINUUM

In order for word study to be effective, teachers must understand that learning about words is a systematic process that is based on a continuum that moves from simple to more complex knowledge. Furthermore, teachers must understand what students already know and what they need to know. According to Dorn and Jones (2012), teachers should ask three questions to inform their decision making:

- What does the reader already know about words?
- What does the reader need to know about words?
- Where is the reader's learning on a word study continuum?

Earlier in this chapter, we shared how phonological and orthographic knowledge progresses along a developmental continuum. Now, in concert with the processing continuum, we provide teachers with three resources for planning systematic instruction. In Figure 7.5 we present a processing scale that teachers can use as a tool for planning word-learning activities within texts. Next, in Figure 7.6 and Resource G.3, Instructional Activities Aligned with Phonological and Orthographic Language Continuum, we share instructional possibilities that align with students' knowledge of letters and words along the processing continuum. Then, later in the chapter, in Figure 7.7, we present an instructional framework for scaffolding students to learn about analogies across words. In subsequent chapters, we'll refer back to these resources as we discuss the letter- and word-building components of the small-group interventions.

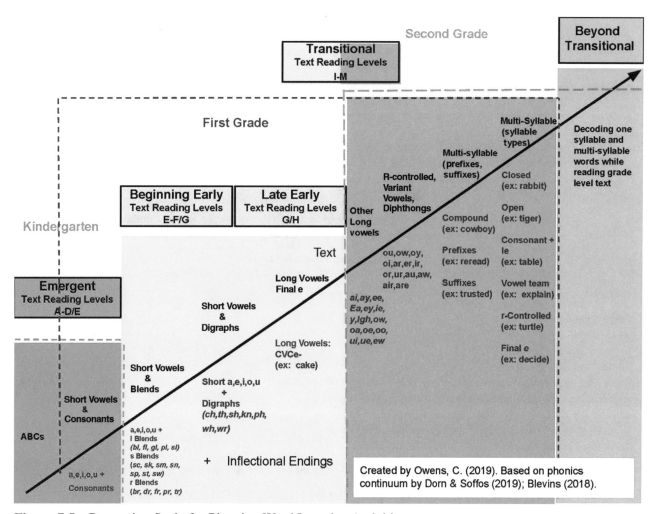

Figure 7.5   Processing Scale for Planning Word Learning Activities

---

Emergent Processing Level

Text Reading Levels: A–D/E, and Decodable Texts

Kindergarten

<u>*Possibilities for Strategic Letter Work*</u>

- Reads ABC chart chorally; reads in a variety of ways (reads consonants, reads vowels, reads every other letter).
- Reads pattern charts chorally.
- Reads letter books chorally.
- Develops knowledge for how to learn letters (describes path of movement).
- Recognizes and sorts distinguishable features of letters.
- Recognizes and names all upper- and lowercase letters fluently.
- Writes most upper- and lowercase letters fluently.

<u>*Possibilities for Strategic Word Learning: Building and Supporting the Decoding and Blending Processes*</u>

- Builds, breaks, and reassembles **high-frequency words** with predictable letter–sound relationships in a left-to-right order; reads words with fluency.

Figure 7.6   Instructional Activities Aligned with Phonological and Orthographic Language Continuum

- Builds simple one-syllable words with easy, predictable letter–sound relationships (**CV, VC and CVC**) in left-to-right sequence; breaks words letter by letter and blends letter sounds back together to read words (*go, g-o, go; at, a-t, at; cat, c-a-t-, cat*); disassembles, reconstructs, and rereads words for fluency.
- Records simple high-frequency words, (**CV, VC, and CVC**) in personal dictionary using first letter **to alphabetize**; reads recorded words with fluency.
- Builds known one-syllable **CVC** words in a left-to-right sequence; breaks words using onset and rime; blends parts back together; reads words with fluency; recognizes, notes, and records simple rime patterns.
- Builds known one-syllable **CVC** words in a left-to-right sequence; breaks words using onset and rime; rebuilds words; generates other words that sound the same (*h-am, f-an*); manipulates onset to make new words; reads words with fluency.
- Builds known words in a left-to-right sequence; adds a simple **inflectional ending** to make new words (*cat, cats; dog, dogs*); reads words with fluency.

Instructional Activities Aligned with Phonological and Orthographic Language Continuum
Increasing Awareness of the Phonological *and* Orthographic Language Systems

Beginning Early Processing Level
Text Reading Levels: E–F/G, Decodable Texts, and Grade-Level Texts

Early First Grade

Possibilities for Strategic Letter Work
- Reads ABC chart chorally.
- Reads pattern charts chorally.
- Reads letter books chorally.
- Develops knowledge for how to form letters (describes path of movement).
- Recognizes and categorizes distinguishable features of letters.
- Identifies and categorizes letters by vowels and consonants.
- Recognizes and names all upper- and lowercase letters fluently.
- Writes most upper- and lowercase letters fluently.

Possibilities for Strategic Word Learning: Building and Supporting the Decoding and Blending Processes During Reading

Note: Review emergent word learning until knowledge is secure before moving into slightly more complex word learning.

- Builds, breaks, and reassembles grade-appropriate **high-frequency words** letter by letter in a left-to-right order; recognizes and notes letter–sound discrepancies if applicable (*was, w-a-s*); reads words with fluency.
- Writes grade-appropriate **high-frequency words** in a personal dictionary using first letter **to alphabetize**; reads recorded words with fluency.
- Builds, breaks, and reassembles known one-syllable **CVC** words in left-to-right sequence; manipulates consonants or vowels in the beginning, middle, or ending position to make new words (*cat, hat; hot, hit; stop, step*); recognizes change in letters and sounds; reads words with fluency.
- Builds one-syllable **CCVC** words in left-to-right sequence; breaks words between **consonant blends** and other letters or patterns; blends consonant blends and letters and/or patterns back together; recognizes, notes, and records consonant blends; reads words with fluency (*flip, clap*).
- Builds one syllable **CCVC** words in left-to-right sequence; breaks words between **consonant digraphs** and other letters and/or patterns; blends consonant digraphs and letters and/or patterns back together; recognizes, notes, and records consonant digraphs; reads words with fluency (*ship, stop*).
- Builds known words in left-to-right sequence with **consonant blends and digraphs** in beginning and ending position; breaks words using onset and rime patterns (*st-ep, f-ish*) or at meaningful and logical units (*sh-i-p, f-i-sh*); reads words with fluency.
- Builds words in a left-to-right sequence with a **CVCe** pattern; breaks words letter by letter; blends letters back together; recognizes, notes, and records long-vowel patterns; reads words with fluency (*have, h-a-v-e, made, m-a-d-e*).
- Builds known words in a left-to-right sequence; adds **inflectional endings** to make new words (*looks, looking, looked*); recognizes, notes, and records inflectional endings; reads words with fluency.

Figure 7.6 *(Continued)*

Instructional Activities Aligned with Phonological and Orthographic Language Continuum
Gaining Control of the Phonological and Orthographic Language Systems

Late Early Processing Level
Text Reading Levels: G/H, Decodable Texts, and Grade-Level Texts
Mid-First Grade

Possibilities for Strategic Letter Work

- Develops speed, fluency, and ease in identifying and writing all upper- and lowercase letters.

Possibilities for Strategic Word Learning: Building and Supporting the Decoding and Blending Processes During Reading

Note: Review beginning early word learning until knowledge is secure before moving into slightly more complex word learning.

- Builds, breaks, and reassembles grade-appropriate **high-frequency words** letter by letter in a left-to-right order; recognizes and notes letter- or pattern-sound discrepancies if applicable; reads words with fluency.
- Builds words with **long-vowel patterns** (vowel teams) in a left-to-right sequence; breaks words at meaningful and logical units (*sheet, sh-ee-t; seat, s-ea-t*); blends letters, consonant blends, digraphs, and long-vowel patterns into sounds to read word; recognizes, notes, and records long-vowel patterns; reads words with fluency.
- Builds known words with **long-vowel patterns** (vowel teams); generates other words that sound the same and look the same or sound the same but are spelled differently; sorts words according to "sound the same and spelled the same" and "sound the same but spelled differently"; recognizes, notes, and records different spellings for long-vowel patterns; reads words with fluency.
- Builds **two-syllable words** in a left-to-right sequence using syllable knowledge, letter–sound knowledge, and pattern-sound knowledge; breaks words into syllables (*rab-bit, un-til*); recognizes, notes, and records spelling change process if applicable; reads words with fluency.
- Builds **compound words** in a left-to-right sequence; breaks compound words into two smaller words (*out-side, sun-shine*); recognizes, notes, and records compound words; reads words with fluency.
- Builds two known words (*I, am*); removes a letter or letters to form **contractions** (*I'm*); recognizes, notes, and records contractions; reads words with fluency.
- Builds known words in a left-to-right order; adds more complex **inflectional endings** that require a spelling change (*stop, stopped, stopping, dash, dashes*); recognizes, notes, and records words and the spelling change process; reads words with fluency.
- Builds known words (*cat, fur*) in a left-to-right order; adds apostrophe + *s* to show ownership (*cat's fur*); recognizes, notes, and records **possessives**; reads words with fluency.

Instructional Activities Aligned with Phonological and Orthographic Language Continuum
Extending Control of the Phonological and Orthographic Language Systems

Transitional Processing Level
Text Reading Levels: I–M and Grade-Level Texts
End of First Grade to End of Second Grade

Possibilities for Strategic Word Learning: Building and Supporting the Decoding and Blending Processes During Reading

Note: Review late early word learning until knowledge is secure before moving into slightly more complex word learning.

- Builds, breaks, and reassembles grade-appropriate **high-frequency words** letter by letter in a left-to-right order; recognizes and notes letter- or pattern-sound discrepancies if applicable; reads words with fluency.
- Builds words with *r-controlled vowels* in a left-to-right sequence; breaks words at meaningful and logical units (*part, p-ar-t, burn, b-ur-n, third, th-ir-d*); blends letters, consonant blends, consonant digraphs, and *r*-controlled vowels into sounds to read word; recognizes, notes, and records *r*-controlled vowel patterns; reads words with fluency.
- Builds words with **irregular vowel patterns** in a left-to-right sequence; breaks words at meaningful and logical units (*draw, dr-aw, broom, br-oo-m*); blends letters, consonant blends, consonant digraphs, and irregular vowel patterns into sounds to read words; recognizes, notes, and records irregular vowel patterns; reads words with fluency.

Figure 7.6 *(Continued)*

- Builds words with **diphthongs** in a left-to-right sequence; breaks words at meaningful and logical units (*shout, sh-ou-t, blow, bl-ow, soil, s-oi-l, boy, b-oy*); blends letters, consonant blends, consonant digraphs, and diphthongs into sounds to read word; recognizes, notes, and records diphthongs; reads words with fluency.
- Builds **complex multisyllabic words** in a left-to-right sequence; breaks words at the syllable level (*joyful, joy-ful, whisper, whis-per flower, flow-er, information, in-for-ma-tion*); blends syllables to read words; recognizes, notes, and records multisyllabic words; reads words with fluency.
- Builds known base words; makes new words by adding common **prefixes or derivational suffixes** to modify meaning of base word; recognizes, notes, and records prefixes or suffixes; reads words with fluency.

Instructional Activities Aligned with Phonological and Orthographic Language Continuum
Extending Control of the Phonological and Orthographic Language Systems

Beyond Transitional Processing Level

Grade-Level Texts

Third Grade and Beyond

***Possibilities* for Strategic Word Learning: Building and Supporting the Decoding and Blending Processes During Reading**

Note: Review transitional word learning until knowledge is secure before moving into slightly more complex word learning.

- Builds, breaks, and reassembles grade-appropriate **high-frequency words** letter by letter in a left-to-right order; recognizes and notes letter- or pattern-sound discrepancies if applicable; reads words with fluency.
- Builds base words; makes new words by adding common **Latin suffixes** (*-tion/-sion*; *-ity, -ment*); recognizes, notes, and records Latin suffixes; reads words with fluency.
- Builds base words; makes new words by adding **suffixes** that form comparatives and modify meaning (*high/higher/highest*); recognizes, notes, and records suffixes that form comparatives; reads words with fluency.
- Builds **multisyllabic** words in a left-to-right sequence; breaks words at meaningful and logical units (*in-ven-tion, pre-ap-pre-hen-sion*) using known word patterns; blends syllables back together to read words; recognizes, notes, and records syllables; reads words with fluency.

Builds **homophones** (same pronunciation but different spelling) or **homographs** (same spelling, different meanings, and sometimes different pronunciations); recognizes, notes, and records homophones or homographs; reads words with fluency.

Figure 7.6   *(Continued)*

Instructional Framework for Scaffolding Students to
Learn About Analogies at Four Points in Time

Instructional Goal 1: Making Analogies Across Words—Drawing Students' Attention to the Process of Noticing Word Parts (Onset and Rime)

Assessment Prompt: What do students need to know in order to learn from instruction? Students must be able to break onset from rime and blend the parts back together, and they must know the word in order to learn the process.

Instructional Framework:
- Have the students build a known word.
- Have the students break the word into parts using onset and rime.
- Have the students blend the parts back together to say the word.
- Have the students generate other words that sound the same in ending position. Record the words on a large chart and underline the ending part. If the students generate a word that sounds the same but doesn't look the same, then tell them that it does sound the same, but it looks different.
- Draw the students' attention to how using known words and word parts provides readers and writers with tools for solving unknown words fluently within continuous texts.

Figure 7.7   Instructional Framework for Scaffolding Students to Learn About Analogies at Four Points in Time

Instructional Goal 2: Making Analogies Across Words—Drawing Students' Attention to the Process of Noticing Word Parts (Onset and Rime or at Meaningful and Logical Units)

Assessment Prompt: What do students need to know in order to learn from instruction? Students must be able to hear and break words into parts, and they must know the word.

Instructional Framework:
- Have the students build the known word _____ (e.g., *start*).
- Have the students break the word _____ using onset and rime or at meaningful and logical units (e.g., *start* into parts: *st-ar-t*).
- Have the students blend the parts together and read the word (e.g., *start*).
- Draw students' attention to how using known parts provides readers and writers with tools for solving unknown words fluently within continuous texts.

Instructional Goal 3: Making Analogies Across Words—Drawing Students' Attention to the Process of Using Word Parts to Read New Words

Assessment Prompt: What do students need to know in order to learn from instruction? Students must be able to break onset from rime and blend the parts back together, and they must know the words to learn the process.

Instructional Framework:
- Have the students build the word _____ (e.g., *jump*) and the word _____ (e.g., *stop*).
- Have the students break off the first part of the word _____ (e.g., *stop*) and the last part of the word _____ (e.g., *jump*).
- Have the students run their finger under the new word and read the word.
- Draw the students' attention to how using known words and word parts provides readers and writers with tools for solving unknown words fluently within continuous texts.

Instructional Goal 4: Making Analogies Across Words—Drawing Students' Attention to the Process of Using Known Word Parts to Read Unknown Multisyllabic Words

Assessment Prompt: What do students need to know in order to learn from instruction? Students must be able to break a multisyllabic word into syllables or parts, and they must know the letter patterns or word parts that are needed to take the word apart.

Instructional Framework:
- Provide the students with an unknown multisyllabic word (write the word on a card for each student or write the word on a whiteboard).
- Have the students draw lines to break the word apart, or have them write the word in parts, to demonstrate how to look for known parts to read an unknown word.
- Have the students blend the parts back together to read the word.
- Draw the students' attention to how known words and word parts provide readers and writers with tools for solving unknown words fluently within continuous texts.

Figure 7.7   *(Continued)*

DESIGNING A WORD STUDY LESSON

The goal of word study is to enable the student to understand how words work in order to apply this knowledge for solving unknown words in connected text. In designing a word study, teachers must ask three questions:

- What does the student understand about words?
- What does the student need to understand about words?
- How much support will the student need to accomplish the new word-solving task?

A well-designed word study intervention includes four instructional elements: (1) predictable framework with some established routines, (2) clear model using exemplar words that illustrate a learning principle, (3) explicit teaching followed by guided practice, and (4) precise language for scaffolding the student's problem-solving actions. The following is an example of an instructional framework for teaching students a new word.

- Draw students' attention to the word by pointing to the word while saying it. Use instructional language (e.g., "This word is . . .").
- Have students observe carefully as you build the word letter by letter in a left-to-right sequence.
- Do not talk, just model. Make sure the students' eyes are scanning left to right across the word.
- Read the newly built word as you run your finger under the word in a left-to-right sequence.
- Provide the students with the correct magnetic letters and ask them to build the word, left to right, paying close attention to the sequence of the letters within the word (provide a model if needed).
- Have the students run their finger under the word in a left-to-right sequence and check the word.
- Provide the students with an opportunity to build, check, break, and rebuild the word several times.
- Provide the students with an opportunity to write the word several times. If they are fluent, have them add the word to their personal dictionary or spelling pattern card.

As we discussed earlier, knowledge about words progresses along a continuum from simple to more complex. As students acquire greater competency, teachers adjust their instruction to accommodate the student's expanding knowledge. In Table 7.1, we illustrated how this might look at four points along a processing continuum. In Figure 7.7, we shared an instructional framework for scaffolding students to learn about analogies. In this example, the goal is that students will understand the process of making analogies by using known patterns (onset and rime) to solve unknown words. Each lesson includes three components:

- Instructional goal for accomplishing the learning task.
- Assessment prompt that is based on what the students will need to know in order to accomplish the learning task.
- Instructional framework for scaffolding the students to acquire the new learning.

CLOSING THOUGHTS

The ultimate goal of word study is to enable students to decode words rapidly and efficiently in order to keep the focus on comprehending the message. If students are unable to transfer their knowledge about words to connected texts, that knowledge serves little purpose for the reading act. Therefore, all word study activities must be aligned with the reading and writing processes.

The purpose of this chapter has been to present the rationale for letter and word study in an intervention group. Each intervention includes a systematic word study component. As you implement these interventions, we encourage you to return to this chapter to assist with the word study component and use the examples to support the use of word study.

Chapter 8

COMPREHENSION FOCUS GROUP FOR INCREASING COMPREHENSION POWER

Why do some students have difficulty learning to read and others do not? For many low-progress readers, the problem does not lie with inadequate decoding skills (Duke, Pressley, and Hilden 2004; Englert and Thomas 1987; Buly and Valencia 2002). Rather, as Gersten and colleagues (2001) explain, "the breakdown occurs in the domain of strategic processing and metacognition (i.e., students' ability to control and manage their cognitive activities in a reflective, purposeful fashion)" (2).

Many problems can arise in the strategic processing of texts. These problems are exacerbated for low-progress readers, who often do not possess the background knowledge or vocabulary they need to recognize when a problem occurs. Or, if they do recognize the problem, they might not know the best strategy for addressing it, which could result in guessing behaviors. This is in contrast to strategic readers, who make deliberate and intentional choices, which they spontaneously monitor in their desire to comprehend the message.

In Chapter 1, we described the strategic reader as a reflective and analytical learner, one who is able to process multiple sources of information with ease and efficiency. How do students become strategic readers? During initial learning, students develop an awareness of strategies for solving problems; then, with successful practice, they become skilled at mobilizing the most efficient strategies for producing faster actions. Economy and flexibility do not happen overnight; rather, these strategic processes are nurtured through challenging opportunities at three points in time:

- Acquisition strategies for learning new information.
- Troubleshooting strategies for solving problems as they arise.
- Accommodating strategies when processing capacity is exceeded (e.g., task is too difficult, learner is fatigued or stressed).

The Comprehensive Focus Group (CFG) intervention is designed to promote the development of strategic activity in low-progress readers, thus supplying them with the tools to learn from experience. In this chapter, we share the principles that support the CFG as an effective intervention, followed by the specialized procedures for implementing the intervention with readers at third grade and beyond.

PRINCIPLES THAT SUPPORT THE CFG INTERVENTION

Background Knowledge. Research indicates that limitations in background knowledge and vocabulary are the primary causes of comprehension failure, especially after third grade (Stanovich 1986). The more students know about a topic, the more deeply they can understand it. For adequate comprehension, according to Nagy and Scott (2000), readers should know between 90 and 95 percent of the words in a text. With this background in place, readers are able to comprehend the main ideas within the text and infer the meanings of unfamiliar words. Comprehension suffers when readers cannot synthesize new and old information and when they are unable to select relevant prior knowledge and apply those sources to the text. Students must possess the necessary content knowledge, along with important cognitive strategies, to comprehend the deeper meanings within texts.

The CFG intervention is designed to build students' content knowledge and academic vocabulary through language-based experiences with texts on a variety of topics. As students revisit complex texts, their knowledge moves from the surface level (key ideas and details within the text) to the deep level (critical analysis of relationships within and across texts). Deep comprehension requires students to understand the structure of a problem and its interrelated components (i.e., causes, consequences, solutions, actors, setting, time, and such). When students are familiar with a problem's deep structure, they are more likely to transfer this information to new reading tasks (Willingham 2017).

Themed Units of Study. Everything we hear or read is automatically interpreted in light of what we already know. If we don't have adequate background knowledge for the topic, our brain will try to make sense of the information by filtering it through something we do know. Inadequate knowledge can result in a misinterpretation of the topic under investigation; when such misinterpretations are overlearned, students develop flawed meanings for important concepts. To acquire deep comprehension, students need lots of opportunities to integrate knowledge from multiple experiences, thus constructing networks of denser meanings through relational knowledge.

The CFG intervention is organized to expose students to a variety of text types and complexities around an important conceptual theme. Through scaffolded instruction, students acquire topical knowledge for comprehending the words, sentences, and ideas within a text. Then, as they encounter this information in different situations, they are able to make evidence-based inferences and think critically about relationships within and across texts. The familiarity of information across themed sets provides a bridge for connecting ideas and expanding knowledge to deeper levels.

Knowledge of Genre and Text Structures. Knowledge of genre and text structures plays an important role in constructing an understanding of text (Purcell-Gates, Duke, and Martineau 2007). This background knowledge assists students in constructing inferences (Duke et al. 2004), making accurate predictions (McIntyre 2007), and selecting strategic actions (Pressley et al. 2007). Further, knowledge of specific genres frees up working memory so that readers can process text at higher levels of comprehension.

The CFG intervention includes explicit instruction in genre and text structures, including the analysis of mentor texts for structural elements to determine how writers organize their texts to support readers' comprehension. Within a language-based framework, students learn that reading and writing share common structures for communicating meanings; therefore, they can transfer what they know from reading to assist their writing and vice versa.

Comprehension Strategies. In Chapter 1, we discussed the six levels of comprehension (Shanahan et. al, 2010) plus the role of texts (both oral and written) in shaping students' higher-level thinking strategies. Students need a repertoire of strategies that they can activate when comprehension breaks down, including monitoring when a problem occurs, connecting known and new information within and across texts, and resolving ambiguities between sources of information (Paris, Wasik, and Turner 1991; Pressley 2002).

The CFG intervention includes opportunities for students to develop and expand their comprehension strategies through listening, speaking, reading, and writing experiences, all of which take place around well-crafted, motivating texts. Additionally, during comprehension minilessons, teachers use mentor texts to highlight specific strategies for understanding complex ideas and language.

Writing About Reading (WAR). Writing instruction helps students make connections between what they read, know, and understand, thus improving their comprehension of text. Results are especially noteworthy when students write personal reactions or interpret ideas from the text. Research implies that writing about a text yields better gains than just reading it, rereading it, studying it, discussing it, or receiving reading instruction (Graham and Herbert 2010). Writing about reading requires students to gather evidence from the text and present that information in writing.

Specific types of writing for increasing reading comprehension are (1) responding to text in writing, (2) writing a summary of a text, (3) writing notes about a text, (4) answering questions about a text in writing, or (5) creating and answering written questions about a text. Questions about the text may address a variety of aspects, including themes and central ideas, knowledge of vocabulary, syntax and structure, and author's craft. In support of the reading-writing connection, Graham and Herbert (2010) offer three recommendations:

● Have students write about the texts they read.
● Teach students the writing skills and processes that go into creating text.
● Increase how much students write.

The CFG includes explicit instruction in writing about reading. In Figure 8.1, we illustrate how the WAR component is aligned with Bloom's taxonomy of higher-level thinking.

Linking the Revised Bloom's Taxonomy with Writing About Reading

Level	Key Words		Description	Sample Prompts
Create	Imagine Compose Design Adapt Create Generate	Integrate Invent Reorganize Rearrange Substitute	**This level refers to the ability to assemble information to produce a new or original whole.** ● *Retell the story as "Goldilocks and the Three Fishes."* ● *Retell the story of Pearl Harbor assuming U.S. armed forces had been ready for the attack.*	● *Pretend you were a participant in the Boston Tea Party and write a diary entry that tells what happened.* ● *Rewrite "Little Red Riding Hood" as a news story.* ● *Design a different way of solving this problem.* ● *Formulate a hypothesis that might explain the results of these three experiments.*
Evaluate	Appraise Assess	Judge Critique	**This level deals with examining components from a critical perspective.** ● *Do you think it was right for Goldilocks to go into the bears' house without having been invited? Why or why not?* ● *Do you feel that the bombing of Pearl Harbor has any effect on Japanese-American relations today? Why or why not?*	● *Which of the two main characters in the story would you rather have as a friend? Why?* ● *Is violence ever justified in correcting injustices? Why or why not?* ● *Which of the environments we studied seems like the best place for you to live?* ● *Create a persuasive piece inspired by your reading.*
Analyze	Analyze Contrast Distinguish Deduce Categorize Diagram	Outline Discriminate Distinguish Illustrate Infer Prioritize	**This is the ability to break material into its component parts to understand its organizational structure and relationships.** ● *What things in the Goldilocks story could have really happened?* ● *What lesson did our country learn from Pearl Harbor?*	● *Which events in the story are fantasy and which really happened?* ● *Compare and contrast the post-Civil War period with post-Vietnam.* ● *Sort this collection of rocks into three categories.* ● *Analyze character traits across more than one text.* ● *Complete a text map.*

Figure 8.1   Linking the Revised Bloom's Taxonomy with Writing About Reading

Level	Key Words		Description	Sample Prompts
Apply	Practice Calculate Apply Execute Discover Produce	Show Use Manipulate Demonstrate Modify	**This level refers to the ability to use learned material in new situations with a minimum of direction.** • *If Goldilocks came to your house today, what things might she do?* • *If you had been responsible for the defense of the Hawaiian Islands, what preparation would you have made against an attack?*	• *Use each vocabulary word in a new sentence.* • *Calculate the area of your classroom.* • *Think of three situations in which we could use this mathematics operation.* • *Use the parts to reassemble this motor.* • *Compare and contrast two different texts.* • *Create a time line of events.*
Understand	Summarize Discuss Explain Outline Infer Interpret Paraphrase	Provide examples Ask questions Translate Predict Rewrite Generalize	**This level describes the ability to make sense of the material. The learning goes beyond mere recall and represents the lowest level of comprehension.** • *Why did Goldilocks like baby bear's things best?* • *Why did the Japanese bomb Pearl Harbor?*	• *Summarize the paragraph.* • *Why are symbols used on maps?* • *Write a paragraph explaining the duties of the mayor.* • *Outline the steps for completing this experiment.* • *Sequence the information.*
Remember	Define Label Recall Recognize Sequence	Retell Describe Match Identify	**Remember refers to rote recall and recognition of previously learned material, from specific facts to a definition or a complete theory.** • *What did Goldilocks do in the three bears' house?* • *What was the date of the bombing of Pearl Harbor?*	• *What is the definition of a verb?* • *Label the three symbols on this map.* • *What are the three branches of government?* • *Which object in the picture is a xylophone?*

Figure 8.1 (*Continued*)

Engagement in Text-Based Discussions. Quality discussions in classrooms impact students' vocabulary and use of comprehension strategies (Kong and Fitch 2002/2003) and are linked to gains in reading comprehension (Murphy et al. 2009). Research on productive book discussions suggests they have six common features (Soter et al. 2008):

• Conversations are structured and focused, yet not dominated by the teacher.
• Students hold the floor for extended periods of time and build on one another's ideas.
• Discussions are based on evidence from the text.
• Students are prompted to discuss texts through open-ended or authentic questions.
• The teacher incorporates student questions and comments into the discussion.
• Teacher scaffolding at strategic points in the discussion facilitates more elaborated forms of reasoning from students.

An essential component of the CFG intervention is the Literature Discussion Group (LDG). The LDG format includes specialized procedures for mediating students' speaking, listening, reading, and writing competencies through text-based discussions of complex ideas.

INTERVENTION FRAMEWORK FOR THE CFG

The CFG intervention is based on a series of reading and writing lessons in a specific genre, text type, or theme. The lessons occur over several weeks and focus on developing students' reading and writing strategies for understanding complex ideas within texts. The CFG aligns with the classroom components of reading workshop, including interactive read-aloud with mentor texts, strategy-based minilessons, LDG, and WAR (see Chapter 4).

The intervention framework for the CFG occurs in three phases (language phase, reading phase, writing phase) with thirty minutes of instruction each day. Each phase includes specialized procedures for building students' knowledge of reading and writing as language-based processes. It is important for students to have daily instruction as they strive to make connections between past and future learning.

Phase One: Language Phase. During the language phase, the students develop the necessary background knowledge for future learning. Teachers create themed sets around conceptual ideas (e.g., relationships, wisdom, challenges) that encompass three text types: (1) literary, (2) expository and informational, and (3) persuasive or argumentative. Themed sets include a range of texts that can be used for multiple purposes: more complex texts for interactive read-aloud, anchor charts, and guided participation; instructional texts for small-group discussions; and easier texts for independent reading. During the language phase, teachers select three to five mentor texts that are revisited for different purposes (e.g., inferring meanings, figurative language and phases, text conventions and structures, author's craft). In Video 8.1, the teacher introduces the genre and mentor texts for the language phase.

Video 8.1   The teacher introduces Genre and Mentor Texts for Language Phase.

Phase Two: Reading Phase (Part 1). The reading phase includes two complementary parts that work together to foster the students' capacity for deep comprehension and transfer. The first part includes six components:

- The teacher provides a comprehension strategy minilesson and engages students in guided practice.
- The teacher orients students to the new text and sets purposes for reading.
- Students read silently and annotate the text in critical areas.
- The teacher conducts one-to-one conferences and provides tailored support.
- Students respond to the reading in their reading log.
- Teacher convenes a group meeting to discuss text meaning, plus comprehension strategies used.

Phase Two: Reading Phase (Part 2). Based on successful experiences in Part 1, the students are ready to expand their knowledge to the next level. Part 2 of the reading phase includes five components:

- The teacher refreshes students' knowledge of the text structure from previous lessons, then provides students with a text map for analyzing a particular structure for the text.
- Students place the text map in their reading logs and complete the map, while the teacher observes their actions and provides scaffolding as needed.
- The teacher prepares students for the text discussion by reviewing conversational moves on the anchor chart and setting a purpose for the text discussion.
- Students engage in the text discussion, and the teacher provides mediating prompts when necessary to keep the discussion at a high level.
- The teacher provides students with a prompt for writing about their reading, and students respond in their reading logs.

Literature Discussion Group. The LDG is considered the heartbeat of the CFG intervention. It mirrors the LDG format for reading workshop that we described in previous texts (Dorn and Jones 2012, Dorn and Soffos 2005, Henderson and Dorn 2011). An important goal of the LDG is to lift the understanding of the group through interactive dialogue and conversational moves (norms) that keep the discussion in motion. Prior to the first text discussion, the teacher introduces the students to conversational norms, such as agreeing or disagreeing with each other, expressing confusion when puzzled, seeking or giving clarification, comparing ideas, and offering evidence. Generally, the teacher introduces one or two moves at a time, records these on an anchor chart, and engages the students in practicing the language during the book discussion. Over time, students become more natural with using conversational moves and employ them as needed to enrich their understanding of the text experience. (See Figure 8.2 for anchor chart of conversational moves.)

In Videos 8.2, 8.3, and 8.4, we illustrate how the components of the LDG are implemented over several days. The learning experience is designed around a broader unit of study on Life's Lessons, which uses varied text types to build students' background knowledge in essential areas. Within this broader theme, the students are learning how authors use language to create mood that influences the readers' comprehension. To support their learning, the students use sticky notes to highlight important information for sharing with one another. In Figure 8.3, the students use a graphic organizer to identify significant events in the story and the use of language for elaborating on these important events. In these examples, the teacher is a participant in the discussion, apprenticing the students in learning how to talk about books at deeper levels.

Video 8.2   These two videos illustrate the teaching and learning interactions over a two-day period of the literature discussion group framework of the CFG. Based on a themed set of texts, the teacher provides a strategy-based minilesson on using sticky notes to highlight the author's language, conducts one-to-one reading conferences, and mediates the book discussions to enable students to construct deeper meanings of important concepts within and across texts.

Video 8.3

Video 8.4   This video occurs a few days later in the themed unit of study. Here, the students are learning how to facilitate the book conversation; the teacher sits outside the circle, observes their interaction, and joins the discussion at critical points to scaffold the learning.

Phase Three: Writing Phase. The writing phase mirrors the components of the Writing Aloud Intervention (see Chapter 5). The reciprocal benefits of language, reading, and writing are highlighted, as students use their knowledge of reading as the raw material for writing. During the writing phase, the teacher engages the students in a group composition that undergoes planning, drafting, revising, and editing for a particular reading audience.

PLANNING FOR INSTRUCTION

Planning is a critical component of a successful CFG intervention. Prior to instruction, the teacher selects the appropriate materials and plans specific activities to meet the instructional goals. In this section, we provide materials to support teachers in this critical step. First, we share the Lesson Planner for Comprehension Focus Group Intervention (see Resource H.1). Then we share the Guide Sheet for Comprehension Focus Group Intervention (Figure 8.4 and Resource H.2), with procedural steps for implementing the intervention with consistency, followed by details on specific components. Within this framework, teachers should base their instructional decisions on systematic observations of students' learning and ongoing assessments (see Chapter 3). Additionally, we provide video links to demonstrations of specific lesson components discussed in the CFG Guide Sheet.

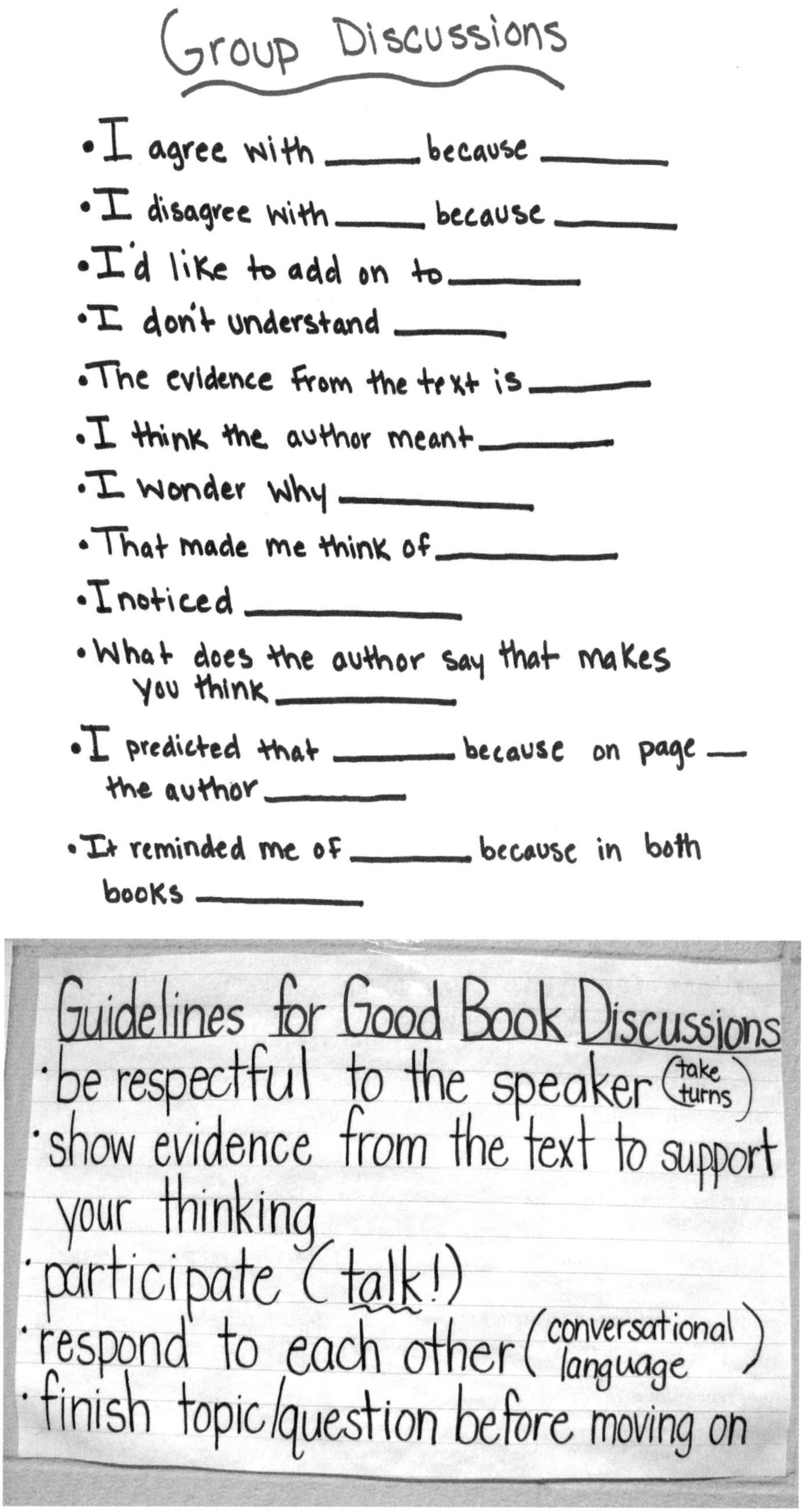

Group Discussions

- I agree with _____ because _____
- I disagree with _____ because _____
- I'd like to add on to _____
- I don't understand _____
- The evidence from the text is _____
- I think the author meant _____
- I wonder why _____
- That made me think of _____
- I noticed _____
- What does the author say that makes you think _____
- I predicted that _____ because on page ___ the author _____
- It reminded me of _____ because in both books _____

Guidelines for Good Book Discussions

- be respectful to the speaker (take turns)
- show evidence from the text to support your thinking
- participate (talk!)
- respond to each other (conversational language)
- finish topic/question before moving on

Figure 8.2 Teacher and students co-construct anchor chart of conversational moves for engaging in interactive dialogue during the CFG intervention.

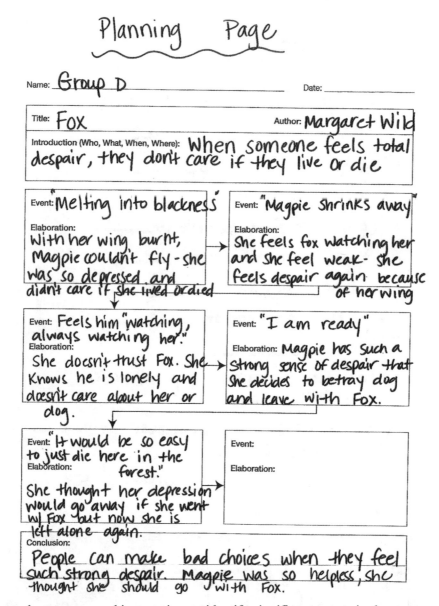

Figure 8.3   The students use a graphic organizer to identify significant events in the story and the use of language for elaborating on these important events.

Section on Planner	Phase 2: Reading *Comprehension Strategy or Word-Learning Minilesson, Reflection and Goal Setting*
Part 1	**Comprehension Strategy, Language Strategy, or Word-Learning Minilesson:** The goal is for students to flexibly initiate comprehension and word-solving strategies before, during, and after reading. **Comprehension Strategy Lesson:** The teacher supports students in the following ways: • Presents comprehension strategy lesson using sections from a mentor text or multiple texts with the goal for students to build a toolbox of comprehension strategies that can be mobilized as needed to solve problems in reading.

Figure 8.4   Guide Sheet for Comprehension Focus Group Intervention

- Models the process by thinking aloud and provides an opportunity for students to apply the strategy or strategies with appropriate levels of scaffolding.
- Engages students in a rich discussion about the process being investigated and learned.
- Records the strategy on a chart to be referred to in future lessons.
- Encourages students to record strategy in log to be revisited when needed.

OR

Video 8.5   The teacher presents a minilesson on comprehension strategies.

Language Strategy Lesson:

The teacher supports students in the following ways:

- Presents a language strategy lesson to develop students' understanding of the functions of the language system, including grammatical structures, text conventions, vocabulary, and crafting techniques.
- Models the process by thinking aloud and provides an opportunity for students to apply the strategy with appropriate levels of scaffolding.
- Engages students in a rich discussion about the process being investigated and learned.
- Records the strategy on a chart to be referred to in future lessons.
- Encourages students to record strategy in log to be revisited when needed.

OR

Word-Learning Lesson:

The teacher supports students in the following ways:

- Presents a word-learning lesson on syllabic, morphemic, and contextual analysis.
- Models the process by thinking aloud and provides an opportunity for students to apply the strategy with appropriate levels of scaffolding.
- Engages students in a rich discussion about the process being investigated and learned.
- Records the word-learning process on a chart to be referred to in future lessons.
- Encourages students to record the word-learning process in log to be revisited when needed.

Reflection and Goal Setting The goal is for students to become metacognitive about their learning and to transfer their knowledge across reading events. The teacher supports students in the following ways:

- Prompts students to discuss the comprehension strategy, language strategy, or word-learning principle studied and provide examples to signal and demonstrate understanding.
- Affords students an opportunity to set a goal for transferring the learning across reading events.
- Provides students with an opportunity to chart their goal with an example on a sticky note or in a log.

Section on Planner	
	Orientation to Text—Set or Scaffold Purpose for Reading
Part 2	**Orientation to Text—Set or Scaffold Purpose for Reading:** The goal is for students to apply their background knowledge of topic, text genre, text structure, language, comprehension, and word-solving strategies to prepare for the reading. The teacher supports students in the following ways: • Reads the title and provides an overview of the text and sets the purpose for reading, or reads the title and prompts or scaffolds the students to set their own purpose for reading. • Uses specific language structures and discusses relevant vocabulary that will support the comprehension process. • Points out important features within text, such as illustrations, text structure, and text features, if needed. • Assigns text, chapter, or pages for silent reading.

Figure 8.4   (*Continued*)

Section on Planner	Independent Reading (Reading may span several days) Reflection and Goal Setting
Part 3	**Independent Reading:** The goal is for students to engage in silent reading and to flexibly apply comprehension and word-solving strategies to read the text with comprehension. The teacher supports students in the following ways: • Provides students with a copy of the text and any annotating tools needed to support the comprehension process. • Conferences with students and provides appropriate levels of scaffolding to ensure comprehension is developing. • Prompts students to read aloud a section of the text, records notes regarding accuracy, fluency, and independent word-solving processes. **Reflection and Goal Setting:** The goal is for students to reflect on their comprehending and/or word-solving strategies while reading. The teacher supports students in the following ways: • Provides an opportunity for students to reflect on their comprehending and problem-solving process and record an example on a sticky note. • Provides students with an opportunity to discuss their reflection and example. • Provides an opportunity for students to set new goals for transferring their learning to other texts and across reading events. Video 8.6 The teacher prompts students to reflect on strategies used during their reading.
Section on Planner	**Phase Two: Reading** *Text Discussion and Writing About Reading*
Part 1	**Literature Discussion:** The goal is for students to use literate discourse to support deeper comprehension of the text. The teacher supports students in the following ways: • Provides students with an opportunity to engage in a rich discussion about the text using conversational language. • Scaffolds the discussion by prompting for active listening and the use of conversational language. • Scaffolds students to discuss important elements of the text to facilitate deeper comprehension of the text. • Records notes about students' participation in the discussion and the change in their depth of comprehension.
Part 2	**Writing About Reading Prompt:** The goal is for students to deepen their comprehension by writing about their reading and providing textual evidence to support their thinking. The teacher supports students in the following way: • Provides appropriate levels of support to ensure students understand the goal of the writing task and the planning, encoding, revising, and editing processes involved in completing the response. **Writing About Reading Lesson—High to Moderate Level of Scaffolding:** The teacher scaffolds students in the following ways: • Models and/or scaffolds the planning process by using a planner or an outline to prepare for Writing About Reading. • Co-constructs the response with the students and scaffolds the thinking as needed (e.g., composing strategies, specific vocabulary, spelling strategies, language principles, and revising and editing techniques). • Engages students at appropriate times in the problem-solving process on their individual dry erase boards. • Provides an opportunity for students to reflect on writing by using a Writing About Reading rubric or checklist; makes revisions if need.

Figure 8.4   (*Continued*)

	OR
	Independent Writing About Reading—Moderate to Low Level of Scaffolding: The teacher scaffolds the students in the following ways: • Provides students with a comprehension prompt that promotes deeper thinking and analysis. • Prompts students to use a planner or outline to plan for their writing about the reading. • Provides students with an opportunity to display their understanding by writing about their thinking, supported by textual evidence. • Provides an opportunity for students to use composing strategies, specific vocabulary, spelling strategies, language principles, and revising and editing techniques while composing their response. **Reflection and Goal Setting:** The goal is for students to reflect on their writing about the reading and to set goals for transferring their knowledge across other Writing About Reading events. The teacher supports students in the following ways: • Provides an opportunity for students to reflect on the writing strategies they used and present an example to demonstrate learning. • Provides an opportunity for students to set goals for transferring successful strategies to other Writing About Reading events.
Section on Planner	**Phase Three: Writing** *Co-Construction of Text or Writing Minilesson, Independent Writing, Reflection and Goal Setting*
Part 1	**Co-Construction of Text:** The goal is for students to acquire knowledge of the writing process through a supportive and engaging context. *The composing of the collaborative group mentor text may span several days.* The teacher supports students in the following ways: • Provides an opportunity for the teacher and students to collaboratively consider the purpose and genre of their writing and plan accordingly. • Provides an opportunity for the teacher and students to co-construct a group text guide or outline to support comprehension of the collaborative mentor text. • Provides an opportunity for the teacher and students to co-construct the group mentor text by participating in the composing, spelling, revising, and editing processes. • Provides an opportunity for students to independently or collaboratively puzzle out word spellings and crafting techniques in their logs or on a whiteboard. • Provides an opportunity for the teacher and students to revisit the text map or outline before beginning the group writing for that particular day. • Provides an opportunity for the teacher and students to continue to co-construct the group mentor text by engaging and participating in the composing, spelling, revising, and editing processes. Video 8.7 The teacher guides the students in completing a text guide for planning a group personal narrative. **OR** **Writing Minilesson:** The goal is for students to use their knowledge of author's purpose, text genre, text structure, and the writing process to independently compose a meaningful piece of writing. The teacher supports students in the following ways: • Presents a writing minilesson that focuses on a writing strategy or strategies that students need to think more about during their own writing. • Uses mentor texts, co-constructed texts, teacher's writing, or student's writing to teach or draw students' attention to the strategy or strategies under investigation. • Provides students with an opportunity to apply a strategy or strategies to their writing or to a co-constructed text and scaffolds as needed.

Figure 8.4   *(Continued)*

Reflection and Goal Setting: The goal is for students to reflect on the writing strategies discussed and investigated and to set goals for transferring the knowledge across other writing events. The teacher supports students in the following ways:

- Provides an opportunity for students to reflect on the writing strategies used during the co-construction of group text or highlighted during the strategy minilesson and to present examples to demonstrate their understanding.
- Provides an opportunity for students to set goals for transferring successful writing strategies to their independent writing and across other writing events.

Part 3

Independent Writing: The goal is for students to use their knowledge of author's purpose, aligned with text structure and the writing process, to complete their own piece of writing. The teacher supports students in the following way:

- Conducts individual conferences; records students' problem-solving processes and use of craft; and records prompts given to support students.

Video 8.8   The teacher conducts individual writing conferences with students.

Reflection and Goal Setting: The goal is for the students to reflect on their writing and to highlight some successful writing strategies they used during independent writing. The goal is achieved through a variety of activities:

- Teacher provides a writing strategy checklist aligned with the strategies discussed and learned during prior lessons.
- Students identify and discuss strategies used and provide evidence to support their thinking.
- Students set writing goals for transferring efficient and effective writing strategies across other writing events.

Video 8.9   Students reflect on strategies used during writing.

Figure 8.4   (*Continued*)

MATERIALS FOR PLANNING THE CFG

The CFG is designed to increase students' background knowledge and comprehension strategies for processing complex texts. It is critical that the teacher be well organized, with all materials easily accessible. The teacher's materials include the following:

- Collection of mentor texts within a themed set
- Sets of student texts for literature discussions
- Student response logs with four tabs
- Chart tablet for anchor charts
- Large text maps for writing minilesson
- Large graphic organizers for writing minilesson
- Large text guides for writing minilesson
- Small text maps for student log
- Small graphic organizers for student log
- Small text guides for student log
- Reproducible strategy prompts, checklists, rubrics

STRATEGY-BASED MINILESSONS

In Chapter 4, we introduced the three types of strategy-based minilessons as they are applied to the integrated workshop in the classroom (see also Dorn and Soffos 2005). Now, with a focus on transfer across classroom and intervention settings, we revisit these essential strategies (language, reading, and writing) as a component of the CFG intervention, including video examples to illustrate particular components. As an additional resource, teachers can use Figure 8.5 to plan minilessons that promote the transfer of knowledge sources across language systems. (See Resource H.3, Teaching for Strategic Activity and Transfer Across Language Systems, for a reproducible copy.)

Teaching for Strategic Activity and Transfer Across Language Systems		
Reading Strategies	**Writing Strategies**	**Language Strategies**
The reading phase includes structured minilessons with explicit modeling and scaffolding around high-quality text experiences that nurture students' potential to become independent, strategic readers. Here are the ten comprehension strategies at the core of CFG minilessons. 1. Apply previewing strategies to gather information about the text and anticipate meanings. 2. Ask questions before, during, and after reading to continually clarify and extend meaning. 3. Reread the text for a closer analysis to refine and enhance meanings. 4. Apply flexible strategies, including visualizing, predicting, summarizing, inferring, and monitoring, to construct meaning for the text. 5. Activate prior knowledge (world experiences and specific academic knowledge) to make sense of the text. 6. Use knowledge of text structures and genres to predict main and subordinate ideas. 7. Highlight and annotate the text to remember content, ask questions, and make connections. 8. Use context and word parts to infer meaning. 9. Reflect on text meanings through Writing About Reading. 10. Engage in focused, high-quality discussions on the meaning of the text.	The writing phase includes minilessons that utilize a group composition for modeling the processes involved in preparing a writing piece for a particular audience. The ten writing strategies and processes form the basis of the writing minilessons, which are also supported by mentor texts that provide exemplary models of author's craft. 1. Apply prewriting strategies (e.g., brainstorming, notetaking, outlining). 2. Utilize various resources to gather, organize, and check information (e.g., graphic organizers, checklists, rubrics, internet, texts, media, interviews) throughout the writing process. 3. Revise message for word choice, clarity of meaning, and writing craft. 4. Apply editing and self-correcting strategies, including technological tools. 5. Use sentence combining to organize short, choppy sentences into longer, more effective sentences. 6. Vary sentence structures (length and complexity) to promote fluency, rhythm, and effect. 7. Use transitional words and phrases to connect ideas and increase readability. 8. Use varied punctuation to communicate meaning. 9. Use descriptive language and sensory details to create mind images (show, not tell). 10. Use appropriate language conventions and text structures to communicate a clear and coherent message for a particular audience and purpose.	The language phase includes interactive read-alouds with memorable texts that provide scaffolded opportunities for students to learn how writers use language to support readers' comprehension. The ten language strategies are the basis of understanding the role of language in reading and writing development. 1. Demonstrate command of grammar; be able to comprehend messages where authors have manipulated language forms for purposes of crafting. 2. Make good word choices that communicate clear messages. 3. Use pronouns to stand for nouns. 4. Use punctuation to clarify meanings and regulate fluency. 5. Examine how authors create rhythms in language by varying phases and sentences to engage readers in fatigueless and meaningful reading. 6. Organize related ideas into paragraphs, chapters, texts, and genres. 7. Use dialogue to carry and extend meaning. 8. Use figurative language to symbolize meanings. 9. Build vocabulary through word relationships and patterns. 10. Use transitional words and phrases.

Figure 8.5   Teaching for Strategic Activity and Transfer Across Language Systems

Comprehension Strategy Minilessons. The reading phase includes structured minilessons with explicit modeling and scaffolding around high-quality text experiences that nurture students' potential to become independent, strategic readers. When planning CFG lessons, teachers design strategy-based minilessons using ten essential, evidence-based practices.

- Apply previewing strategies to gather information about the text and anticipate meanings (see Video 8.10).
- Ask questions before, during, and after reading to continually clarify and extend meaning.
- Reread the text for a closer analysis to refine and enhance meanings.
- Apply flexible strategies, including visualizing, predicting, summarizing, inferring, and monitoring, to construct meaning for the text.
- Activate prior knowledge (world experiences and specific academic knowledge) to make sense of the text.
- Use knowledge of text structures and genres to predict main and subordinate ideas.
- Highlight and annotate the text to remember content, ask questions, and make connections.
- Use context and word parts to infer meaning.
- Reflect on text meanings through writing about reading.
- Participate in focused, high-quality discussions on the meaning of the text.

Video 8.10   The students apply strategies for previewing and surveying books.

Writing Strategy Minilessons. The writing phase includes minilessons that utilize a group composition for modeling the processes involved in preparing a writing piece for a particular audience. Ten writing strategies and processes form the basis of the writing minilessons, which are also supported by mentor texts that provide exemplary models of author's craft. The ten writing strategies are highlighted below in relation to the writing phase of the CFG intervention.

- Apply prewriting strategies (e.g., brainstorming, notetaking, outlining).
- Utilize various resources (e.g., graphic organizers, checklists, rubrics, internet, texts, media, interviews) to gather, organize, and check information throughout the writing process.
- Revise message for word choice, clarity of meaning, and writing craft (see Video 8.11).
- Apply editing and self-correcting strategies, including technological tools.
- Use sentence combining to organize short, choppy sentences into longer, more effective sentences (see Video 8.1).
- Vary sentence structure (length and complexity) to promote fluency, rhythm, and effect.
- Use transitional words and phrases to connect ideas and increase readability.
- Use varied punctuation to communicate meaning.
- Use descriptive language and sensory details to create mind images (show, not tell).
- Use appropriate language conventions and text structures to communicate a clear and cohesive message for a particular audience and purpose.

Video 8.11   The teacher supports the student in sentence combining.

Video 8.12   The teacher uses a mentor text for a minilesson on writer's craft.

Language Strategy Minilessons. The language phase in the CFG includes ten high-impact language strategies that highlight the role of language in reading and writing development. With a focus on integrating reading, writing, and language systems, teachers design strategy-based minilessons using mentor texts that illustrate how authors use language to activate and expand the reader's comprehension of the text.

- Manipulate forms of speech for expressing meaning.
- Make good word choices that communicate clear messages.
- Use pronouns to stand for nouns.
- Use punctuation to clarify meanings and regulate fluency.
- Combine simple sentence structures into more complex sentence structures.
- Organize related ideas into paragraphs, chapters, and text genre.
- Use dialogue to carry and extend meaning.
- Use figurative language to symbolize meanings.
- Build vocabulary knowledge through relationships with other words.
- Use transitional words and phrases to connect ideas.

READING RESPONSE LOG FOR ORGANIZING, ASSESSING, AND EXPANDING KNOWLEDGE

The reading log is an essential tool for increasing students' reading comprehension and also serves as a literacy resource for new learning. The log includes four predictable tabs with unique purposes.

- **Tab 1: Meaning.** Responses to the text are recorded in this section, for example, asking questions, summarizing information, taking notes, making inferences, and providing evidence.
- **Tab 2: Language.** Words, definitions, phrases, conventions, vocabulary activities, and such are stored in this section.
- **Tab 3: Strategies.** Strategy prompts, checklists, activities, and explanations are recorded here (see examples below).
- **Tab 4: Organizers.** Texts maps, graphic organizers, and drawings are filed in this section.

It is important for struggling readers to develop metacognition of useful strategies for reflecting on their reading. During minilessons, teachers model comprehension strategies within mentor texts, followed by opportunities for students to apply these strategies to new passages within the text. The strategies are written on large anchor charts, which are referred to as needed during text reading activities. Additionally, teachers prompt students to reflect on their strategic processes in their reading response logs. Taken together, these varied experiences over time and situations are essential in fostering students' strategic processing. Here are a few examples of strategy prompts for developing metacognition.

- **Strategy Prompt for Visualization:** For the last week, we have been working on making pictures in our heads from our books. How often were you able to apply the visualization strategy to help you with your reading today? Give at least one example of a picture you made in your head today while you were reading.
- **Strategy Prompt for Figurative Language:** Reread this passage from your book *Up North at the Cabin*, by Marsha Wilson Chall: "From the dock I dive head first, skimming over sand that swirls behind me. Anchored to the bottom upside down, I am an acrobat in a perfect handstand. Then rising in a sea of air-balloon bubbles, I float on a carpet of waves." Respond to the prompt: "What words does the author use to paint images in your mind? Underline the words and draw a picture of the image."
- **Checklist of Strategies Used:** Underline all the strategies you used today to help you understand the text you are reading. Circle the strategy you used the most. Give an example of how you used this strategy to help

Name: _____

Date: _____

Underline all the reading strategies you used today to help you comprehend the article.
- I previewed the title to get a better idea of the topic.
- I turned headings into questions.
- I took notes in an organized manner.
- I looked at pictures and captions to extend my thinking.
- When I came to an unfamiliar word, I looked for parts I knew that could help.
- I located important facts.

Circle the strategy that helped you the most today. Give an example of how it helped you comprehend the informational text.

_____

_____

_____

_____

_____

_____

_____

How would you apply the taking notes of important facts into your other classes?

_____

_____

_____

_____

Figure 8.6   Example of Strategy Checklist for Response Log

you understand the text. (See Figure 8.6 for a strategy checklist and Video 8.13 for an example of strategy use during writing.)
- **Strategy Prompt for Study Elements.** What are the elements of a fable? Draw a fable map. Name one fable we have read.
- **Participating in Text Discussions.** How much did you participate in the text discussion today (about the right amount, too much, not at all, too little)? What was an important contribution you made to the group discussion? What was an important idea expressed by someone else in the group discussion? Explain why you think this idea helped you to understand the author's message better.

Video 8.13   Checklist of Strategies Used During Writing. Teacher prompts students to reflect on strategies used during writing.

TYPES OF TEXTS

We use the term *literature* in a broad sense to describe any type of written publication that communicates knowledge about a topic, for example, traditional books, articles, brochures, reports, and newsletters. Under this umbrella, the CFG includes three types of texts:

- **Literary Texts:** Story narrative, personal narrative, poetry, plays.
- **Informational Texts:** Literary nonfiction (e.g., biography, autobiography, memoir), scientific reports, articles, brochures, newspapers.
- **Persuasive and/or Argumentative Texts:** Essays, speeches, opinion, letters.

In order to build students' content knowledge of historical and scientific information, the CFG intervention is organized around themed sets with a range of complexity. A typical themed unit lasts four to six weeks and includes a variety of text types. With deeper comprehension as the goal, teachers build students' background knowledge of complex topics through scaffolded instruction during interactive read-alouds, followed by structured opportunities for students to expand their knowledge through strategic minilessons, independent readings with teacher conferences, written responses, and LDGs.

CLOSING THOUGHTS

Interventions that are appropriate for early readers may not be suitable for older readers. Many low-progress readers have adequate decoding skills but lack the knowledge for applying this information to continuous texts. This is especially notable for students beyond third grade. The problem is further exacerbated when struggling readers habituate guessing behaviors, which then become resistant to instruction. The first step in reversing this ineffective pattern is to create the conditions for students to develop self-monitoring behaviors through meaningful, motivating experiences with texts. The CFG intervention incorporates the elements of reading and writing workshops in the classroom, thus making transfer more observable across classroom and intervention settings.

Chapter 9

STRATEGIC PROCESSING INTERVENTION FOR STUDENTS WITH READING DISABILITIES

Clearly, all children do not learn to read in the same way (Clay 1987, 2019; Hatcher and Snowling 2002; Vellutino et al. 1996; Reid 2016); furthermore, children have different combinations of cognitive skills and individual styles of processing information (Hatcher and Snowling 2002, Pohlman 2008). To promote accelerated learning, an intervention should utilize learners' strengths as a scaffold for remediating their weaknesses. This is especially relevant for children with reading disabilities, since presenting these learners with isolated information without a known source can create confusion. Therefore, reading programs should focus on the integration of visual, phonological, and contextual aspects of reading simultaneously at all stages in reading, from early development to competencies (Gavin 2016).

Clay (1987) argued it is difficult to distinguish between the learning behaviors of low-achieving and learning-disabled readers through conventional assessment methods. Similarly, Vellutino (2010) advised that conventional approaches to classifying children as learning disabled do "little or nothing to inform instruction or remedial planning" and typically lead to "low expectations of children assigned an LD label" (6). Vellutino and colleagues proposed that early reading difficulties in most children are caused by experiential and instructional deficits rather than biologically based cognitive deficits (Vellutino et.al. 1996; Vellutino, Scanlon, and Lyon 2000). This theory suggests that teachers must be expert observers of developmental changes in children's literacy behaviors in response to instruction. Simultaneously, teachers must understand what constitutes effective instruction and be able to scaffold students in ways that accommodate their strengths and needs.

The Strategic Processing Intervention (SPI) is designed for students with the greatest difficulties in reading. The intent of the SPI is to help children acquire efficient word recognition and decoding skills, along with flexible strategies that can be transferred to reading and writing tasks. As discussed in Chapter 1, transfer requires intentional thinking, which is stimulated by motivation to solve a meaningful problem in correlation with item knowledge and a powerful strategy. This theory implies that interventions for struggling readers should include a focus on metacognition and strategic activity with opportunities for students to transfer their knowledge, skills, and strategies across changing contexts and for different purposes.

In this chapter, we share a brief overview of the research on phonological processing, followed by additional references to transfer and scaffolding, as mentioned in all chapters. Then, we'll describe the SPI as an effective intervention for the hardest-to-teach readers—those with reading disabilities, including dyslexic readers. Finally, we'll share practical details, including assessments, for implementing the SPI as a component of the CIM portfolio.

PHONOLOGICAL PROCESSING

Students with dyslexia have difficulty with decoding and spelling words, indicating a deficit in their phonological processing system (Shaywitz, Morris, and Shaywitz 2008). The relationship between orthography and phonology is essential in the development of automatic reading skills, which subsequently leads to reading fluency (Hatcher and Snowling 2002). This finding suggests that reading interventions should include a systematic phonics approach (Torgesen et al. 2007; Torgesen, Alexander, and Wagner 2001), along with opportunities to read for meaning (Reid 2016). Systematic, explicit phonics methods fall into two categories:

- **Synthetic:** Converting letters into sounds and blending sounds to form words.
- **Analytic:** Breaking words apart by transferring known phonetic patterns to unknown words and, if necessary, analyzing these patterns into smaller graphemes.

Research on these two approaches reveals no significant difference in their effectiveness (Torgersen et al. 2006). The SPI includes systematic phonics instruction, along with opportunities for students to integrate their phonological and visual information with their language skills in order to construct meaning from the text. Using explicit teacher-guided phonics procedures, students are taught how to become metalinguistically aware and reflective of word-reading strategies (Berninger and Nagy 2008). The goal of instruction is achieved when readers understand the structure and function of language as a literacy tool for learning from printed messages. This strategic process is a complex interaction of several language systems working together, allowing the reader to infer deeper meanings from text, thus creating the conditions for transfer to occur.

TEACHING FOR TRANSFER

As discussed in Chapter 1, transfer does not happen by chance. It requires an intentional design for mediating the transfer of knowledge from one situation to another, all for the purpose of learning from experience. To create the conditions for transfer, teachers should observe what students know, then introduce a new task within their cognitive control to encourage students to retrieve relevant information, integrate that information with other sources, monitor the outcome, and self-correct if necessary, while keeping all systems working together in flexible ways to understand the message (Clay 2001; Singer 1994). In the process, new structures are created out of old ideas. Texts provide struggling readers with rich opportunities to build the kind of effective neural processing systems that successful readers use as they read without problems (Clay 2001).

In the SPI, teachers use a predictable framework with specialized procedures and language prompts that emphasize transferable knowledge across a range of language, reading, and writing tasks. At the same time, the effectiveness of the SPI is dependent on the teacher's skill in adjusting degrees of scaffolding that enable students to apply flexible strategies for dealing with complexity within continuous texts.

SCAFFOLDING FOR STRATEGIC ACTIVITY WITHIN TEXTS

Teachers can use Wood's levels of scaffolding (2002) to plan their instructional moves for supporting the student's ability to accomplish a new task. Using instructional-level texts, students are taught how to employ cognitive strategies for monitoring their word-solving actions in the service of comprehending the text. For example, in support of the transfer principle, when the learning is new, the teacher could write the comprehension strategy on a sticky note, which is then placed in the child's reading log and referred to, as needed, for activating the strategy in a different situation. Through repeated and successful practice, the reader acquires greater flexibility with strategies for solving problems within texts.

Teaching and assessing for transfer are essential principles of the SPI; therefore, the teacher assesses readers' ability to transfer their knowledge, skills, and strategies to novel tasks at designated intervals. To promote transfer, teachers should select meaningful texts with increasing gradients of difficulty that provide readers with strategic opportunities for "reading work" (Clay 2001, 128). The SPI framework is intentionally designed to nurture students' capacity to acquire, consolidate, and generalize phonological information across lesson components for purposes of constructing meaning.

STRATEGIC PROCESSING INTERVENTION (SPI)

In Chapter 1, we described the research on evidence-based practices and how all interventions in the CIM portfolio are aligned with these practices. An important feature of the CIM relates to the teacher's ability to use data to inform decisions about the best intervention for the student. If a student qualifies for the SPI, the student's intervention will include more time for phonological processing, word fluency, spelling strategies, and decoding practice, along with opportunities to transfer this information to reading and writing in continuous texts. The SPI aligns with the four essential elements of evidence-based interventions as outlined in Scammacca et al. 2007:

- Phonological awareness, decoding, and word study
- Independent reading of progressively more difficult text
- Writing activities
- Engaging students in practicing comprehension while reading meaningful texts

In keeping with the CIM phases, the SPI emphasizes listening and speaking comprehension through read-aloud activities and strategy-based instruction during reading and writing, plus formative assessments at designated intervals to monitor the students' capacity to transfer their knowledge, skills, and strategies to new texts.

INTERVENTION FRAMEWORK

The SPI includes three language-based phases that work together to build students' control of oral and written language. Each phase is thirty to forty-five minutes long, depending on the size of the group, and includes systematic activities that align with evidence-based practices for teaching children with reading difficulties. Additionally, the SPI includes an assessment phase at two-week intervals for monitoring students' ability to transfer their knowledge and skills to new tasks. Teachers can access the SPI lesson planner in Resource I.1, Lesson Planner for Strategic Processing Intervention.

Phase One: Language Phase. As discussed in Chapter 4, all interventions begin with Phase 1, the language phase, which focuses on building the students' listening and speaking comprehension through an interactive read-aloud with a complex text. Additionally, the language phase provides students with multiple opportunities to revisit the text for a closer analysis of vocabulary, inferred meanings, text structures, and author's craft. During this phase, the teacher engages students in the creation of large anchor charts that highlight important elements of texts, including comparing common features across multiple texts, with subsequent opportunities for students to transfer this knowledge to small-group and independent literacy activities. The language phase also includes time for students to respond to the read-aloud text through writing.

Phase Two: Reading Phase. The instructional goal of the reading phase is for students to develop skills in phonological and orthographic processing, fast word recognition, decoding strategies within continuous text, reading for meaning, and fluent reading. As reflected in columns one and two of Table 9.1, the teacher designs sequential and systematic activities for building students' knowledge of letters, sounds, and words, including the reading of decodable sentences that contain these phonological elements. Then, as reflected in column three, the teacher selects meaningful texts with gradients of difficulty that provide students with opportunities to apply decoding skills and flexible problem-solving strategies, along with semantic and syntactic information, to comprehend the text meaning. During the reading, the teacher provides scaffolding, as needed, to create a successful experience. To illustrate this process, we provide three video excerpts of the reading phase with a chapter book at three points during the text reading component:

- **Before the reading.** The teacher orients the student to the text by revisiting the previous chapter, while encouraging the student to articulate the big ideas. Then the teacher introduces three new vocabulary words within the text that she suspects might be troublesome to the student and prompts the student to read the vocabulary in the sentence context.

Table 9.1.   Progress Monitoring Assessments for Automaticity of Skills and Transfer to Novel Texts

Optional Assessment Checks as Needed (can be embedded into intervention procedures)			Two-Week Interval Assessment for Transfer to New Reading/Writing Tasks
Phonological/ Phonemic Skills	Phonics Skills	Spelling Skills	

Phonological
• Fluent Sentence Segmentation
• Fast Rhyme Identification
• Fast Rhyme Production
• Fast Rhyme Manipulation
• Fast Identification of Long- and Short-Vowel Sounds
 	
Phonemic
• Fast Phoneme Identification (beginning, middle, and end of words)
• Fast Phoneme Segmentation
• Fast Phoneme Blending
• Fast Phoneme Substitution
• Fast Phoneme Manipulation
• Fast Phoneme Deletion
	• Reading Decodable Text/Sentences
	• Fast Reading of Words
	• Fast Reading of Letters
	• Fast Letter/Sound Production
	• Fast Identification of Consonants and/ or Vowels
	• Fast Reading of Spelling Patterns
	• Fast Spelling Pattern Sound Production
	• Identifying Syllable Types in Words
		• Fast Spelling of Words
		• Fluent Writing of a Dictated Decodable Sentence
			Reading Process
			• Listening Comprehension on New Read-Aloud Text
			  ◦ Vocabulary
			  ◦ Text-Based Inferences
			• Reading Comprehension on New Text
			  ◦ Accuracy Rate
			  ◦ Strategic Activity
			  ◦ Fluency
			  ◦ Oral and/or Silent Comprehension
			
			Writing Process
			• Writing About Text Reading
			  ◦ Writing Strategies
			  ◦ Composing
			  ◦ Comprehension
			  ◦ Language Structure
			  ◦ Spelling

- **During the reading.** The student applies decoding and comprehension strategies while reading the next chapter. The teacher observes the student's reading behaviors for evidence of strategic activity at points of difficulty and intervenes only when necessary. With comprehension as the ultimate goal of reading, the teacher is prepared to scaffold if needed to ensure the reader's state of flow (i.e., a balance of easy and challenging work that engages the reader in fatigueless reading).
- **After the reading.** The teacher prompts the student to reflect on the reading by highlighting specific examples to illustrate productive work. The teacher concludes the lesson by stating a purpose for the next day's reading of the following chapter.

Video 9.1   The teacher and student interact during the reading phase of the intervention.

Video 9.2   The teacher and student interact
during the reading phase of the intervention.

Video 9.3   The teacher and student interact
during the reading phase of the intervention.

Phase Three: Writing Phase. The instructional goal is for students to develop skills for matching sounds to letters in sequence, for spelling words with greater speed and accuracy, and for fluently writing decodable sentences. As reflected in columns one and two of Table 9.1, the teacher designs sequential and systematic instruction in writing development. As reflected in column three, the teacher assesses the students' independent reading behaviors on a previously read text, followed by a collaborative discussion of the text. Next, the teacher provides explicit feedback and direct instruction on specific cognitive strategies used or neglected during reading and, when appropriate, records the strategy with an example on a sticky note to place in the student's reading log. Finally, the teacher prompts the student to write about the text.

ASSESSMENT

As discussed in Chapter 3, each intervention phase includes systematic observation and ongoing assessments to monitor students' responsiveness to instruction. As part of a comprehensive diagnostic, teachers should collect and triangulate a variety of measures to identify students' strengths and needs. For children with characteristics of dyslexia, teachers should administer one or more appropriate standardized measures, for example, the Comprehensive Test of Phonological Processing (CTOPP), the Gray Oral Reading Test (GORT), the Slosson Written Expression Test (SWET), the Developmental Spelling Analysis (DSA), and/or the Developmental Reading Assessment 2 (DRA2).

During the intervention, the teacher should collect ongoing assessments of reading and writing progress, including running records of reading behaviors, Writing About Reading samples, fluency scales, and word tests. In Table 9.1, we illustrate the types of word-level checks that can be embedded into the SPI procedures. For example, if the teacher needs to confirm the student's fast recognition of important high-frequency words, she could administer this assessment during the intervention. Also, the teacher can use a Dynamic Assessment protocol within intervention components to help determine the student's optimal level for performing a task with assistance.

In addition to ongoing assessments, the teacher administers a reading and writing measure at two-week intervals to monitor students' ability to transfer their knowledge, skills, and strategies to novel reading and writing tasks. This component includes three assessments:

- Listening comprehension for understanding vocabulary and for making text-based inferences in a more complex text
- Oral and/or silent reading comprehension and problem-solving strategies on a new text
- Writing strategies for responding to the text just read

GUIDE SHEET FOR STRATEGIC PROCESSING INTERVENTION

The SPI Guide Sheet provides teachers with an instructional framework for designing systematic lessons based on evidence-based practices. In Figure 9.1/Resource I.2, Guide Sheet for Strategic Processing Intervention, we outline the procedures within the reading and writing phases.

Section on Planner	**Phase Two: Reading** *Attaining Speed and Accuracy of Previously Taught Concepts* *Fast Reading of ABC or Word Pattern Chart, Fast Phonological Awareness, Fast Letter or Word Pattern Naming, Fast Letter or Word Pattern Sound Production and Blending, Fast Word Reading, Fast Reading of Decodable Sentences or Text*
Part 1	**Fast Reading of ABC or Word Pattern Chart:** The goal is for students to read all letters of the alphabet or word patterns while pointing to the corresponding pictures with speed and accuracy. The teacher supports students in the following ways: • Provides students with an opportunity to practice reading the letters of the alphabet while pointing to the corresponding picture. • Provides students with an opportunity to practice reading the ABC chart in a variety of ways to develop print knowledge (e.g., read all the vowels, read all the consonants). • Provides students with an opportunity to practice reading the word pattern chart with fluency while pointing to the corresponding picture. **Fast Phonological Awareness:** The goal is for students to hear and manipulate **previously taught** units of sound within the sound structure of spoken words—i.e., word boundaries, syllables, rhyming (onset and rime), and individual phonemes within words—with speed and accuracy. The teacher supports students in the following ways: • Provides students with an opportunity to practice hearing and identifying individual words within spoken language. • Provides students with an opportunity to practice hearing and identifying syllables within a spoken word. • Provides students with an opportunity to practice hearing, identifying, generating, and manipulating onset and rime in spoken words. • Provides students with an opportunity to practice hearing, segmenting, blending, deleting, substituting, and adding individual phonemes within words. **Fast Letter or Fast Word Pattern Naming:** The goal is for students to read **previously taught** letters and word patterns with speed and accuracy. The teacher supports students in the following ways: • Provides students with an opportunity to practice naming previously taught letters. • Provides students with an opportunity to practice naming previously taught word patterns. **Fast Letter or Fast Word Pattern Sound Production and Blending:** The goal is for students to produce **previously taught** letter or word pattern sounds and to blend the sounds together smoothly with speed and accuracy. The teacher supports students in the following ways: • Provides students with an opportunity to practice producing the sounds of all previously taught letters. • Provides students with an opportunity to practice producing the sounds of all previously taught word patterns. • Provides students with an opportunity to practice blending letter and/or word pattern sounds together smoothly and effortlessly. **Fast Word Reading:** The goal is for students to read **previously taught** words with speed and accuracy. The teacher supports students in the following ways: • Provides an opportunity for students to practice reading **previously taught** words with speed and accuracy. • Provides an opportunity for students to match pictures with known words. **Fluent Reading of Decodable Sentences or Text:** The goal is for students to use meaning and structure and to independently apply **previously taught** decoding strategies with speed and accuracy. The teacher supports students in the following ways: • Provides students with an opportunity to practice reading sentences or texts that coordinate with previously learned phonetic principles with speed and accuracy. • Provides students with an opportunity to decode words as needed that reflect previously taught phonetic principles. • Provides students with an opportunity to practice reading for meaning and decoding as needed with speed and accuracy.

Figure 9.1 Guide Sheet for Strategic Processing Intervention

Section on Planner	**Providing Explicit Instruction in New Concepts** *Phonological Awareness, Letter or Word Pattern Identification, Letter or Word Pattern–Sound Production and Blending, Word Learning, Reading of Decodable Sentences or Text, Cut-Up Decodable Sentences and Words, Reflection and Goal Setting*
Part 2	**Instruction of Phonological Awareness:** The goal is for students to hear and manipulate both larger and smaller units of sound within the sound structure of spoken words—i.e., word boundaries, syllables, rhyming (onset and rime), and individual phonemes within words—with speed and accuracy. The teacher supports students in the following ways: ● Provides explicit instruction in hearing and identifying individual words within spoken language. ● Provides explicit instruction in hearing and identifying syllables within a spoken word. ● Provides explicit instruction in hearing, identifying, generating, and manipulating onset and rime in spoken words. ● Provides explicit instruction in hearing, segmenting, blending, deleting, substituting, and adding individual phonemes within words. ● Provides students with explicit instruction in manipulating individual phonemes in different ways. **Instruction in Letter or Word Pattern Identification:** The goal is for students to be able to name all the letters in the alphabet and to read word patterns as units with speed and accuracy. **Letter Identification:** The goal is for students to identify and name all the letters in the alphabet and to distinguish between consonants and vowels with speed and accuracy. The teacher supports students in the following ways: ● Provides students with explicit instruction in understanding spatial and sequential aspects of letter learning. ● Provides explicit instruction in letter learning by teaching students about the features of letters and how they come together in a specific order to give the letter its name. ● Provides kinesthetic experiences (salt, sandpaper, shaving cream) to help students learn the directionality principle of the features of the letters. ● Directs students' attention to the features of letters by providing them with an opportunity to trace over letters, describe the path of movement, and name the letters. ● Provides students with an opportunity to sort letters by letter features, similarities and differences, uppercase and lowercase, letter sounds, and letter name. ● Provides an opportunity for students to read and write the letters with accuracy and speed. **Word Pattern Identification:** The goal is for students to read all word patterns as units with speed and accuracy. The teacher supports students in the following way: ● Provides students with explicit instruction in noticing and seeing word patterns as units rather than as individual letters. **Instruction in Letter–Sound or Word Pattern–Sound Production and Blending:** The goal is for students to produce the sounds of known letters and word patterns with speed and accuracy. **Letter–Sound Production and Blending:** The goal is for students to produce the letter sounds for all the letters in the alphabet and to blend the letter sounds together to make meaningful words with speed and accuracy. The teacher supports students in the following ways: ● Provides explicit instruction in matching letter–sound relationships. ● Provides an opportunity for students to use picture cards, letters, and letter sounds to support meaning and letter–sound relationship. ● Provides explicit instruction in blending letter sounds together smoothly to produce meaningful words. **OR** **Word Pattern–Sound Production and Blending:** The goal is for students to produce word pattern sounds and to blend the word pattern sounds together to make meaningful words with speed and accuracy. The teacher supports students in the following ways: ● Provides students with explicit instruction in word pattern–sound relationships.

Figure 9.1   (*Continued*)

- Provides an opportunity for students to use picture cards, word patterns, and sounds to support meaning and letter–sound relationship.
- Provides explicit instruction in blending word pattern sounds together smoothly to produce meaningful words.

Instruction in New Words: The goal is for students to build word knowledge along a continuum from simple to more complex with speed and accuracy. The teacher supports students in the following ways:

- Provides students with explicit instruction in the sequence of letters, letter–sound relationships, and the decoding and blending processes.
- Provides students with explicit instruction in the sequence of word patterns, word pattern–sound relationships, and decoding and blending and processes.
- Provides students with explicit instruction in the morphology (base words, root words, affixes) of words.
- Provides students with explicit instruction in the six syllable types and concrete rules for dividing syllables.

Read Decodable Sentences or Text: The goal is for students to read for meaning a decodable sentence or text that includes known words and **previously taught** words with speed and accuracy. The teacher supports students in the following ways:

- Provides students with an opportunity to read for meaning a sentence or text that coordinates with the phonics scope and sequence and previously learned phonetic principles with speed and accuracy.
- Provides students with an opportunity to apply their decoding strategies as needed when reading.
- Provides scaffolding prompts and tools as needed during the reading to support transfer.

Cut-Up Decodable Sentence (optional): The goal is for students to reassemble, with speed and accuracy, a meaningful cut-up decodable sentence that has been previously read. The teacher supports students in the following ways:

- Provides an opportunity for students to read the sentence prior to cutting the sentence and words into parts.
- Provides an opportunity for students to rebuild the cut-up decodable sentence, orchestrating multiple sources of information, including their phonological, orthographic, and morphological knowledge.
- Provides scaffolding prompts and tools as needed during the reconstruction process to support orchestration and transfer.

Video 9.4   The teacher engages a third-grade student in specialized procedures for learning about letters and words at weeks 5, 7, and 9.

Video 9.5   Learning About Letters and Words

  Video 9.6   Learning About Letters and Words

Reflection and Goal Setting: The goal is for students to reflect on the learning and to become more metacognitive about how words work and how to apply the decoding and blending processes when encountering unknown words in reading. The teacher supports students in the following ways:

- Provides students with an opportunity to reflect on the prior word-learning principle and provide an example to demonstrate understanding.
- Provides students with an opportunity to set new goals for transferring the phonetic principle to problem-solving on unknown words in reading.
- Scaffolds the reflection and goal-setting process as needed.

Figure 9.1   (*Continued*)

Section on Planner	Transferring Strategic Knowledge to Reading—Building Reading Power *Read Familiar or Easy Texts, Read Instructional Text,* *Before Reading—Orientation to Text,* *After Reading—Discussion of Text,* *Reflection and Goal Setting*
Part 3	**Reading of Familiar or Easy Texts:** The goal is for students to exercise efficient processing, including flexible strategy use, through the rereading of previously read texts. The teacher supports students in the following ways: • Provides students with an opportunity to reread a familiar or easy text with fluency and comprehension. • Provides students with an opportunity to apply decoding and blending processes as needed with fluency, speed, and accuracy. • Provides students with an opportunity to discuss text with deeper comprehension and to highlight decoding strategies used or neglected at the point of difficulty. **Reading Instructional Text:** The goal is for students to set a meaningful purpose for reading and use flexible comprehension and word-solving strategies as needed to comprehend both instructional and complex text. **Before Reading—Orientation to New Text:** The goal is for students to apply their background knowledge of topic, text genre, text structure, language, and decoding strategies to prepare for the reading. The teacher supports students in the following ways: • Provides an overview of the text or scaffolds students to apply their background knowledge of the concept or topic and use previewing strategies to build a meaningful framework for reading. • Uses specific language structures and provides students with an opportunity to repeat and/or read the unfamiliar language structures within the text. • Points out important features within the text (e.g., illustrations, text structure, and text features) to support comprehension. • Discusses relevant or new vocabulary that will enable students to read the text with understanding. • Guides the students to locate known and/or unknown words using their knowledge of letters, sounds, words, and word patterns. **During Reading:** The goal is for students to use meaning, structure, decoding strategies, and visual searching strategies in an orchestrated way to read with fluency and comprehension. The teacher supports students in the following ways: • Holds one-to-one conferences; listens as students read orally and notes their reading fluency and use or neglect of problem-solving strategies; checks on comprehension through a brief discussion. • Prompts students to apply decoding, blending, and searching strategies as needed and provides appropriate levels of scaffolding. • Prompts students to use morphological units to support word meaning and comprehension of text. **Figure 9.2** Student transfers a decoding strategy to an unknown word during the text reading component of the SPI intervention.

Figure 9.1   (*Continued*)

Video 9.7   A student applies strategies for reading an informational text. First, the student rereads part of the text from the previous day's lesson to practice decoding and comprehension strategies. Then the student reads the new sections of the text. The teacher prompts the student to integrate multiple cues as she reads for meaning.

After Reading—Discussion of Text and Strategy Reflection: The goal is to enhance students' comprehension of the text by allowing them to engage in a meaningful conversation about the reading and to lift strategy use through precise teaching and reflection. The teacher supports students in the following ways:

- Engages students in a discussion about the text at the meaning level.
- Encourages students to discuss and provide examples for their thinking about the reading.
- Encourages students to reflect on the problem-solving strategies they used or neglected.
- Identifies a common problem-solving strategy neglected by students and explicitly teaches how to use that strategy to support comprehension.

Reflection and Goal Setting: The goal is for students to become more metacognitive about efficient strategy use by reflecting on their reading and problem-solving during reading. The teacher supports students in the following ways:

- Prompts students to reflect on their use or neglect of comprehension strategies and/or word-solving strategies and to provide an example on a sticky note.
- Provides students with an opportunity to discuss their reflection and example.
- Provides an opportunity for students to set new goals for transferring their learning to other texts and across reading events.

Section on Planner	**Phase Three: Writing/Spelling and Reading Assessment** *Attaining Speed and Accuracy of Previously Taught Concepts* *Fast Writing of Letters or Word/Spelling Patterns,* *Fast Sound–Letter or Sound–Spelling Pattern Production,* *Fast Writing/Spelling of Words, Fluent Writing of Decodable Sentences*
Part 1	**Fast Writing of Letters or Word/Spelling Patterns:** The goal is for students to write **previously taught** letters or word/spelling patterns with speed and accuracy. The teacher supports students in the following ways: • Provides students with an opportunity to practice writing partially known letters to promote speed and fluency. • Provides students with an opportunity to practice writing partially known word/spelling patterns to promote speed and fluency. **Fast Sound–Letter or Fast Sound–Spelling Pattern Production:** The goal is for students to produce the sound for **previously taught** letters or word/spelling patterns with speed and accuracy. The teacher supports students in the following ways: • Provides students with an opportunity to practice producing the sounds of known letters. • Provides students with an opportunity to practice producing the sounds of known word/spelling patterns. **Fast Spelling/Writing of Words:** The goal is for students to spell **previously taught** words with speed and accuracy. The teacher supports students in the following way: • Provides students with an opportunity to practice writing and accurately spelling previously taught words.

Figure 9.1   *(Continued)*

	Fluent Writing of Decodable Sentences: The goal is for students to orchestrate their phonological, orthographic, and morphological knowledge to spell and write known words and **previously taught** words with speed and accuracy. The teacher supports students in the following ways: • Provides students with a dictated sentence or passage that includes known words as well as **previously taught** words. • Provides students with an opportunity to spell and write words in a dictated sentence or passage with speed and accuracy.
Section on Planner	**Providing Explicit Instruction in New Concepts** *Instruction in Letter Writing, Spelling, Writing of Dictated Decodable Sentences and* *Cut-Up Decodable Sentences; Reflection and Goal Setting*
Part 2	**Instruction in Letter Writing:** The goal is for students to write letters with speed and accuracy. The teacher supports students in the following ways: • Provides students with explicit instruction in how to form letters systematically for letter-writing fluency. • Provides students with an opportunity to review the features of the targeted letters by using multisensory techniques. • Provides students with an opportunity to write the targeted letters for fluency. **Spelling Instruction:** The goal is for students to write and spell known words and **previously taught words** with speed and accuracy when composing a message. The teacher supports students in the following ways: • Provides students with explicit instruction in how to use their phonological, orthographic, and morphological knowledge when writing and spelling words. • Provides students with explicit instruction in how to use spelling strategies, including phonological and orthographic knowledge, to produce the correct orthographic representation of a written word. **Writing of Dictated Decodable Sentences:** The goal is for students to orchestrate their phonological, orthographic, and morphological knowledge to spell and write known and **previously taught** words with speed and accuracy. The teacher supports students in the following ways: • Provides students with an opportunity to accurately spell and write known words and **previously taught** words when writing a sentence or sentences. • Provides scaffolding prompts and tools as needed during the spelling and writing process to support accurate spelling. 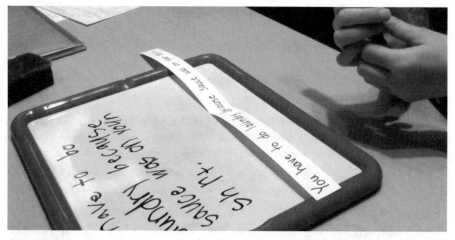 **Figure 9.3** Teacher dictates a sentence for the student to write based on previously taught words and spelling patterns. Then the teacher writes the sentence on a sentence strip for the student to check for accuracy. Last, the teacher cuts the sentence apart at known spelling patterns for the student to assemble.

Figure 9.1   (*Continued*)

Cut-Up Decodable Sentence (optional): The goal is for students to reassemble with speed and accuracy a cut-up decodable sentence that has recently been written. The teacher supports students in the following ways:

● Provides an opportunity for students to read the sentence or sentences prior to cutting the sentence and words into parts.

● Provides an opportunity for students to rebuild the cut-up decodable sentence, orchestrating multiple sources of information including their phonological, orthographic, and morphological knowledge.

● Provides scaffolding prompts and tools as needed during the reconstruction process to support orchestration and transfer.

Figure 9.4   Student assembles a cut-up version of his decodable sentence.

Reflection and Goal Setting: The goal is for students to reflect on the learning in order to become more metacognitive about how to use their knowledge to support the encoding processes when writing. The teacher supports students in the following ways:

● Provides students with an opportunity to reflect on the spelling process and to supply examples from their writing to demonstrate their learning.

● Provides students with an opportunity to set new goals for transferring the spelling and writing processes to their independent writing.

● Scaffolds the reflection and goal-setting process as needed.

Section on Planner	**Assessing and Scaffolding for Transfer** *Assessment of Reading Processing on Instructional Text,* *Writing About Reading Prompt with Levels of Scaffolding,* *Reflection and Goal Setting*
Part 3	**Assessment of Reading Processing on Instructional Text:** The goal is for the teacher to code, score, and analyze the students' reading behaviors and to use the collected data to plan for instruction. The teacher makes the following assessments: ● Takes a running record on two or more students reading the text or passage from the previous day's session. ● Analyzes the behaviors used and/or neglected during reading. ● Provides students with an opportunity to discuss the text at the meaning level. ● Uses language and scaffolding tools to validate and/or activate strategic processing behaviors used or neglected while reading.

Figure 9.1   (*Continued*)

Writing About Reading Prompt: The goal is for students to deepen their comprehension by writing about their reading and providing textual evidence to support their thinking. The teacher supports students in the following way:

- Provides appropriate levels of support to ensure students understand the goal of the writing task and the planning, encoding, revising, and editing processes involved in completing the response.

Writing About Reading Lesson—High to Moderate Level of Scaffolding:
The teacher scaffolds students in the following ways:

- Models and/or scaffolds the planning process by using language and a practice page or planner to prepare for writing about their reading.
- Co-constructs the response with the students and scaffolds the thinking as needed (e.g., composing strategies, specific vocabulary, spelling strategies, language principles, and revising and editing techniques).
- Engages the students at the appropriate time in the problem-solving processes on their individual dry erase boards.
- Provides an opportunity for students to reflect on writing by using a Writing About Reading rubric or checklist; makes revisions if needed.

OR

Independent Writing About Reading—Moderate to Low Level of Scaffolding:
The teacher scaffolds students in the following ways:

- Provides students with a comprehension prompt that stimulates deeper thinking.
- Prompts students to use practice page or planner to prepare for writing about their reading.
- Prompts students to use composing strategies, specific vocabulary, spelling strategies, language principles, and revising and editing techniques while writing.

Figure 9.5   Student uses the practice page of her writing journal to solve unknown words while composing a meaningful text in the WAR component of the SPI lesson.

    Video 9.8   The SPI teacher scaffolds the student in writing about an informational text, suggesting composing and spelling strategies for constructing the message.

Video 9.9   The SPI teacher prompts the student to use evidence from the text to respond to his reading from yesterday's text.

Figure 9.1   (*Continued*)

Reflection and Goal Setting: The goal is for students to reflect on their writing about the reading and to set goals for transferring their knowledge across other Writing About Reading events. The teacher supports students in the following ways:

- Provides an opportunity for students to reflect on writing strategies used and to supply examples to demonstrate their learning.
- Provides an opportunity for students to set goals for transferring successful planning and writing strategies to other Writing About Reading events.

Figure 9.1 (*Continued*)

CLOSING THOUGHTS

Transfer, which is the ultimate goal of instruction, can be observed in students' capacity to explain the knowledge and processes they are acquiring and to make flexible use of this information to learn something new (Campione et al. 1995). This observation implies that what students bring to the reading act will have a profound influence on their ability to learn from texts. Although students' word-level knowledge is essential to reading, they must understand how to integrate this knowledge, along with flexible strategies, to construct meaning from the text. To stimulate this neural process, instructional design must balance word-level goals with tailored opportunities to practice efficient strategies on texts that gradually increase in complexity and difficulty.

Grounded in evidence-based practices and research in phonology, transfer, and scaffolding, the Strategic Processing Intervention is a viable approach for teaching children with characteristics of dyslexia. In sum, the SPI intervention framework provides teachers with a manageable structure for implementing complex activities across language systems that nurture the development of strategic readers and writers.

Chapter 10

IMPLEMENTING THE COMPREHENSIVE INTERVENTION MODEL FOR LITERACY IMPROVEMENT

The Comprehensive Intervention Model is a systemic approach to Response to Intervention. This approach is grounded in the belief that teachers are the agents of literacy improvement, and that professional development creates an authentic context for shaping teacher expertise, thus increasing student achievement (Owens 2015; Schaefer 2015). In contrast to simplistic approaches that rely on quick fixes to complex problems, a systemic method is a slower, more intentional process that emphasizes collaborative planning, curriculum alignment, layered interventions, ongoing progress monitoring, and meaningful professional development. This design requires management structures within the school for nurturing teacher leadership and decision-making expertise that yield increases in student learning (Dorn and Layton 2016). Most importantly, a systemic approach to RTI emphasizes sustainable improvement by changing the culture of the school (Dorn and Henderson 2010a).

TEN PRINCIPLES OF CIM PROFESSIONAL DEVELOPMENT DESIGN

The CIM is grounded in ten principles of professional development that emphasize the comprehensive and systemic nature of the design. These principles are embedded in the theories and practices represented in this book.

- **Principle One:** The first wave of literacy defense occurs at the classroom level. High-quality classroom instruction includes evidence-based practices for all students with targeted support for students who are not responding to instruction.
- **Principle Two:** All interventions in the CIM portfolio include explicit practices that mirror high-quality classroom instruction, thus enabling low-progress readers to transfer their knowledge, skills, and strategies across different settings.
- **Principle Three:** Interventions must emphasize reading for meaning at all grade levels, with the expectation that students will demonstrate more advanced reading strategies for comprehending a broad range of high-quality texts as they progress through the grades.
- **Principle Four:** All interventions include similar components with distinctions made in the proportion of time devoted to particular activities. Interventions are selected based on the strengths and needs of the individual. If a student is not progressing at the expected rate, the RTI team evaluates the effectiveness of the intervention based on the three decision rules. (See Chapter 1.)
- **Principle Five:** The processing behaviors of students with reading confusions (as a result of environmental influences) and students with reading disabilities (as a result of biological factors) look similar. RTI provides a systemic framework for observing changes over time in students' processing behaviors in response to teaching and for making adjustments to promote acceleration.

- **Principle Six:** Low-progress readers have developed weak monitoring systems that have led to guessing behaviors. Therefore, all interventions in the CIM portfolio emphasize well-designed activities for fostering students' metacognition and problem-solving strategies for dealing with challenges.
- **Principle Seven:** Assessments are systematic, comprehensive, and multidimensional, with established benchmarks for charting growth over time. Progress monitoring points are established to assess the effectiveness of a particular intervention for narrowing the literacy gap.
- **Principle Eight:** Decision-making teams enable teachers to collaborate on student learning and make informed decisions about interventions.
- **Principle Nine:** Transfer across classroom and supplemental settings does not occur by accident. Transfer requires an intentional design that utilizes four essential elements: alignment, congruency, common language, and collaboration.
- **Principle Ten:** Teachers who are more knowledgeable about teaching and learning are more likely to use evidence-based practices that are associated with increased student achievement. The CIM is an investment in teacher knowledge, in contrast to scripted programs.

To illustrate the ten principles in action, we share the stories of literacy educators from California, Washington State, Wisconsin, and Missouri who have implemented the CIM as a systemic RIT approach. In each case, professional development serves to empower teachers with the knowledge and strategies to make effective data-based decisions for accelerating student learning. As teachers become more knowledgeable about literacy learning and as they observe their students' responsiveness to their teaching, they develop a "sense of moral purpose" (Fullan 1993) that guides their decision-making processes.

With this in mind, we view professional development as the driver for systemic change that occurs along a continuum of five phases: awareness, initiation, implementation, institutionalization, and transformation. (See Figure 10.1; see also Resource J.1, Continuum of Change as Influenced by Professional Development in the CIM Portfolio of Interventions.) Here, systemic change is both a generative and recursive process that can be fostered as educators initiate and implement one or more interventions in the CIM portfolio and continuously evaluate the effectiveness of the interventions on literacy improvement within the school system. As changes move through the various phases, educators make data-based adjustments in the types of professional development that empower teachers as agents of school change. Within these phases of change, educators utilize the ten principles of the CIM to plan professional development and evaluate steps for continuous improvement. As you read the stories, we encourage you to consider the implications for your own school's implementation, specifically, the impact of collaboration on teacher efficacy, moral purpose, and student achievement.

BOWERS ELEMENTARY SCHOOL, SANTA CLARA UNIFIED SCHOOL DISTRICT, CALIFORNIA

VICKI WONG, READING RECOVERY TEACHER LEADER AND LITERACY COACH

Santa Clara Unified School District sits squarely in the middle of Silicon Valley, surrounded by tech giants. Although the district is in one of the most affluent areas in California, there are many challenges. Currently, five of the district's eighteen elementary schools receive Title I funds and 42 percent of the incoming kindergarteners are classified as English Learners (EL).

To explore a promising solution to these challenges, the district piloted the CIM as a framework for increasing teacher efficacy and student achievement. Two of the four pilot sites were Title 1 schools, and one had an EL population greater than 50 percent, heightening the need for teacher training in language and literacy interventions. Toward that goal, the district's CIM coach provided the Reading Recovery teachers

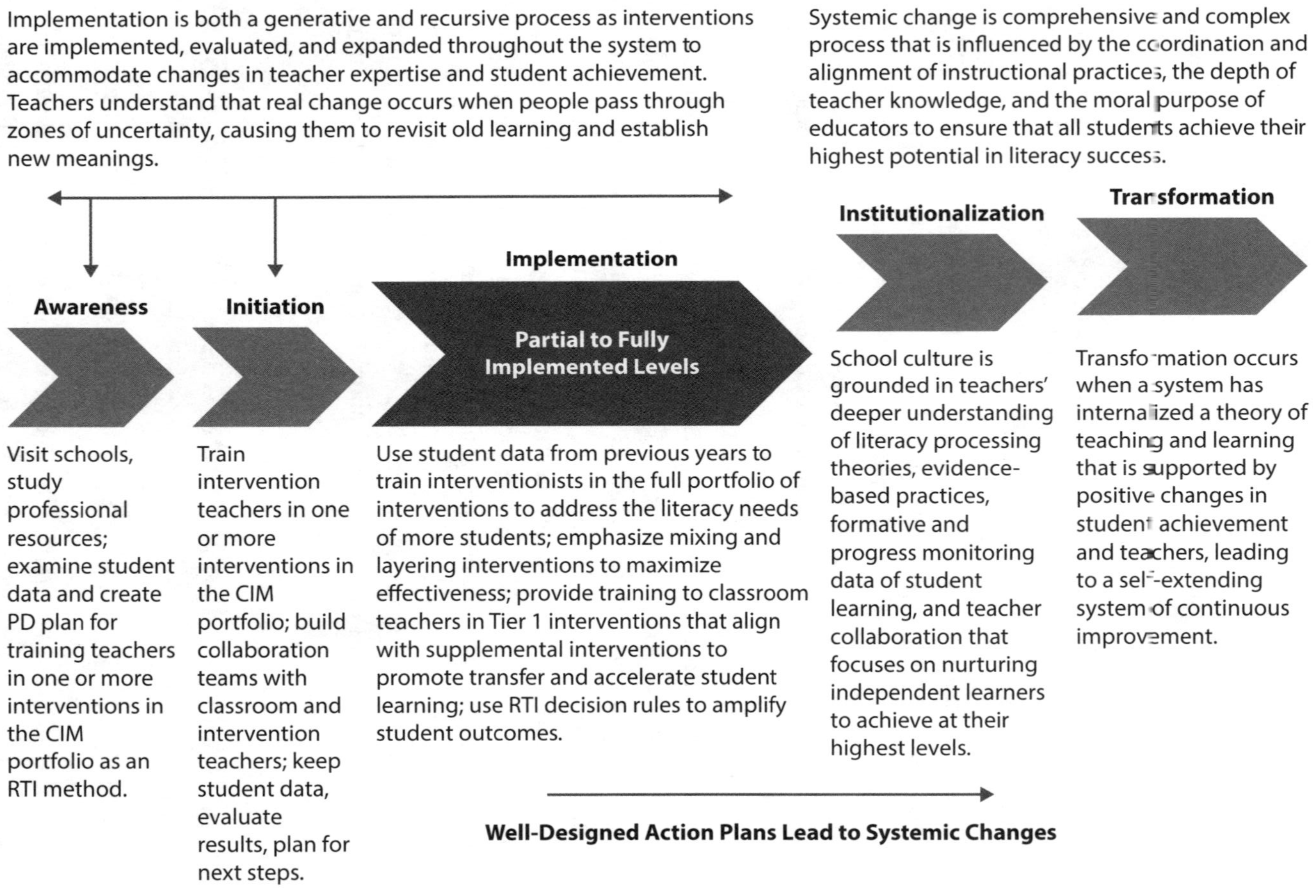

Implementation is both a generative and recursive process as interventions are implemented, evaluated, and expanded throughout the system to accommodate changes in teacher expertise and student achievement. Teachers understand that real change occurs when people pass through zones of uncertainty, causing them to revisit old learning and establish new meanings.

Systemic change is comprehensive and complex process that is influenced by the coordination and alignment of instructional practices; the depth of teacher knowledge, and the moral purpose of educators to ensure that all students achieve their highest potential in literacy success.

Awareness

Initiation

Implementation

Partial to Fully Implemented Levels

Institutionalization

Transformation

Visit schools, study professional resources; examine student data and create PD plan for training teachers in one or more interventions in the CIM portfolio as an RTI method.

Train intervention teachers in one or more interventions in the CIM portfolio; build collaboration teams with classroom and intervention teachers; keep student data, evaluate results, plan for next steps.

Use student data from previous years to train interventionists in the full portfolio of interventions to address the literacy needs of more students; emphasize mixing and layering interventions to maximize effectiveness; provide training to classroom teachers in Tier 1 interventions that align with supplemental interventions to promote transfer and accelerate student learning; use RTI decision rules to amplify student outcomes.

School culture is grounded in teachers' deeper understanding of literacy processing theories, evidence-based practices, formative and progress monitoring data of student learning, and teacher collaboration that focuses on nurturing independent learners to achieve at their highest levels.

Transformation occurs when a system has internalized a theory of teaching and learning that is supported by positive changes in student achievement and teachers, leading to a self-extending system of continuous improvement.

Well-Designed Action Plans Lead to Systemic Changes

Figure 10.1 A Continuum of Change as Influenced by Professional Development in the CIM Portfolio of Interventions

with specialized training in the CIM portfolio, including the use of decision-making protocols for selecting the most appropriate intervention based on student needs. Simultaneously, classroom teachers received professional development in literacy processing theory, reading and writing continuum, transfer principles, and evidence-based practices.

Teacher collaboration around student data is a central feature of the CIM professional development framework (Principle 8). With that in mind, the CIM teachers worked closely with classroom teachers to analyze student data on a range of assessment tasks, then determine which intervention in the CIM portfolio would be the most appropriate to accelerate students' literacy gains. In accordance with CIM guidelines, teachers delivered eight-week rounds of instruction, focusing on one intervention group while training as CIM teachers. This procedure had an unexpected impact on teachers' knowledge. With only eight weeks in any given round of instruction, CIM teachers taught with a greater sense of urgency and precision. As a result, students made significant gains within a shorter period. At the same time, classroom and CIM teachers kept a watchful eye on the students' progress and were prepared to provide additional support, as needed, to ensure continuous literacy improvement.

PROMISING RESULTS

The pilot study was initiated to explore the impact of CIM professional development on teacher efficacy and student achievement. In keeping with Principle 10, the district believed that teachers who are more knowledgeable about teaching and learning are more likely to use evidence-based practices associated with increased student achievement. At the end of the pilot year, the data provided evidence that as teacher knowledge increased, the students made considerable gains in specific literacy areas. With only eight weeks of instruction, most first- and second-grade students showed reading gains of at least two text levels, while kindergarten students made gains in letter identification, text-level reading, and letter–sound analysis in writing. The teachers concluded that assessing student gains at eight-week intervals provided formative-assessment data for examining student growth and rate of learning, while simultaneously fostering a greater sense of urgency and precision teaching.

As a professional development model, the CIM had a positive effect on all literacy instruction when both classroom and intervention teachers were simultaneously trained in the interventions. The intervention teachers enhanced their decision-making skills by teaching intervention students as their CIM colleagues observed the lessons and provided feedback. In the process, they refined their ability to observe patterns in students' literacy behaviors and to adjust their scaffolding to promote students' independence. In a similar way, classroom teachers learned to differentiate instruction and use formative assessments for instructional decisions that enabled all students to achieve their highest potential in literacy. Additionally, as teachers acquired greater knowledge of literacy theory and research, they began to assert themselves as literacy leaders in their school.

MNO GRANT ELEMENTARY SCHOOL, ANITOCH SCHOOL DISTRICT, CALIFORNIA

JANEEN ZUNIGA, PRINCIPAL

With a focus on literacy acquisition and oral language development, Principal Janeen Zuniga and her teaching staff designed and implemented the Comprehensive Language and Literacy Model (CLLM). These educators were concerned that only 3 percent of their English Learners had gained enough English proficiency to be redesignated as Fluent English Proficient, and the school did not have a school-wide formative assessment system in place to document reading and writing growth for all students. The CLLM provided Multiple Tiers of Student Support (MTSS), with four tiers of intervention. This arrangement allowed teachers to expand their professional knowledge as they worked with students, including those with low language competencies, rather than simply implementing a packaged program. The professional development design consisted of five layers of teacher support:

- Whole-staff training for building awareness and understanding of the model.
- Small-group training that included university coursework.
- Individual learning that included coaching from a teacher leader or a peer coach.
- Collaborative learning teams that made data-based decisions based on students' responsiveness to instruction.
- Virtual learning experiences with CIM colleagues across the county, including real-time observations of literacy lessons and constructive dialogue for linking cognitive theories to instructional decisions.

TEACHER COLLABORATION FOR STUDENT SUCCESS

During the school year, the team met monthly for three hours after school to discuss core instruction (Tier 1) within an integrated workshop in grades K–5. The team also discussed the theory and evidence-based practices of the CIM layered interventions (Tiers 2, 3, and 4). With transfer in mind, the school team abandoned the long-standing practice of delivering intervention services outside of the classroom. Using a differentiated approach, the classroom teacher provided all students with evidence-based core instruction, plus a small-group classroom intervention for students with mild literacy challenges (Tier 1), while the CIM specialist delivered a Tier 2 supplemental intervention within the classroom setting for students with greater challenges. Conceptually, the layering principle provided more transfer opportunities from intervention group to whole-class activities for students, as well as greater transfer opportunities of learning between teacher colleagues (see Figure 10.2).

COLLABORATION AROUND STUDENT DATA

All classroom teachers, interventionists, and special educators worked collaboratively in monthly meetings to analyze the literacy progress of the lowest-performing students. During these collegial discussions, the goal was to build transfer of student learning across classroom and intervention settings, along with

Figure 10.2   Intervention teacher provides Tier 2 small-group intervention in the classroom as classroom teachers observe.

increasing congruence of teaching strategies and teacher language (Principle 9). Toward that goal, the teachers utilized a large assessment wall of pocket charts that held an index card for each individual student. At benchmark points in the school year, the teachers recorded reading-level information and tiers of service on the cards. They then placed each card on the wall, based on the student's instructional reading level at any given point in the school year. As a professional development tool, the assessment wall served five unique purposes:

- It created whole-staff awareness of reading benchmarks that progress along a behavioral continuum of difficulty and complexity.
- It provided a visual for observing changes over time in individual rates of learning in comparison to established benchmarks and in response to specific interventions.
- It fostered a common language for describing reading and writing behaviors in observable terms that can be linked to instructional goals.
- It engaged classroom and intervention teachers in problem-solving discourse about intervention procedures that promote integration and transfer of student knowledge across multiple contexts.
- It promoted the sense of urgency that is required, along with sensitive observation and intentional teaching, to enable low-progress readers to catch up with average-performing peers as quickly as possible.

At the conclusion of each analysis of the assessment wall, teachers moved into grade-level groups with their intervention colleagues to determine specific strengths and areas of need, plus common language and strategies to use with the students they shared.

PROMISING RESULTS

In support of systems change, the school team created a professional development design for increasing teachers' knowledge of evidence-based practices, layered interventions, and theories of language and literacy development. Through these authentic experiences, all teachers improved in their ability to observe students' literacy behaviors, set learning targets, and scaffold students in their zone of proximal development. As a result, the students demonstrated increased knowledge and strategies in the following areas: academic vocabulary, use of text-based evidence, Writing About Reading, independent reading stamina, and writing more complex sentences. Moreover, the school's literacy data included the following promising results:

- 70 percent of students reached proficiency on Beaver and Carter's (2011) *Reading Assessment.*
- English Learner redesignation rate soared from 3 percent to 25 percent.
- There were no retentions for any students, two years in a row.
- Special education identification dropped from 12 percent to 8 percent.
- State assessment ELA scores rose by 5 percent.

SPOKANE PUBLIC SCHOOLS, WASHINGTON

MOLLY BOZO, READING RECOVERY TEACHER LEADER; DANA MYERS, SPOKANE PUBLIC SCHOOLS K-4 SPECIAL PROGRAMS CIM COORDINATOR; PEGGY EKLOF, SPOKANE PUBLIC SCHOOLS DISTRICT CIM FACILITATOR

Twelve years ago, the Spokane Public Schools implemented the CIM as a professional development design for continuous literacy improvement. The professional development plan was formed in reaction to district concerns about the over-identification of students for special education and the absence of alternative services for students below grade level. This reality required a comprehensive and systemic plan for school improvement, including collaborative structures for changing teacher perceptions, instructional practices, intervention approaches, and assessment processes.

Based on district data, the professional development plan included two simultaneous components. As the first line of literacy defense, classroom teachers engaged in training that emphasized evidence-based practices within a differentiated workshop framework, including Tier 1 targeted interventions for below-basic students. At the same time, the district's interventionists received specialized training in the CIM interventions and utilized data for monitoring student progress over time and across settings. All PD included frameworks for aligning instruction and engaging in collaborative meetings to maximize student learning across classroom and intervention settings. To achieve this goal, the schools created management structures that embedded collaboration into the school day at two levels:

- Workshop framework that enabled the CIM specialist to deliver supplemental interventions within the classroom structure. (See Video 10.1 and Figure 10.3 for Writing Aloud (WA) intervention planner for photo.)
- RTI framework that allowed CIM specialists and classroom teachers to select students for interventions and monitor student growth. (See Figure 10.4 and Videos 10.3–10.5 for examples of RTI meetings.)

 Video 10.1   During the WA intervention, the classroom teacher teaches her third graders how to write an argumentative response to the text, while the CIM specialist scaffolds a small group of striving writers to achieve the same goal using evidence from the text.

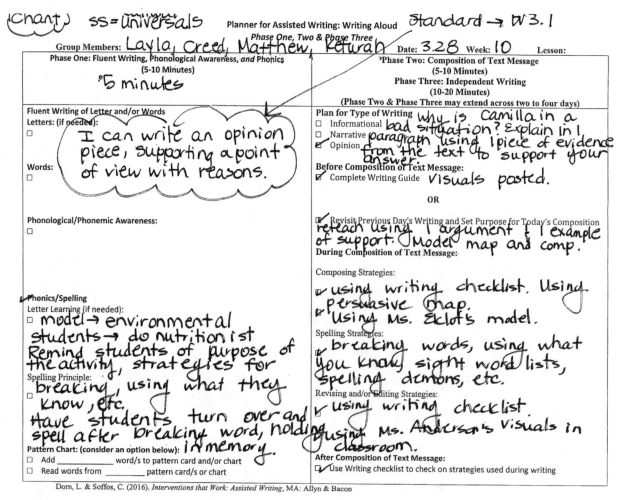

Dorn, L. & Soffos, C. (2016). *Interventions that Work: Assisted Writing*, MA: Allyn & Bacon.

Figure 10.3   The CIM teacher uses the WA planner to design her intervention lesson.

Figure 10.4   The CIM teacher supports a small group of third grade students in writing an opinion piece during the Writing Aloud intervention graders while the classroom teacher works with the rest of the class on the same goal.

Example 1. The RTI process begins with the classroom teacher, who administers the San Diego Quick Word Assessment as a screener for students who appear to be at risk for reading problems. Then, the CIM specialists examine students' reading and writing data for grouping in the most appropriate intervention. If a student is not progressing at the expected rate of learning, the team examines student data more closely to inform decisions about duration, intensity, and layering effects.

Video 10.2

Example 2. The RTI team discusses grouping configurations for students, including cases in which an individual student does not fit into a group structure. In this example, the intervention teacher agrees to provide one-to-one targeted instruction (Tier 3), as well as collaborating with the classroom teacher for a Tier 1 classroom intervention.

Video 10.3

Example 3. In schools without literacy coaches, the CIM specialists provide additional support for the classroom teacher, including a resource kit of reading and writing activities for low-progress readers.

Video 10.4

Example 4. The interventionists share how they use a mobile data wall to facilitate collaborative discourse at staff meetings and to monitor students' progress in response to particular interventions.

Video 10.5

LITERACY IMPROVEMENT FOR CHILDREN WITH LEARNING DISABILITIES

As the district moved through the implementation phases (see Figure 9.1), the professional development goals were expanded to incorporate training classes in the CIM portfolio for special educators. There were three significant training events that impacted teacher knowledge, thus leading to positive outcomes for students with learning disabilities.

Major Event 1: During Year 3 implementation, the CIM coaches trained sixty special education resource teachers in the CIM. These teachers used the small-group interventions with their students who were labeled as Learning Disabled (LD). For the first time in the history of the district, 205 LD students were discontinued from special education services because they had reached grade-level standards in literacy. As a result, ten speech and language pathologists were trained in CIM and provided intervention to small groups of kindergarten children.

Major Event 2: In Year 5, four schools participated in action research for studying the effects of the CIM on the literacy gains of low-progress readers. Based on previous results, the school board approved the hiring of new intervention teachers at eight schools, along with two CIM coaches to train intervention teachers and work with school teams. Also, principals were trained about what to look for in the small-group when they were used for observing teaching and learning interactions during small-group reading instruction within the core literacy block, as well as for observing targeted interventions for low-performing readers. From a systems perspective, the CIM framework was a lever for building teacher knowledge, fostering a common language, and analyzing students' responsiveness to instruction across the district, thus leading to increases in students' literacy performance.

Major Event 3: In Year 8, the speech and language pathologists participated in an action research study that examined the effects of the Early Language Intervention (ELI) for low-progress kindergarten children. Instructional coaches became intervention teachers, and professional development opportunities were expanded for intervention teachers, speech and language pathologists, and school coaches. Results indicated that the kindergarten children who participated in the ELI made significant gains in language and literacy areas.

SUSTAINABLE RESULTS

Over twelve years of the CIM implementation, the Spokane School District has sustained its improvement efforts through a professional development design that fosters intellectual discourse grounded in observations of students' responsiveness to instruction. Program evaluation, which is a critical aspect of the district's implementation plan, provides a historical timeline of K–3 professional events and the subsequent impact on student achievement. Currently, the district employs seventy-five CIM teachers who provide the most appropriate interventions within the CIM portfolio. In support of transfer, intervention teachers collaborate with classroom teachers on the literacy curriculum and deliver intervention within the classroom setting. Using professional development as the driver for literacy improvement, all teachers across the district have developed a deeper understanding of literacy theory and evidence-based practices, thus leading to significant gains for low-progress readers.

SCHOOL DISTRICT OF FORT ATKINSON, WISCONSIN

AMY OAKLEY, DIRECTOR OF INSTRUCTION; CANDICE SAYRE, DISTRICT LITERACY COORDINATOR AND LITERACY COACH; AND JENNIFER SOEHNER, DISTRICT CIM COACH, READING RECOVERY TEACHER, AND LITERACY INTERVENTIONIST

Through systemic implementation of the CLM and the CIM, the School District of Fort Atkinson (SDFA) achieved significant increases in student learning, as evidenced by formative assessments and progress monitoring measures, as well as externally on the Wisconsin Accountability School Report Card. Over a two-year period, the district increased the overall score on the Wisconsin School Report Card from 69.0—Meets Expectations to 82.5—Exceeds Expectations. Furthermore, the Achievement subscore increased 10 points, the Growth subscore increased 19.7 points (leading to a perfect score in this area), and the Closing Gaps subscore increased 15.6 points. These data provide evidence of the transformational growth experienced as a result of systemic change and are compelling, especially the increases in the Growth and Closing Gaps scores.

Demonstrating the success and power of this model, the SDFA earned two highly competitive International Literacy Association awards, namely, the Exemplary Reading Program of the Year for 2013, honoring all four of the district's elementary schools, and same award for 2017, honoring the Fort Atkinson Middle School. These awards not only recognize the collective work of the professionals in the district, who strive for excellence in literacy through rigorous professional learning, collaboration, and high-quality instruction; they also spotlight the power of the CLM and CIM implementation, and the power of aligned instruction in core and intervention to accelerate student learning. (See Video 10.6 for SDFA's implementation in Year 1.)

Acting on the belief that the first wave of literacy defense occurs at the classroom level (Principle 1), the district established strong core instruction by defining evidence-based instructional practices and using observational protocols to support continuous improvement. Simultaneously, intervention teachers were trained in the CIM portfolio and collaborated with classroom teachers on aligning instructional goals across classroom and intervention settings. In keeping with Principle 2, the goal of intervention was to prepare low-progress readers with the knowledge, skills, and strategies to learn from core instruction; therefore, all interventions in the portfolio included explicit practices that mirrored literacy tasks from the classroom.

Video 10.6   During Year 1, the district implements the CLM in all elementary schools.

CIM FRAMEWORK FOR ALIGNMENT AND ACCOUNTABILITY

When the SDFA began work in the CLM, the CIM was simultaneously adopted. Having both models in place is integral to systemic success. The CIM framework established a system for interventionists to study and grow as professionals alongside classroom teachers. The model inherently provided classroom teachers, coaches, principals, and reading interventionists with a sense of joint responsibility for all of the students.

COLLABORATIVE PROCESS FOR SUPPORTING INTERVENTION STUDENTS

The first casting of the intervention net identified students who performed in the below basic (minimal) category. Classroom teachers administered assessment tasks for the most up-to-date information, then CIM specialists administered additional assessments to provide more comprehensive information. At team meetings, results were discussed, and determination of the most appropriate intervention for each student was made. The team considered the group size when placing students, realizing that some students would require more intensive help while others might need a slightly larger group to foster richer conversations with peers about texts. Since the interventions are supplemental to classroom instruction, the timing of the group was also examined to ensure that students would not miss any core instruction from the classroom.

Teacher collaboration around student data is critical to the success of readers and writers. Therefore, shared AIM line forms were completed every two weeks for primary students who received intervention. These forms included a grade-level line, an intervention line, and a classroom line (see Figure 10.5). The sharing of the information allowed both the classroom teacher and the interventionist to see where the student was performing across the two settings. Being able to compare the lines and note rates of acceleration over time offered information for collaborative conversations.

SCHEDULING MEETINGS

Time was built into the elementary schedules to allow for collaborative conversations. Intervention Collaboration Meetings (ICMs) occurred once every ten days with each grade level in the K–5 buildings. These meetings followed a systematic format to discuss two previously selected students. The meetings followed a protocol to ensure that fidelity was maintained. This was beneficial because interventionists worked with more than one grade level, more than one type of intervention, and in more than one building. Literacy checklists were completed independently by the classroom teacher and the interventionist. The checklists, along with student work samples from both classroom and intervention, were brought to the ICM and provided additional information. A collaborative goal sheet (see Resource K.3) was filled out, documenting what the student successfully controlled in the classroom and in intervention, thus providing written evidence of transfer between the settings. The ICM grade-level team then decided collectively what the next steps for the child should be based on the data shared. Lastly, the team set a learning goal for the student and identified the teachers' instructional goals, including the use of common language for scaffolding the student's capacity for transfer across multiple settings.

In addition to providing a framework for discussing students in interventions, the CIM also provided a structure for discussing other learners who may have fallen behind in their classroom success. While conversations regarding specific students were addressed in ICMs, conversations with coaches about evidence-based classroom practices and how to reach all learners were embedded into the school day. Frequently, those conversations resulted in a literacy diagnostic to determine if the student should receive intervention. ICMs provided a time to compare classroom and intervention data, and when transfer was consistently occurring between both settings with supporting data, the student was dismissed from reading intervention, and a plan for monitoring classroom performance was created.

SCHEDULING ISSUES

Educators realized that scheduling was critical for the success of the CLM and CIM. Therefore, the ICM meetings occurred during the school day and did not affect student contact minutes. Interventionists attended the meetings only of the grade levels in which they were serving students. Teachers attended grade-level meetings even if their student was not being discussed, because of the "universality of need." That is, each teacher was likely to have a student in their classroom who was performing in about the same range, or doing the same inefficient processing, as the student being reviewed. Their own teaching could benefit from the discussion, and they could contribute to the conversation about their colleague's student, offering insight and recommendations for next steps.

Another aspect of ICM was the coordination of teaching schedules. Interventionists served multiple grade levels and sometimes were in multiple buildings. The intervention students came from multiple classrooms, and scheduling of groups could be difficult. Intervention and classroom teachers always tried to work the schedules out, but sometimes the conflicts were hard to resolve. In these instances, principals were always willing to assist with scheduling difficulties, for example by moving a recess, flipping a gym class, or suggesting that teachers talk to the IMC director for assistance.

The last component of scheduling is intervention fidelity and reflection. Most small-group interventions are thirty minutes long and are full of literacy work. Lessons are planned, and records, both anecdotal and formalized, are kept. In Fort Atkinson, the district allowed interventionists to schedule a ten- to fifteen-minute reflection time after each lesson. Interventionists reflected on several key questions:

- What behavioral evidence indicates students are transferring their knowledge and strategies across varied reading and writing tasks?

● Are students progressing at the expected rate of learning? If not, where is the breakdown in literacy processing?

● What next step should occur to get a shift in the student's literacy processing in order to have continued acceleration and therefore dismissal from intervention services?

TRANSFORMATIVE RESULTS

Transformative results can be characterized as accumulated and sustainable gains along a learning continuum, internal accountability with flexible guidelines, and coordinated interactions between people and the environment (Dorn 2016). Within the SDFA, educators worked together within apprenticeship-type settings, where they asked questions, identified problems, created solutions, and transformed knowledge through active testing. This complex process required a management framework for coordinating and aligning the CLM and CIM components into a unified, holistic design. The district's professional development was supported by on-site coaching using an apprenticeship approach, in which teachers were empowered to make evidence-based decisions to accelerate student learning. Here, the teachers were in charge, not the "boxed" program, and the fidelity to instruction was based on teachers' firsthand knowledge of readers and writers, not on what the manual said to do next. In keeping with the commitment to empowering educators. professional development was organized in three broad areas: (a) building teacher beliefs that were grounded in sound learning theory and tested against observations of student learning, (b) honoring the gradual release process for both professional and student learning, and (c) balancing urgency with attainable growth.

NIXA PUBLIC SCHOOLS, MISSOURI

CINDY OWENS, PH.D., ELA TITLE 1 COORDINATOR, READING RECOVERY TEACHER LEADER, AND DYSLEXIA THERAPIST

Some children experience extreme difficulty in learning to read and write. Among this group are students who have characteristics of dyslexia. Nixa Public Schools (NPS) prides itself on creating learning environments that promote academic excellence for all students; yet some children still struggle with literacy acquisition. Dr. Stephen Kleinsmith, former Nixa superintendent, led with the philosophy that "the true measure of a district's success is the achievement of the lowest student." In keeping with this philosophy, teachers were viewed as the real agents of change, and high-quality professional development was considered a tool for supporting teacher knowledge. To address the needs of students with characteristics of dyslexia, NPS provided teachers with specialized training in the theories and evidence-based practices of the Strategic Processing Intervention (SPI).

INSTRUCTIONAL ALIGNMENT ACROSS LITERACY PROGRAMS

Instructional alignment across classroom and supplemental intervention facilitates the learners' capacity to generalize their knowledge and strategies across multiple contexts and similar learning tasks. With classroom instruction as the first line of literacy defense, core instruction (Tier 1) utilizes an integrated workshop framework with intentional activities that promote students' transfer of knowledge and strategies across the three language systems. Additionally, classroom teachers design systematic word study activities that align with the processing continuum of orthographic and phonological knowledge, as discussed in Chapter 7.

The integrated language workshop includes structures for balancing rigor and support, while recognizing that some students (approximately 20 percent) will need additional scaffolding to learn from core instruction.

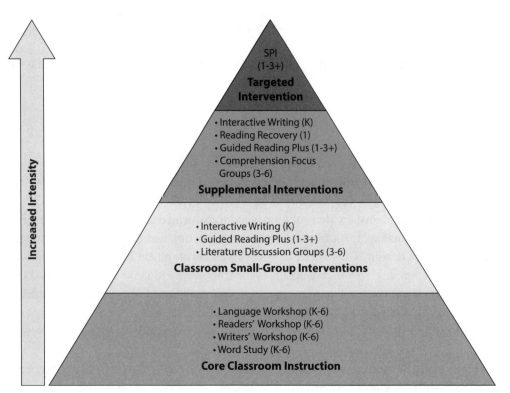

Figure 10.5   The district uses a decision-making model with layers of instructional support and degrees of intensity to meet the unique needs of striving readers.

For students who are not responding to classroom instruction, the classroom teacher and interventionist examine student data and make decisions about the intensity and duration of the intervention for closing the literacy gap as quickly as possible. The students who show characteristics of a reading disability, specifically dyslexia (approximately 2.5 to 5 percent), receive intensive, targeted instruction in the SPI from the SPI specialist. Simultaneously, the classroom teacher provides explicit procedures in areas of phonological and orthographic processing. This layering of interventions across classroom and intervention settings, including collaborative planning among teachers, enables low-progress readers to apply their knowledge with greater accuracy and flexibility. A decision-making model with layers of instructional support and degrees of intensity provides a framework for meeting the unique needs of students with reading problems. At Tier 1, the integrated workshop provides a framework for fostering flexibility and transferability of students' knowledge across language systems. At Tiers 2 and 3, the CIM specialists provide supplemental interventions to low-progress readers, and at Tier 4, they provide targeted instruction in the Strategic Processing Model to students with learning difficulties, such as dyslexia. (See Figure 10.5.)

STRATEGIC PROCESSING INTERVENTION

As discussed in Chapter 9, the SPI is a three-phase intervention designed for the students with the greatest difficulties in reading. The effectiveness of the SPI is dependent on the teacher's ability to assess student knowledge, teach new skills explicitly and systematically, and set up conditions for students to transfer skills to authentic reading and writing tasks.

The SPI training model is a blend of theory, practice, and assessment that enables teachers to implement the intervention concurrently with their own training. Using an apprenticeship approach within a clinical setting, the year-long training consists of three full days of assessment training followed by four-hour weekly classes, as

Table 10.1.   Class Structure and Purpose for Training Activities During Weekly Classes

Class Activity	Purpose
View *yesterday's* videotaped lessons	Teachers capture student data used to make necessary adjustments
Plan *today's* lesson collaboratively	Teachers practice planning with intentionality based on observation
Observe live lesson and collect student data	Teachers use reflective practice to observe for change in student processing
Discuss learning theory as related to instructional decisions	Teachers develop an understanding of cognitive learning theories used to created optimal learning environments
Collaborate on analyzing student data	Teachers learn to balance word-level skills with the integration of those skills into reading and writing tasks

summarized in Table 10.1 below. Furthermore, the clinical design utilizes a balance of face-to-face and virtual teaching demonstrations, supported by collegial discourse that examines the effect of instructional decisions on student learning. Through collaboration and reflection, teachers learn to maintain a balance between word-level skills and the integration of those skills into reading and writing tasks.

PLANNING SPI LESSONS

Accelerative academic gains are dependent upon a teacher's ability to link what a student knows to the new skill or concept that is being taught. SPI teachers use student data, targeted activities, and varied texts to plan individualized lessons. Moreover, teachers use student data to regulate the pacing and intensity of the intervention and to track how many lessons a student might need before being able to transfer a new skill to a reading or writing task. For example, NPS teachers used weekly reflection forms to analyze their instructional decisions for linking decoding aspects (from columns 1 and 2 of the SPI planner) to the overall goal of transfer (see Table 10.2).

In planning for instruction, SPI teachers ask reflective questions, such as the following:

- What is the particular instructional sequence that is most effective in assisting the student with acquiring new skills?
- What behaviors indicate the student is consolidating the learning—a prerequisite to transfer?
- Is there a combination of multisensory techniques that enables the student to demonstrate mastery?
- What is the role of texts in facilitating the student's capacity to transfer skills and strategies for different purposes? (See Table 10.3 for types of texts.)

DATA ANALYSIS

Planning was also facilitated by the analysis of student data in both reading and writing. Electronic AIM lines were used to capture changes in the student's encoding and composition skills during the WAR component of

Table 10.2. The teacher uses weekly reflection around the SPI planner to design systematic instruction across the reading and writing phases.

Column 1 Review Concepts	Column 2 New Concepts	Columns 1 & 2 Decodable Sentence(s)	Column 3 New Book and WAR Reflections on Transfer
Long-vowel pattern chart	**Known:** "ow" "show" "grow" Touch spell, what part says "ow"? **New:** window, throw, rainbow (letter boxes) Cut-up strip: rain/bow	**Col 1:** Do you know if the seed can grow in the snow? (read fluently w/no errors). **Col 2:** The yellow crew can stand still in the snow (35/35). BWA "st-and" with voice.	**What opportunities for transfer did I plan for?** New book "know." Student broke unknown word in parts with eyes, voice, and fingers and read "kn-ow" on the run. Student solved word with letter boxes (f-o-l-l-o-w). Noticed "ew" said "ow" like in "know" during new book reading; wrote "snow" quickly (dictated word) **Where was there evidence of transfer?** Dictated sentence, "snow" BWA with eyes, voice, and fingers; linked new words, "show," "flow," "pillow" in Column 2 ("on," "own"); Finger spell and knew which sound said "ow." Facilitated "follow" in composing message; student solved with letter boxes "f-o-l-l-o-w." **What evidence, if any, was needed for transfer to occur?** Teacher prompt "What do you hear at the end of "foll-ow" and wrote the known word "gr-ow" as link; student then wrote "follow" in letter boxes. "What part said "ow"? Student underlined "ow" in "follow" and "grow."

Table 10.3. Types and Purposes of Texts Used in SPI

Type of Text	Purpose of Text
Decodable Sentence (Review)	Provide an opportunity for student to practice reading a controlled text with speed and accuracy.
Decodable Sentence (New Skill)	Provide an opportunity for student to transfer a newly learned skill in a controlled text.
Familiar Reading	Provide an opportunity for student to fluently read an independent leveled text.
New Books	Provide an opportunity for student to transfer skills learned and read an instructional-level text for meaning.
Grade-Level Text	Provide an opportunity for student to build background knowledge and listening and comprehension skills on a grade-level text.

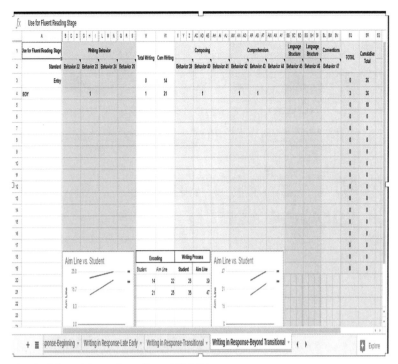

Figure 10.6   Electronic Writing About Reading AIM Line

the SPI lesson (see Figure 10.6). Additionally, patterns of the student's miscues were analyzed to document the changes over time in processing efficiency (see Chapter 3). Using these data tools, teachers observed a marked increase in the use of visual information after just four weeks of the SPI intervention. In order to monitor the progression of changing behaviors in multiple areas, CIM teachers were trained to note patterns of growth across reading, writing, and word-level processes.

In Video 10.7, the CIM teacher and SPI coach use the electronic AIM line to discuss student progress and to plan next steps for improvement. We encourage teachers to create data systems that allow them to triangulate student growth in multiple areas and to monitor the effectiveness of particular interventions for closing the literacy gap as quickly as possible.

Video 10.7   The electronic AIM line provides a valuable tool for monitoring students' progress in response to the intervention and for planning next steps for continuous improvement.

COLLABORATION TOOLS

Collaboration between the SPI interventionist and the classroom teacher is vital to maximize student achievement. Collaborative meetings focus on alignment of instruction, materials, and teacher language. Common ABC charts, blends charts, and vowel charts are used in both classrooms (Resource K1.a, b, and c). A phonics continuum is another tool used for tracking progress and planning sequence of skills taught (see Chapter 7 and Resource G.3).

To promote transfer of skills, the classroom teacher and SPI interventionist jointly analyze WAR prompts using the three steps below. Figure 10.7 illustrates the rapid growth of one student after only four weeks of instruction in the SPI.

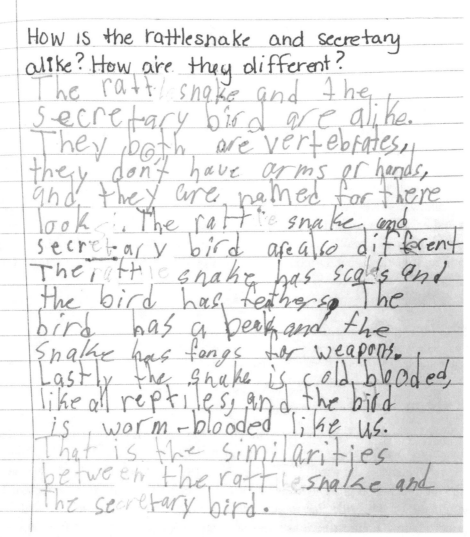

A sentence in the story says, "Suddenly, Wesley's thoughts shot sparks." What does this **mean**? Please explain your answer.

It means that he had a great idea and he felt exe excited

How is the rattlesnake and secretary alike? How are they different? The rattlesnake and the secretary bird are alike. They both are vertebrates, they don't have arms or hands, and they are named for there looks. The rattle snake and secretary bird are also different. The rattle snake has scales and the bird has feathers. The bird has a beak and the snake has fangs for weapons. Lastly the snake is cold blooded, like all reptiles, and the bird is warm-blooded like us. That is the similarities between the rattlesnake and the secretary bird.

Figure 10.7   Example of one student's growth in writing after four weeks of instruction in the SPI.

Step 1: Describe

- What strengths did the student demonstrate?
- What confusions does the student need to overcome?

Step 2: Interpret

- Did the student fully understand and respond appropriately to the written response?
- Did the student plan efficiently and follow through with the plan?
- Did the student monitor for completion of the process?

Step 3: Implications for Instruction

- What instructional focus is needed for the student to progress?
- What modality or instructional support will be most effective for supporting the student's learning?

PROMISING RESULTS

By integrating assessment, theory, and practice into a training model that promoted daily analysis and reflection, teachers were able to teach responsively to meet the diverse needs of students who were struggling to enter the literate world. Schools were able to meet the instructional needs of dyslexic students by empowering teachers with tools of knowledge. SPI teachers collected and analyzed student data that captured patterns of change over time in the student's ability to integrate information, use flexible strategies to solve problems, instantly recognize high-frequency words, apply decoding skills to unknown words, and read for meaning on varied texts with degrees of complexity.

After only one year of training in the SPI design, NPS teachers documented that all students had made gains of at least one grade level. Furthermore, teachers were more knowledgeable about the theories, research, and evidence-based practices for teaching children with learning disabilities. As these results indicate, the SPI is a promising model for ensuring the literacy success of dyslexic readers.

CONCLUDING THOUGHTS

As we collaborated with the educators featured in this chapter, we were reminded of Fullan's six domains of teacher leadership: (1) knowledge of teaching, learning, and assessment, (2) knowledge of collegiality, (3) knowledge of educational contexts, (4) opportunities for continuous learning, (5) management of the change process, and (6) sense of moral purpose (Fullan 1993). Without a doubt, each case story exemplifies these six domains—and also provides other educators with promising data for examining the CIM effectiveness. Moreover, Fullan's six domains align with the phases of implementation that we describe in Figure 9.1. Now, we encourage teachers to apply these ideas to their own implementation of the CIM, designing a PD model that builds teacher expertise in literacy processing theory, while concurrently creating a data system for monitoring students' responsiveness to interventions and making adjustments according to decision rules (described in Chapter 1).

Over several decades, our work with teachers has focused on creating an apprenticeship culture within the school that promotes intellectual collaboration. In authentic problem-solving situations, teachers' moral purpose is guided by students' needs; thus, change agency drives us to develop better strategies for accomplishing moral goals (Dorn & Layton 2016, p. 9). Throughout this book, we have provided teachers with a wealth of resources for implementing the most appropriate intervention within the CIM portfolio, and we have contextualized these interventions around specific learning principles that are grounded in literacy processing theories. Now that we have the foundation, let's do the work that brings us together to make the greatest difference in the literacy lives of the students we teach.

REFERENCES

Aaron, P. G. 1997. "The Impending Demise of the Discrepancy Formula." *Review of Educational Research* 67 (4): 461–502.

Adams, Marilyn Jager. 1994. *Beginning to Read: Thinking and Learning about Print*. 9th ed. Cambridge, MA: MIT Press.

Afflerbach, Peter, and Adria F. Klein. 2020. *Meaningful Reading Assessment*. New Rochelle, NY: Benchmark Education Company.

Allington, Richard L. 2002a. "Research on Reading/Learning Disability Interventions." In *What Research Has to Say About Reading Instruction*, ed. Alan E. Farstrup and S. Jay Samuels. 3rd ed. Newark, DE: International Reading Association.

____. 2002b. "What I've Learned About Effective Reading Instruction: From a Decade of Studying Exemplary Elementary Classroom Teachers." *Phi Delta* Kappan 83 (10): 740–747.

Allington, Richard L., and Peter H. Johnston. 1989. "Coordination, Collaboration, and Consistency: The Redesign of Compensatory and Special Education Interventions." In *Effective Programs for Students at Risk*, ed. Robert E. Slavin, Nancy L. Karweit, and Nancy A. Madden. Boston: MA: Allyn and Bacon.

____. 2015. Foreword to *Changing Minds, Changing Schools, Changing Systems: A Comprehensive Literacy Design for School Improvement*, ed. Linda J. Dorn, Salli Forbes, Mary Ann Poparad, and Barbara Schubert. Los Angeles, CA: Hameray.

Allington, Richard L., and Anne McGill-Franzen. 2009. "Comprehension Difficulties Among Struggling Readers." In *Handbook of Research on Reading Comprehension*, ed. Susan E. Israel and Gerald G. Duffy. New York: Routledge.

Batsche, George, Judy Elliott, L. Graden, J. Grimes, J. F. Kovaleski, D. Prasse, D. J. Reschly, J. Schrag, and D. Tilly III 2005. *Response to Intervention: Policy Considerations and Implementation*. Alexandria, VA: National Association of State Directors of Special Education.

Beaver, Joetta, and Mark Carter, M.A. 2001. Developmental Reading Inventory 2, K-8, 2nd edition. Glenview, IL: Pearson.

Bereiter, Carl, and Marlene Scardamalia. 1989. "Intentional Learning as a Goal of Instruction." In *Knowing, Learning, and Instruction: Essays in Honor of Robert Glaser*, ed. Lauren B. Resnick. Hillsdale, NJ: Lawrence Erlbaum.

Berninger, Virginia W., and William E. Nagy. 2008. "Flexibility in Word Reading: Multiple Levels of Representations, Complex Mappings, Partial Similarities, and Cross-Modality." In *Literacy Processes: Cognitive Flexibility in Learning and Teaching*, ed. Kelly B. Cartwright. New York: Guilford.

Blevins, Wiley. 2016. *A Fresh Look at Phonics, Grades K–2: Common Causes of Failure and 7 Ingredients for Success*. Thousand Oaks: CA: Corwin Literacy.

____. 2017. *Teaching Phonics and Word Study in the Intermediate Grades*. 2nd ed. New York: Scholastic.

____. 2021. *Meaningful Phonics and Word Study: Lesson Fix Ups for Impactful Teaching*. New Rochelle, NY: Benchmark Education Company.

Briceño, Allison, and Adria F. Klein. 2019. "A Second Lens on Formative Reading Assessment with Multilingual Students." *The Reading Teacher*. Vol. 72, No. 5. March/April, 2019.

Buly, Marsha Riddle, and Sheila W. Valencia. 2002. "Below the Bar: Profiles of Students Who Fail State Reading Assessments." *Educational Evaluation and Policy Analysis* 24: 219–239.

Campione, Joseph C., Amy M. Shapiro, and Ann L. Brown. 1995. "Forms of Transfer in a Community of Learners: Flexible Learning and Understanding." In *Teaching for Transfer: Fostering Generalization in Learning*, ed. Anne McKeough, Judy Lupart, and Anthony Marini. Hillsdale, NJ: Lawrence Erlbaum.

Caravolas, Marketa, Charles Hulme, and Margaret J. Snowling. 2001. "The Foundations of Spelling Ability: Evidence from a 3-Year Longitudinal Study." *Journal of Memory and Language* 45: 751–774.

Cartwright, Kelly B. 2012. "Insights from Cognitive Neuroscience: Importance of Executive Function for Early Reading Development and Education." *Early Education and Development* 23 (1): 24–36.

Clay, Marie M. 1975. *What Did I Write?* Portsmouth, NH: Heinemann.

____. 1987. "Learning to Be Learning Disabled." *New Zealand Journal of Educational Studies* 22: 155–173.

____. 2013. *Observation Survey of Early Literacy Development*. Portsmouth, NH: Heinemann.

____. 2014. *By Different Paths to Common Outcomes*. Portsmouth, NH: Heinemann.

____. 2015a. *Becoming Literate: The Construction of Inner Control*. Portsmouth, NH: Heinemann.

Clay, Marie M., Malcom Gill, Ted Glynn, Tony McNaughton, and Ted Salmon. 2015b. *Record of Oral Language*. Portsmouth, NH: Heinemann.

Clay, Marie M. 2015c. *Change Over Time in Children's Literacy Development*. Portsmouth, NH: Heinemann.

____. 2016. *Literacy Lessons Designed for Individuals*. 2nd ed. Portsmouth, NH: Heinemann.

D'Agostino, Jerome V., and Judith A. Murphy. 2004. "A Meta-Analysis of Reading Recovery in United States Schools." *Educational Evaluation and Policy Analysis* 26: 23–28.

Denton, Carolyn A., Jack M. Fletcher, Jason L. Anthony, and David J. Francis. 2006. "An Evaluation of Intensive Intervention for Students with Persistent Reading Difficulties." *Journal of Learning Disabilities* 39: 447–466.

Dorn, Linda J. 2015. "Meaningful Change: Wisdom Comes from Seeing the Whole." In *Changing Minds, Changing Schools, Changing Systems: A Comprehensive Literacy Design for School Improvement*, ed. Linda J. Dorn, Salli Forbes, Mary Ann Poparad, and Barbara Schubert. Los Angeles, CA: Hameray.

Dorn, Linda J., Brian Doore, and Carla Soffos. 2015. "Comprehensive Intervention Model: A Diagnostic Decision-Making Process for Closing the Literacy Gap." In *Changing Minds, Changing Schools, Changing Systems: A Comprehensive Literacy Design or School Improvement*, ed. Linda J. Dorn, Salli Forbes, Mary Ann Poparad, and Barbara Schubert. Los Angeles, CA: Hameray.

Dorn, Linda J., and Shannon C. Henderson. 2010a. "The Comprehensive Intervention Model: A Systems Approach to RTI." In *Successful Approaches to RTI: Collaborative Practices for Improving K–12 Literacy*, ed. Marjorie Y. Lipson and Karen K. Wixon. Newark, DE: International Reading Association.

____. 2010b. "A Comprehensive Assessment System as a Response to Intervention Process." In *RTI in Literacy: Responsive and Comprehensive*, ed. Peter H. Johnston. Newark, DE: International Reading Association.

Dorn, Linda J., and Tammy Jones. 2012. *Apprenticeship in Literacy: Transitions Across Reading and Writing, K–4*. 2nd ed. Portland, ME: Stenhouse.

Dorn, Linda J., and Kent Layton. 2016. "Teachers as Agents of Change." *Illinois ASCD Journal* 62 (4): 8–15.

Dorn, Linda J., and Barbara Schubert. 2010. "A Comprehensive Intervention Model for Preventing Reading Failure: A Response to Intervention Process." In *RTI in Literacy: Responsive and Comprehensive*, ed. Peter H. Johnston. Newark, DE: International Reading Association.

Dorn, Linda J., and Carla Soffos. 2002. *Scaffolding Young Writers: A Writers' Workshop Approach*. Portland, ME: Stenhouse.

____. 2005. *Teaching for Deep Comprehension: A Reading Workshop Approach*. Portland, ME: Stenhouse.

____. 2009. *Small Group Intervention: Linking Word Study to Reading and Writing*. Portland, ME: Stenhouse.

____. 2011. *Interventions That Work: A Comprehensive Intervention Model for Preventing Reading Failure in Grades K–3*. Boston, MA: Pearson.

Duffy, Gerald G., and Susan E. Israel. 2009. "Where to from Here? Themes, Trends, and Questions." In *Handbook of Research on Reading Comprehension*, ed. Susan E. Israel and Gerald G. Duffy. New York: Routledge.

Duke, Nell K., and P. David Pearson. 2002. "Effective Practices for Developing Reading Comprehension." In *What Research Has to Say About Reading Instruction*, ed. Alan E. Farstrup and S. Jay Samuels. 3rd ed. Newark, DE: International Reading Association.

Duke, Nell K., Michael Pressley, and Katherine R. Hilden. 2004. "Difficulties with Reading Comprehension." In *Handbook of Language and Literacy Development and Disorders*, ed. C. Addison Stone, Elaine R. Silliman, Barbara J. Ehren, and Ken Apel. New York: Guilford.

Dunn, Michael W. 2007. "Diagnosing Reading Disability: Reading Recovery as a Component of a Response-to-Intervention Assessment Method." *Learning Disabilities: A Contemporary Journal* 5 (2): 31–47.

Durlak, Joseph A., Roger P. Weissberg, Allison B. Dymnicki, Rebecca D. Taylor, and Kriston B. Schellinger. 2011. "The Impact of Enhancing Students' Social and Emotional Learning: A Meta-Analysis of School Based Universal Interventions." *Child Development* 82 (1): 405–432.

Ehri, Linnea C. 1998. "Grapheme-Phoneme Knowledge Is Essential for Learning to Read Words in English." In *Word Recognition in Beginning Literacy*, ed. Jamie L. Metsala and Linnea C. Ehri. New York: Routledge.

Elkonin, D.B. 1973. "USSR." In *Comparative Reading: Cross-National Studies of Behaviour and Process in Reading and Writing*, ed. John Downing. New York: Macmillan.

Engle, Randi A. 2012. "The Resurgence of Research into Transfer: An Introduction to the Final Articles of the Transfer Strand." *Journal of the Learning Sciences* 21 (3): 347–352.

Englert, Carol Sue, and Carol Chase Thomas. 1987. "Sensitivity to Text Structure in Reading and Writing: A Comparison Between Learning Disabled and Non–Learning Disabled Students." *Learning Disability Quarterly* 10 (2): 93–105.

Felton, Rebecca H. 1992. "Early Identification of Children at Risk for Reading Disabilities." *Topics in Early Childhood Special Education* 12: 212–229.

Fischer, Kurt W. 1980. "A Theory of Cognitive Development: The Control and Construction of Hierarchies of Skills." *Psychological Review* 87 (6): 477–531.

____. 2008. "Dynamic Cycles of Cognitive and Brain Development: Measuring Growth in Mind, Brain, and Education." In *The Educated Brain: Essays in Neuroeducation*, ed. Antonio M. Battro, Kurt W. Fischer, and Pierre J. Léna. Cambridge UK: Cambridge University Press.

Fletcher, Ralph, and JoAnn Portalupi. 2001. *Writing Workshop: The Essential Guide*. Portsmouth, NH: Heinemann.

Foorman, Barbara et al. 2016. *Foundational Skills to Support Reading for Understanding in Kindergarten Through 3rd Grade* (NCEE 2016-4008). Washington, DC: National Center for Education Evaluation and Regional Assistance (NCEE), Institute of Education Sciences, US Department of Education. Retrieved from the NCEE website: http://whatworks.ed.gov.

Fountas, Irene, and Gay Su Pinnell. 1996. *Guided Reading: Good First Teaching for All Children*. Portsmouth, NH: Heinemann.

Fullan, Michael. 1993. *Change Forces: Probing the Depths of Educational Reform*. London: Falmer.

Gambrell, Linda B., Robert M. Wilson, and Walter N. Gantt. 1981. "Classroom Observations of Task-Attending Behaviors of Good and Poor Readers. *Journal of Educational Research* 24: 400–404.

Gankse, Kathy. 2000. *Word Journeys: Assessment-Guided Phonics, Spelling, and Vocabulary Instruction*. New York: Guilford.

Gersten, Russel, and Joseph A. Dimino. 2006. "RtI (Response to Intervention): Rethinking Special Education for Students with Reading Difficulties (Yet Again)." *Reading Research Quarterly* 41: 99–108.

Gersten, Russel, Lynn S. Fuchs, Joanna P. Williams, and Scott Baker. 2001. "Teaching Reading Comprehension Strategies to Students with Learning Disabilities: A Review of Research." *Review of Educational Research* 71: 279–320.

Gindis, Boris. 2003. "Remediation Through Education: Sociocultural Theory and Children with Special Needs." In *Vygotsky's Educational Theory in Cultural Context*, ed. Alex Kozulin, Boris Gindis, Vladimir S. Ageyev, and Suzanne M. Miller. New York: Cambridge University Press.

Goldenberg, Claude. 1992. "Instructional Conversations: Promoting Comprehension through Discussion." *Reading Teacher* 46: 316–326.

Goswami, Usha, and Peter Bryant. 1990. *Phonological Skills and Learning to Read*. New York: Routledge.

Graham, Steve, and Karen R. Harris. 2005. "Improving the Writing Performance of Young Struggling Writers: Theoretical and Programmatic Research from the Center on Student Learning." *Journal of Special Education* 39 (1): 19–33.

Graham, Steve, and Michael Hebert. 2010. *Writing to Read: Evidence for How Writing Can Improve Reading*. A Report from the Carnegie Corporation of New York: Alliance for Excellent Education.

Gunning, Thomas G. 2000. *Building Words: A Resource Manual for Teaching Words and Spelling Strategies*. Boston, MA: Allyn and Bacon.

———. 2012. *Reading Success for All Students: Using Formative Assessments to Guide Instruction and Intervention*. San Francisco, CA: Jossey-Bass.

———. (2018) *Assessing and Correcting Reading Difficulties*. 6th ed. Glenview, IL: Pearson,

Hatcher, Peter J. and Margaret J. Snowling. (2002). "The Phonological Representations Hypothesis of Dyslexia: From Theory to Practice." In *Dyslexia and Literacy: Theory and Practice*, ed. Gordon Reid and Janice Wearmouth. Hoboken, NJ, John Wiley & Sons.

Hattie, John. 2012. *Visible Learning for Teachers: Maximizing Impact on Learning*. New York: Routledge.

Healy, Jane. 2004. *Your Child's Growing Mind: Brain Development and Learning from Birth to Adolescence*. New York: Broadway Books.

Henderson, Shannon C., and Linda J. Dorn. 2011. "Supporting Students Who Struggle with Comprehension of Text: Using Literature Discussion Groups in Grades 3–6." In *After Early Intervention, Then What? Teaching Struggling Readers in Grades 3 and Beyond*, ed. Jeanne R. Paratore and Rachel L. McCormack. Newark, DE: International Reading Association.

Immordino-Yang, Mary Hellen, and Antonio Damasio. 2007. "We Feel, Therefore We Learn: The Relevance of Affective and Social Neuroscience to Education." *Mind, Brain, and Education* 1 (1): 3–10.

Jenkins, Joseph R., and Rollanda E. O'Connor. 2000. "Early Identification and Intervention for Young Children with Reading Learning Disabilities." In *Identification of Learning Disabilities*, ed. Renée Bradley, Louis Danielson, and Daniel P. Hallahan. Hillsdale, NJ: Erlbaum.

Johnston, Peter. Richard Allington, and Peter Afflerbach. 1985. "The Congruence of Classroom and Remedial Reading Instruction." *Elementary School Journal* 85: 465–478.

Klein, Adria F. 2019. *Workshop Plus: Comprehensive Literacy Design*. New Rochelle, NY: Benchmark Education Company.

Klein, Adria. F., and Peter Afflerbach. 2018. *Whole-Group Reading Instruction*. New Rochelle, NY: Benchmark Education Company.

Klein, Adria. F., Barbara Andrews, and Peter Afflerbach. 2018. *Small-Group Reading Instruction*. New Rochelle, NY: Benchmark Education Company.

Kong, Ailing, and Ellen Fitch. 2002/2003. "Using Book Club to Engage Culturally and Linguistically Diverse Learners in Reading, Writing, and Talking About Books." *The Reading Teacher* 56: 352–362.

Kozulin, Alex, Boris Gindis, Vladimir S. Ageyev, and Suzanne M. Miller, eds. 2003. *Vygotsky's Educational Theory in Cultural Context*. New York: Cambridge University Press.

Lidz, Carol S., and Boris Gindis. 2003. "Dynamic Assessment of the Evolving Cognitive Functions in Children." In *Vygotsky's Educational Theory in Cultural Context*, ed. Alex Kozulin, Boris Gindis, Vladimir S. Ageyev, and Suzanne M. Miller. New York: Cambridge University Press.

Liew, Jeffrey. 2012. "Effortful Control, Executive Functions, and Education: Bringing Self-Regulatory and Social-Emotional Competencies to the Table." *Child Development Perspectives* 6 (2): 105–111.

Lipson, Marjorie Y., and Karen K. Wixson, eds. 2010. *Successful Approaches to RTI: Collaborative Practices for Improving K–12 Literacy*. Newark, DE: International Reading Association.

Luria, Aleksandr R. 1980. *Higher Cortical Functions in Man*. New York: Basic Books.

Mathes, Patricia G., and Joseph K. Torgesen. 1998. "All Children Can Learn to Read: Critical Care for Students with Special Needs." *Peabody Journal of Education* 73: 317–340.

McIntyre, Ellen. 2007. "Story Discussion in the Primary Grades: Balancing Authenticity and Explicit Teaching." *The Reading Teacher*, 60: 610–620.

McKeough, Anne, Judy Lee Lupart, and Anthony Marini. 1995. *Teaching for Transfer: Fostering Generalization in Learning*. Hillsdale, NJ: Lawrence Erlbaum.

McKinney, James D., Susan S. Osborne, and Ann C. Schulte. 1993. "Academic Consequences of Learning Disability: Longitudinal Prediction of Outcomes at 11 Years of Age." *Learning Disabilities Research and Practice*, 8: 19–27.

Meichenbaum, Donald, and Andrew Biemiller. 1998. *Nurturing Independent Learners: Helping Students Take Charge of Their Learning*. Cambridge, MA: Brookline Books.

Meyer, Kathryn E., and Brian L. Reindl. 2010. "Spotlight on the Comprehensive Intervention Model: The Case of Washington School for Comprehensive Literacy." In *Successful Approaches to RTI: Collaborative Practices for Improving K–12 Literacy*, ed. Marjorie Y. Lipson and Karen K. Wixon. Newark, DE: International Reading Association.

Murphy, P. Karen, Ian A. G. Wilkinson, Anna O. Soter, Maeghan N. Hennessey, and John F. Alexander. 2009. "Examining the Effects of Classroom Discussion on Students' High-Level Comprehension of Text: A Meta-Analysis." *Journal of Educational Psychology* 101: 740–764.

National Academies of Sciences, Engineering, and Medicine. 2018. *How People Learn II: Learners, Contexts, and Cultures*. Washington, DC: The National Academies Press. https://doi.org/10.17226/24783.

National Early Literacy Panel. 2008. *Developing Early Literacy: Report of the National Early Literacy Panel: A Scientific Synthesis of Early Literacy Development and Implications for Intervention*. Washington, DC: National Institute for Literacy.

Neuman, Susan B., and David K. Dickinson, eds. 2011. *Handbook of Early Literacy Research*. Vol. 3. New York: Guilford.

Owens, Cynthia. 2015. "Changing Children's Lives through Kindergarten Intervention." In *Changing Minds, Changing Schools, Changing Systems: A Comprehensive Literacy Design for School Improvement*, ed. Linda J. Dorn, Salli Forbes, Mary Ann Poparad, and Barbara Schubert. Los Angeles, CA: Hameray.

Paris, Scott G., Barbara A. Wasik, and Julianne C. Turner. 1991. "The Development of Strategic Readers." In *Handbook of Reading Research*, ed. Rebecca Barr, Michael L. Kamil, Peter Mosenthal, and P. David Pearson. New York: Longman.

Pedhazur, Elazar J., and Liora Pedhazur Schmelkin. 1991. *Measurement, Design, and Analysis: An Integrated Approach*. Hillsdale, N.J.: Lawrence Erlbaum.

Perfetti, Charles A., Isabel Beck, Laura C. Bell, and Carol Hughes. 1987. "Phonemic Knowledge and Learning to Read Are Reciprocal: A Longitudinal Study of First Grade Students." *Merrill Palmer Quarterly Journal of Developmental Psychology* 33 (3): 283–319.

Perkins, David N., and Gavriel Salomon. 1988. "Teaching for Transfer." *Educational Leadership* 46 (1): 22–32.

——. 2012. "Knowledge to Go: A Motivational and Dispositional View of Transfer." *Educational Psychologist* 47 (3): 248–258.

Pinnell, Gay S., John J. Pikulski, Karen K. Wixson, Jay R. Campbell, Phillip B. Gough, and Alexandra S. Beatty. 1995. *Listening to Children Read Aloud*. Washington, DC: Office of Educational Research and Improvement, US Department of Education.

Pohlman, Craig. 2008. *Revealing Minds: Assessing to Understand and Support Struggling Learners*. San Francisco, CA: Jossey-Bass.

Pressley, Michael. 2002. "Metacognition and Self-Regulated Comprehension." In *What Research Has to Say About Reading Instruction*, ed. Alan E. Farstrup and S. Jay Samuels. 3rd ed. Newark, DE: International Reading Association.

Pressley, Michael, Alison K. Billman, Kristen H. Perry, Kelly E. Reffitt, and Julia Moorhead Reynolds. 2007. *Shaping Literacy Achievement: Research We Have, Research We Need*. New York: Guilford.

Purcell-Gates, Victoria, Nell K. Duke, and Joseph A. Martineau. 2007. "Learning to Read and Write Genre-Specific Text: A Comparison of Low-SES Children in Skills Based and Whole Language Classrooms." *American Educational Research Journal* 32: 659–685.

Reid, Galvin. 2016. *Dyslexia: A Practitioner's Handbook*. 5th ed. Hoboken, NJ: Wiley-Blackwell.

Roth, Froma P., Deborah L. Speece, and David H. Cooper. 2002. "A Longitudinal Analysis of the Connection Between Oral Language and Early Reading." *The Journal of Educational Research* 95 (5): 259–272.

Sadoski, Mark, and Allan Paivio. 2004. "A Dual Coding Theoretical Model of Reading." *Theoretical Models and Processes of Reading* 5: 1329-1362.

——. 2007. "Toward a Unified Theory of Reading." *Scientific Studies of Reading* 11 (4): 337–356.

——. 2013. *Imagery and Text: A Dual Coding Theory of Reading and Writing*. New York: Routledge.

Scammacca, Nancy, Sharon Vaughn, Greg Roberts, Jeanne Wanzek, and Joseph K. Torgeson. 2007. *Extensive Reading Interventions in Grades K–3: From Research to Practice*. Portsmouth, NH: RMC Research Corporation, Center on Instruction.

Scanlon, Donna M., and Kimberly L. Anderson. 2010. "Using the Interactive Strategies Approach to Prevent Reading Difficulties in an RTI Context." In *Successful Approaches to RTI: Collaborative Practices for Improving K–12 Literacy*, ed. Marjorie Y. Lipson and Karen K. Wixson. Newark, DE: International Reading Association.

Schwartz, Robert M. 2005. "Literacy Learning of At-Risk First-Grade Students in the Reading Recovery Early Intervention." *Journal of Educational Psychology* 97 (2): 257–267.

Scott, Karen J., Karen Hood, Sonia Beth, Linda Fugate, and Craig Carson. 2015. "Creating a Learning Culture for Changing Schools Using the ESAIL." In *Changing Minds, Changing Schools, Changing Systems: A Comprehensive Literacy Design for School Improvement*, ed. Linda J. Dorn, Salli Forbes, Mary Ann Poparad, and Barbara Schubert. Los Angeles, CA: Hameray.

Schaefer, Julie. 2015. "Developing Teacher Expertise Through Inquiry-Based Professional Development." In *Changing Minds, Changing Schools, Changing Systems: A Comprehensive Literacy Design for School Improvement*, ed. Linda J. Dorn, Salli Forbes, Mary Ann Poparad, and Barbara Schubert. Los Angeles, CA: Hameray.

Siegler, Robert S. 1996. *Emerging Minds: The Process of Change in Children's Thinking*. New York: Oxford University Press.

——. 2000. "The Rebirth of Children's Learning." *Child Development* 71: 26–35.

Singer, Harry. 1994. "The Substrata-Factor Theory of Reading." In *Theoretical Models and Processes of Reading*, ed. Robert B. Ruddell, Martha Rapp Ruddell, and Harry Singer. 4th ed. Newark, DE: International Reading Association.

Shanahan, Timothy. 2006. "Relations Among Oral Language, Reading, and Writing Development." In *Handbook of Writing Research*, ed. Charles A. MacArthur, Steve Graham, and Jill Fitzgerald. New York: Routledge.

Shanahan, Timothy, Kim Callison, Christine Carriere, Nell K. Duke, P. David Pearson, Christopher Schatschneider, and Joseph Torgesen. 2010. *Improving Reading Comprehension in Kindergarten Through 3rd Grade: A Practice Guide* (NCEE 2010-4038). Washington, DC: National Center for Education Evaluation and Regional Assistance, Institute of Education Sciences, US Department of Education. Retrieved from whatworks.ed/gov/publications/practiceguides.

Shaywitz, Sally, E., Robin Morris, and Bennett A. Shaywitz. 2008. "The Education of Dyslexic Children from Childhood to Young Adulthood." *Annual Review of Psychology* (59): 451–475.

Snow, Catherine E. 1991. "The Theoretical Basis for Relationships Between Language and Literacy in Development." *Journal of Research in Childhood Education* 6 (1): 5–10.

Soter, Anna O., Ian A. Wilkinson, P. Karen Murphy, Lucila Rudge, Kristin Reninger, and Margaret Edwards. 2008. "What the Discourse Tells Us: Talk and Indicators of Higher-Level Comprehension." *International Journal of Educational Research* 47: 272–391.

Spear-Swerling, Louise, and Robert J. Sternberg. 1996. *Off Track: When Poor Readers Become "Learning Disabled."* Boulder, CO: WestView Press.

Stanovich, Keith E. 1986. "Cognitive Processes and the Reading Problems of Learning-Disabled Children: Evaluating the Assumption of Specificity." In *Psychological and Educational Perspectives on Learning Disabilities*, ed. Joseph K. Torgesen and Bernice Y. L. Wong. Orlando, FL: Academic Press.

Tharp, Roland G., and Ronald Gallimore. 1988. *Rousing Minds to Life*. New York: Cambridge University Press.

Togerson, Carole J., Greg Brooks, and Jill Hall. 2006. *A Systematic Review of the Research Literature on the Use of Phonics in the Teaching of Reading and Spelling*. London: Department for Education and Skills.

Torgesen, Joseph K. 1982. "The Learning-Disabled Child as an Inactive Learner: Educational Implications." *Topics in Learning and Learning Disabilities* 2 (1): 45–52.

Torgesen, Joseph K., Ann W. Alexander, Richard K. Wagner, Carol A. Rashotte, Kytja K. S. Voeller, and Tim Conway. 2001. "Intensive Remedial Instruction for Children with Severe Reading Disabilities: Immediate and Long-Term Outcomes from Two Instructional Approaches." *Journal of Learning Disabilities* 34 (1): 33–58.

Torgesen, Joseph, Allen Schirm, Laura Castner, Sonia Vartivarian, Wendy Mansfield, David Myers, Fran Stancavage, Donna Durno, Rosanne Javorsky, and Cinthia Haan. 2007. *Closing the Reading Gap: Findings from a Randomized Trial of Four Reading Interventions for Striving Readers. National Assessment of Title 1 Final Report. Vol. II*. Jessup, MD: National Center for Education Evaluation and Regional Assistance.

Torgesen, Joseph K., and Richard K. Wagner. 1999. "Preventing Reading Failure in Young Children with Phonological Processing Disabilities: Group and Individual Responses to Instruction." *Journal of Educational Psychology* 91 (4): 579.

Vadeboncoeur, Jennifer A., and Rebecca J. Collie. 2013. "Locating Social and Emotional Learning in Schooled Environments: A Vygotskian Perspective on Learning as Unified." *Mind, Culture, and Activity* 20 (3): 201–225.

Vellutino, Frank R. 2010. "Learning to be Disabled: Marie Clay's Seminal Contribution to the Response to Intervention Approach to Identifying Specific Reading Disability." *Journal of Reading Recovery (Fall)*: 5–23.

Vellutino, Frank R., Donna M. Scanlon, Edward R. Sipay, Sheila G. Small, Alice Pratt, RuSan Chen, and Martha B. Denckla. 1996. "Cognitive Profiles of Difficult-to-Remediate and Readily Remediated Poor Readers: Early Intervention as a Vehicle for Distinguishing between Cognitive and Experiential Deficits as Basic Causes of Specific Reading Disability." *Journal of Educational Psychology* 88 (4): 601–638.

Vellutino, Frank R., Donna M. Scanlon, and G. Reid Lyon. 2000. "Differentiating Between Difficult-to-Remediate and Readily Remediated Poor Readers: More Evidence Against the IQ-Achievement Discrepancy Definition of Reading Disabilities." *Journal of Learning Difficulties* 33 (3): 223–238.

Vellutino, Frank R., Donna M. Scanlon, Haiyan Zhang, and Christopher Schatschneider. 2008. "Using Response to Kindergarten and First Grade Intervention to Identify Children At-Risk for Long-Term Reading Difficulties." *Reading and Writing* 21: 437–480.

Vygotsky, L. S. 1978. *Mind in Society: The Development of Higher Psychological Processes*. Cambridge, MA: Harvard University Press.

Willingham, Daniel T. 2017. *The Reading Mind: A Cognitive Approach to Understanding How the Mind Reads*. San Francisco, CA: Jossey-Bass.

Wonder-McDowell, Carla, D. Ray Reutzel, and John A. Smith. 2011. "Does Instructional Alignment Matter?: Effects on Struggling Second Graders' Reading Achievement." *Elementary School Journal* 112 (2): 259–279.

Wood, David. 2002. "The Why? What? When? And How? Of Tutoring: The Development of Helping and Tutoring Skills in Children." *Literacy, Teaching, and Learning* 7 (1,2): 2–30.

Wood, David, Jerome S. Bruner, and Gail Ross. 1976. "The Role of Tutoring in Problem Solving." *Journal of Child Psychology and Psychiatry* 17 (2): 89–100.

INDEX